... the

... Deputy Governor.

...TTEE of the

... Company

MAP

... the Rivers and Lakes

... and Pacifick OCEANS

By Your most obedient & dutiful Servant,

Philip Turner

Mapmaker

Philip Turnor in Rupert's Land in the Age of Enlightenment

Barbara Mitchell

University of Regina Press

Printed and bound in Canada at Friesens. The text of this book is printed on 100% post-con-
sumer recycled paper with earth-friendly vegetable-based inks.

COVER AND TEXT DESIGN: Duncan Campbell, University of Regina Press
COPY EDITOR: Marionne Cronin
PROOFREADER: Kristine Douaud
INDEXER: Sergey Lobachev, Brookfield Indexing Services
COVER ART: Final pages in Turnor's journal from his northward expedition, 1790–92 (HBCA,
B.9/A/3), and eighteenth-century surveyor's field compass by George Adams, London
(Collection of Historical Scientific Instruments, Harvard University, DW0687).
ENDPAPERS: Turnor's 1794 map: "Hudson's Bay and the Rivers and Lakes Between the Atlan-
tick and Pacifick Oceans." Hudson's Bay Company Archives, Archives of Manitoba, Hudson's
Bay Company manuscript maps collection, HBCA G.2/32.

Library and Archives Canada Cataloguing in Publication

Mitchell, Barbara, 1944-, author
        Mapmaker : Philip Turnor in Rupert's Land in the Age of Enlightenment
/ Barbara Mitchell.

Includes bibliographical references and index. Issued in print and electronic formats. ISBN
978-0-88977-503-9 (hardcover).--ISBN 978-0-88977-504-6 (PDF).—ISBN 978-0-88977-505-3
(HTML)

1. Turnor, Philip, 1752–1800. 2. Hudson's Bay Company—Employees—Biography.
3. Surveyors—Canada—Biography. 4. Cartographers—Canada—Biography. 5. Explorers—
Canada—Biography. 6. Fur traders—Canada—Biography.
7. Canada—Discovery and exploration. I. Title.

FC.1.T87M58 2017   971.03'092   C2017-905003-6   C2017-905004-4

10 9 8 7 6 5 4 3 2

University of Regina Press, University of Regina
Regina, Saskatchewan, Canada, S4S 0A2
TEL: (306) 585-4758 FAX: (306) 585-4699
U OF R PRESS   WEB: www.uofrpress.ca

We acknowledge the support of the Canada Council for the Arts for our publishing program.
We acknowledge the financial support of the Government of Canada. / Nous reconnaissons
l'appui financier du gouvernement du Canada. This publication was made possible with
support from Creative Saskatchewan's Creative Industries Production Grant Program.

In honour of my Cree, English, and Orkney ancestors,
the Turnor, Harper, Loutit, and Goff families,

&

especially for Orm, who travelled with
me on my journey of discovery

Contents

List of Illustrations

LIST OF FIGURES

Author's Note

My intent in this first full-length biography of Philip Turnor is to tell his story as truthfully and as compellingly as possible. To do so, I have chosen two narrative voices. The primary voice is that of the biographer, narrating Turnor's story based on the historical record—particularly journals, maps, and correspondence. When, on occasion, I have dramatized a scene, it is prompted by Turnor's own dramatic telling of events as found in his journals and duly noted in the endnotes.

A secondary narrative line is written in my personal voice. Introduced as JOURNAL ONE, JOURNAL TWO, etc., these sections are set off with a dotted line in the margin, and they begin and end with a decorative ornament. These diary-like journals, placed throughout the book, allowed me the latitude to imagine Turnor's interior life, to speculate, to speak about the biographic process, and to make history personal.

Regarding terminology, I want to note that in Philip Turnor's time, the word "Indian" was the common term used to refer to the original peoples of the lands that we now know as Canada. Respecting the more preferred and accurate naming practices of today, I have used this word only when quoting primary material. Where possible I have provided the names of Indigenous individuals.

Similarly, the female partner of a fur trader was called by the French and English traders a "country wife" and the ceremony by which she became his "country wife" as marriage à la façon du pays. These women were seldom named in fur trade documents, and my four-times-great-grandmother's name remains unknown to us. I will refer to her as Turnor's Cree wife.

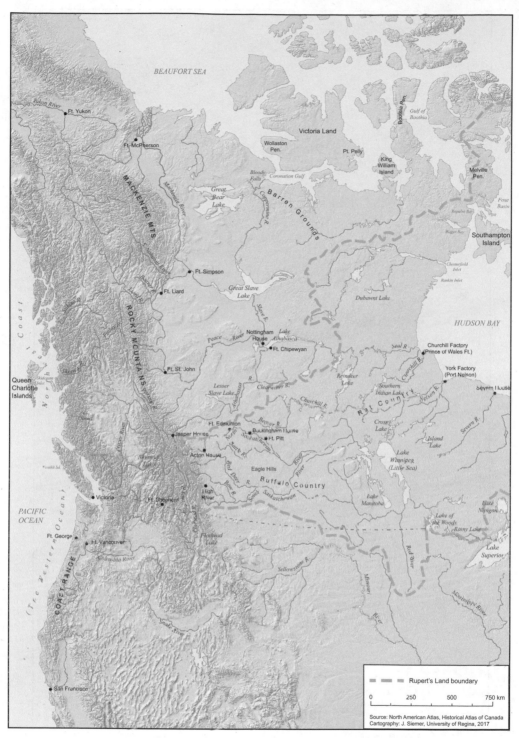

Map 1. West of Hudson Bay and the Arctic
Shores. Adapted from Ruggles (1991).

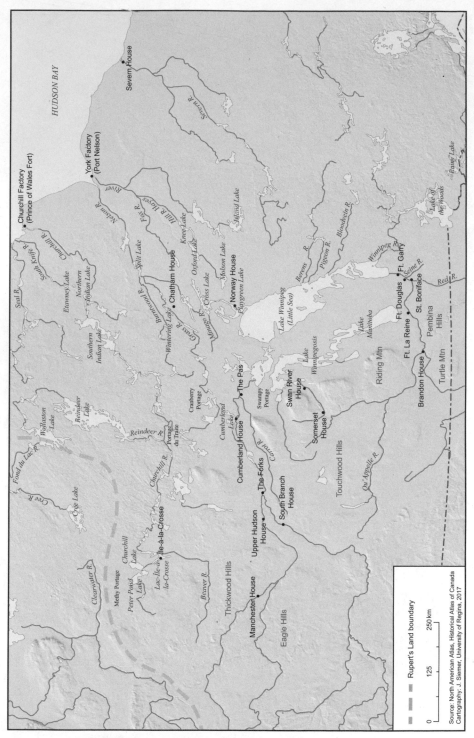

HUDSON BAY

Severn House

York Factory
(Port Nelson)

Churchill Factory
(Prince of Wales Fort)

Severn R.

Seal R.

South Knife

Churchill R

Nelson R.

Fox R.

Hill R.

Hayes R.

Island Lake

Split Lake

Northern Indian Lake

Etawney Lake

Burntwood R.

Chatham House

Knee Lake

Oxford Lake

Cross Lake

Molson Lake

Playgreen Lake

Norway House

Beavers R.

Pigeon R.

Bloodvein R.

Winnipeg R.

Ft. Garry

Seine R.

Red R.

Rainy Lake

Lake of the Woods

Southern Indian Lake

Gods R.

Wintering Lake

Mingoe R.

Lake Winnipeg (Little Sea)

Ft. Douglas

St. Boniface

Ft. La Reine

Pembina Hills

Lake Manitoba

Reindeer Lake

Wollaston Lake

Reindeer R.

Portage du Traite

Cranberry Portage

Cumberland Lake

The Pas

Swampy Portage

Swan River House

Lake Winnipegosis

Riding Mtn

Brandon House

Turtle Mtn

Fond du Lac R.

Cree R.

Cree Lake

Churchill R.

Cumberland House

Somerset House

Touchwood Hills

Qu'Appelle R.

Clearwater R.

Methy Portage

Peter Pond Lake

Churchill Lake

Île-à-la-Crosse

Lac-Île-à-la-Crosse

Beaver R.

The Forks

Upper Hudson House

South Branch House

Carrot R.

Thickwood Hills

Manchester House

Eagle Hills

Rupert's Land boundary

0   125   250 km

Source: North American Atlas, Historical Atlas of Canada
Cartography: J. Siemer, University of Regina, 2017

Map 2. The Nelson and Churchill River Systems.
Adapted from Ruggles (1991).

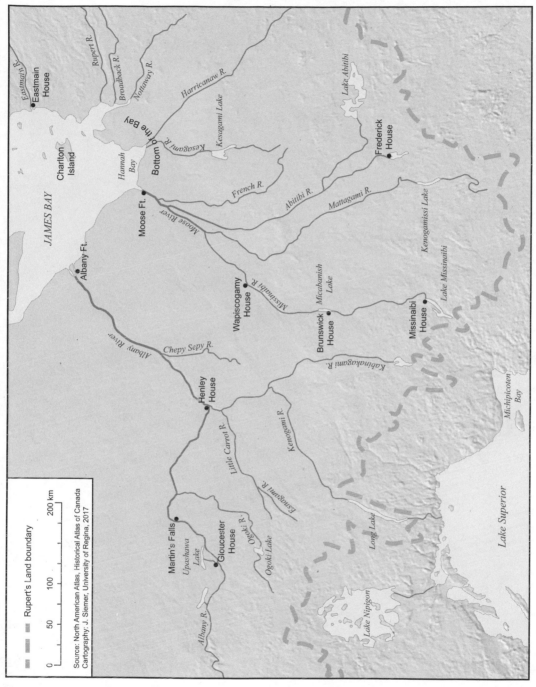

Map 3. Between Lake Superior and James Bay.
Adapted from Ruggles (1991).

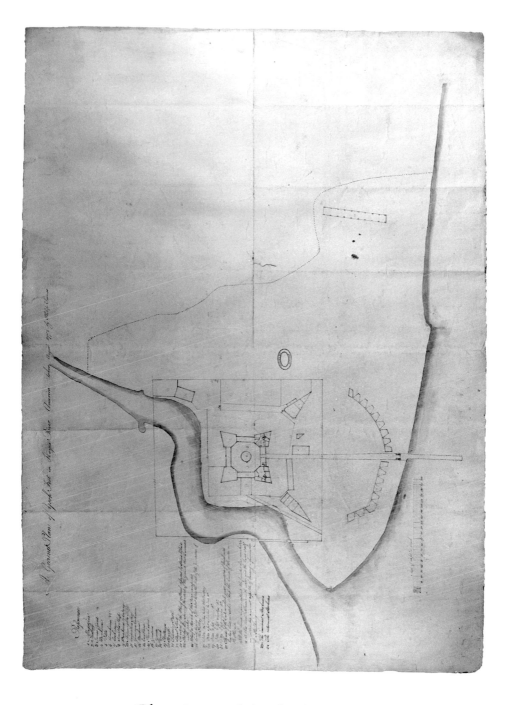

Plate 1. "A Ground Plan of York Fort," 1778

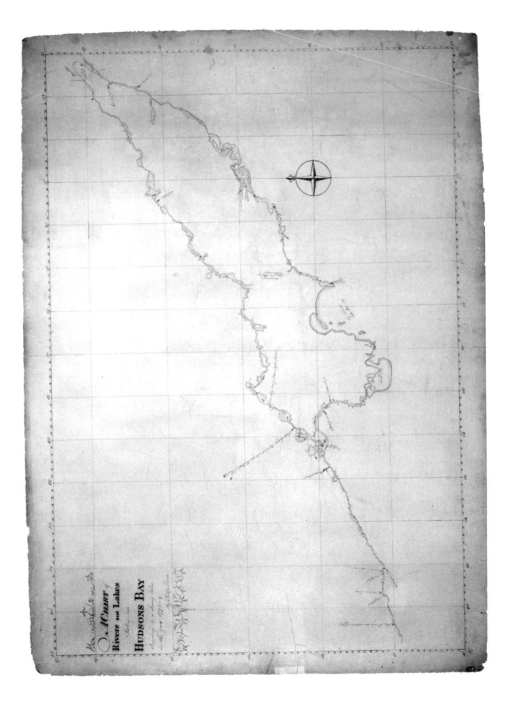

Plate 2. "A CHART of Rivers and Lakes Falling into HUDSONS BAY," 1778 & 79

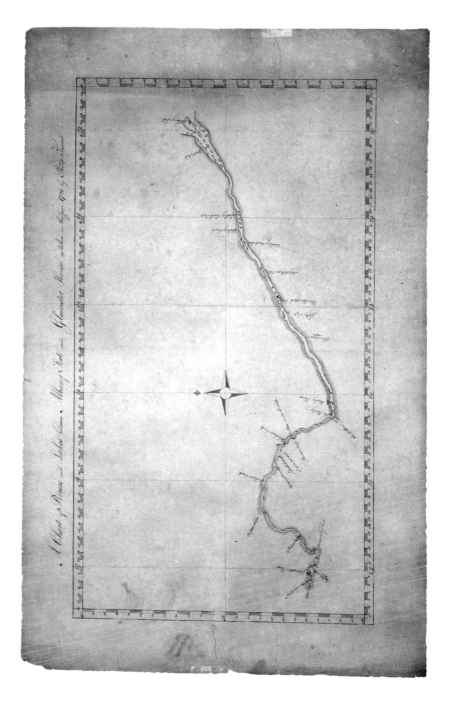

Plate 3. "A Chart of Rivers and Lakes between
Albany Fort and Gloucester House," 1780

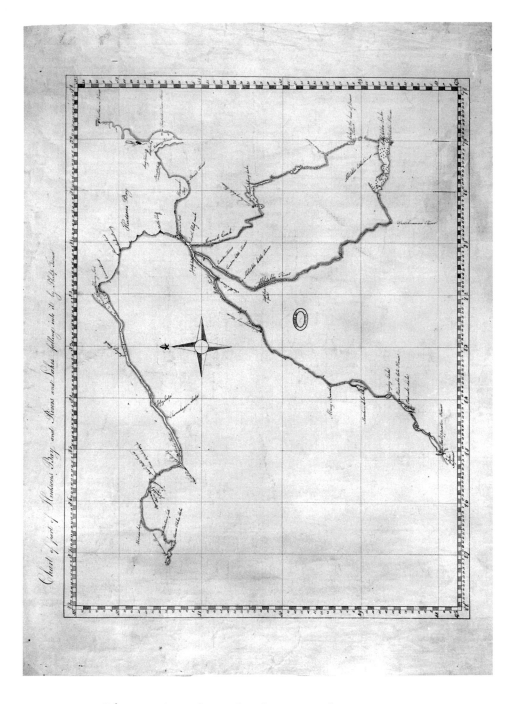

Plate 4. "Chart of part of Hudsons Bay and Rivers," 1782-83

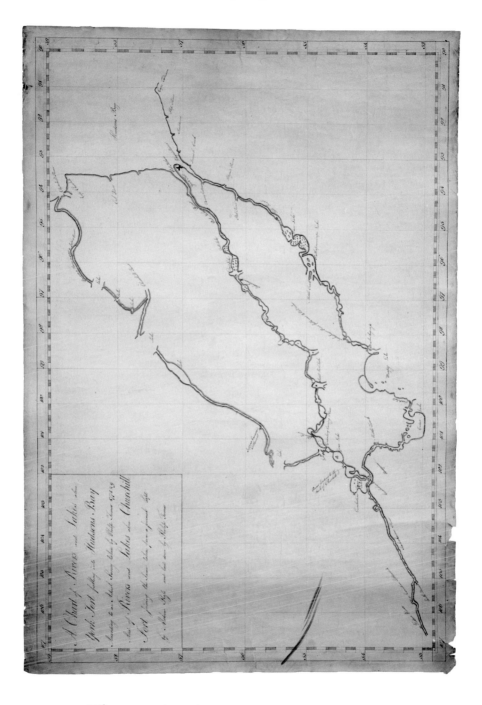

Plate 5. "A Chart of Rivers and Lakes above York Fort…
And of Rivers and Lakes above Churchill Fort," 1787-88

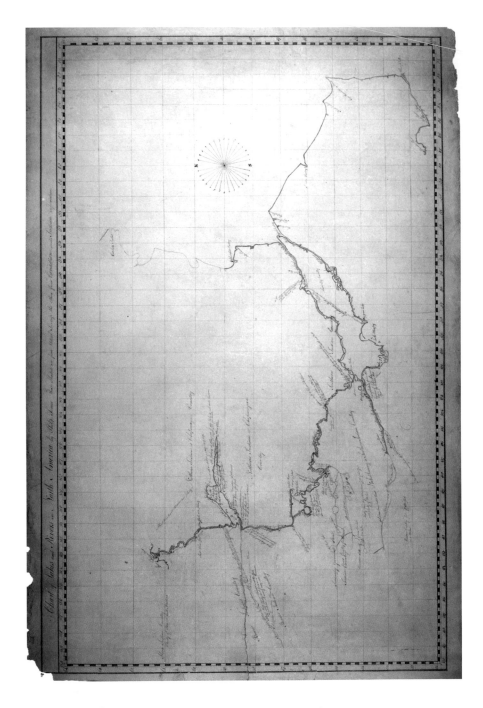

Plate 6. "Chart of Lakes and Rivers in North America," 1792

Plate 7. Cartouche for Turnor's 1794 map

Plate 8. Author viewing Turnor's 1794 map for the first time.

Prologue

Discovery, 24 October 1992

I knew nothing of my family lineage beyond my grandparents, but on this day in 1992 my family multiplied astronomically. I was forty-eight years old.

It was Thanksgiving -the annual family gathering of the eastern branch of the Goff family. Bob, my uncle by marriage and an amateur genealogist, brought a family tree he had been working on for several years. He unfolded it and tacked it on the wall—it was five feet wide, three and a half feet high. A hundred names, with their birth, marriage and death dates, spread out and down the wall. I began with my mother, Dorothy Goff, and her siblings, two of whom, Anna and Vivian, were at the unveiling. I moved upstream through the Goff parents, to the Loutit and then the Harper tributaries, to Joseph Turner Sr., and finally to the source, Philip Turnor, the first name on the chart "Born in England in 1751," I read, he was a mapmaker who "produced the first good maps for the company" and who "took his Indian wife back to England."[1]

That day I discovered a wealth of information I had never known: I was a sixth generation Canadian; I had Orkney-Scots connections as well as English, my ancestors worked in the fur trade; Philip Turnor, whose name I had never heard before, was a significant figure in the Hudson's Bay Company's history. And I had Cree roots. Philip Turnor, my great-great-great-great-grandfather, had come to Rupert's Land in 1778 from Middlesex, England, as a surveyor, in fact the first inland surveyor for the Hudson's Bay Company. His Cree wife[2] was my great-great-great-great-grandmother.

My uncle Bob recalled the day he was checking the 1901 Canadian Census records and discovered "Cree" listed as my grandmother's ancestry. Aunt Anna and Aunt Vivian were astonished that they had not known this about their own mother.[3] When I questioned them, Aunt Anna reported, "No one ever spoke of it. It never occurred to me that she was Cree." Aunt Vivian agreed, "If Mother did know about her Cree ancestry, she didn't say. I wish I had asked her more."[4] In fact, my grandmother was of mixed heritage. Her grandfather, John Low Loutit, and her great-grandfather, James Harper, had been born in Rupert's Land to Orkney HBC servants and Cree women (Figure 1).[5]

So, in 1901 when my grandmother was nineteen and still living at home with her parents in St. Andrew's Parish (Lockport, near Selkirk, Manitoba), it was acknowledged and recorded that she was Cree, but in 1904, when she married an Englishman, that was kept quiet. She did however mention her Cree ancestry to her male children, Barney and Haig. But, like their mother, they did not discuss it openly in the family.[6]

Aunt Anna recalled that there were "always Cree women around. They would bring their lard pails full of saskatoons to Aunt Jennie's and sit down for tea." As young girls my aunts absorbed more than they realized. One New Year's Day on a phone call, my Aunt Vivian recalled hearing a New Year's greeting in Cree when she was a child. "Happy Noot Shey," she said to me. She apologized for her attempt and said she did not know how to spell these words. I asked what else she remembered, and she began counting in what she thought was Cree: "Hanika, banika, dib boose, day"—and she continued to twenty.[7] Although I have not been able to identify her numbering as either Cree or Bungee, a Red River dialect, my questions had awakened in my aunt some long-ago memories of hearing an Indigenous language being spoken by her family and friends.

My aunts recalled for me various traditions of their Cree-Scots upbringing that were practiced in the family during the 1930s. One of their aunts made bannock on top of the old cook stove, and my grandmother told her children stories about the place they went during the summer months, which they lovingly called Buttertown. It was not truly a town, only a pasture area out on their land a few kilometres away where they brought the cattle to graze during the summer. It was one of the great pleasures of her young life, my grandmother told her daughters. They picked berries—wild strawberries, saskatoons, and high bush cranberries. The women made red and purple jellies for the winter and churned butter, which they stored in gallon granite crocks and placed in a hole, dug in the ground, so they would stay cool in the hot prairie summers. Pound blocks would be measured out in a butter pat to sell to their neighbours and relatives.

Unfortunately, this was all my aunts could tell me about this side of my family. The furthest back they could go was to my great-grand-mother, Nancy Ann Harper.

Philip Turnor was just as much a mystery to them as he was to me.

W ork prevented me from pursuing my family history for a num-ber of years, and then I received a letter from my uncle Bob: "At last I've looked up some information about Philip Turnor," he wrote.[8] He had discovered Pearl Weston's family history, *Across the River,* and sent me a few pages. At the beginning of her book is this wisp of a story passed down through six generations: "Our Grandma Campbell remembered, when a little girl, her grandfather, Joseph Turner, speaking about stories he'd heard of his Grandfather Philip Turnor travelling rivers in Northern Canada with only the stars to guide him."[9] Reading that passage, I began to imagine Turnor with his sextant, compass, and watch, and with his Cree guides and my great-great-great-great grandmother, surveying the rivers of Rupert's Land. This started me on my own travels—to the Hudson's Bay Company Archives, to the Orkney Islands, to England, to Moose Factory—to discover who Philip Turnor was and what he contributed to the surveying and mapping of Rupert's Land, the territory that came to be the Canadian north.

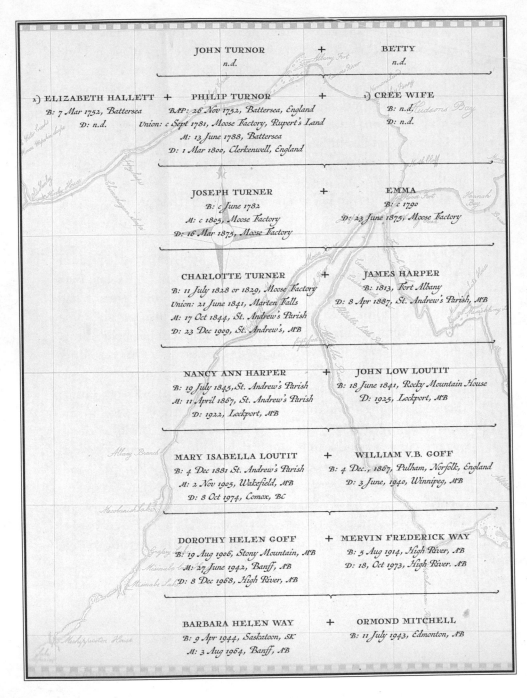

JOHN TURNOR + **BETTY**
n.d. *n.d.*

2) **ELIZABETH HALLETT** + **PHILIP TURNOR** + 1) **CREE WIFE**
B: 7 Mar 1752, Battersea *BAP: 26 Nov 1752, Battersea, England* *B: n.d.*
D: n.d. *Union: c Sept 1781, Moose Factory, Rupert's Land* *D: n.d.*
M: 13 June 1788, Battersea
D: 1 Mar 1800, Clerkenwell, England

JOSEPH TURNER + **EMMA**
B: c June 1782 *B: c 1790*
M: c 1805, Moose Factory *D: 23 June 1875, Moose Factory*
D: 16 Mar 1875, Moose Factory

CHARLOTTE TURNER + **JAMES HARPER**
B: 11 July 1828 or 1829, Moose Factory *B: 1813, Fort Albany*
Union: 21 June 1841, Marten Falls *D: 8 Apr 1887, St. Andrew's Parish, MB*
M: 17 Oct 1844, St. Andrew's Parish
D: 23 Dec 1909, St. Andrew's, MB

NANCY ANN HARPER + **JOHN LOW LOUTIT**
B: 19 July 1845, St. Andrew's Parish *B: 18 June 1841, Rocky Mountain House*
M: 11 April 1867, St. Andrew's Parish *D: 1925, Lockport, MB*
D: 1922, Lockport, MB

MARY ISABELLA LOUTIT + **WILLIAM V.B. GOFF**
B: 4 Dec 1881 St. Andrew's Parish *B: 4 Dec., 1867, Pulham, Norfolk, England*
M: 2 Nov 1905, Wakefield, MB *D: 3 June, 1940, Winnipeg, MB*
D: 8 Oct 1974, Comox, BC

DOROTHY HELEN GOFF + **MERVIN FREDERICK WAY**
B: 19 Aug 1906, Stony Mountain, MB *B: 5 Aug 1914, High River, AB*
M: 27 June 1942, Banff, AB *D: 18, Oct 1973, High River. AB*
D: 8 Dec 1968, High River, AB

BARBARA HELEN WAY + **ORMOND MITCHELL**
B: 9 Apr 1944, Saskatoon, SK *B: 11 July 1943, Edmonton, AB*
M: 3 Aug 1964, Banff, AB

Figure 1. Genealogical chart.

1.

From Farming to Mapmaking

London, *1778*

"War horrid war," read the headline in the *St. James's Chronicle*.[1] America and England had been at war for three years. Five years earlier, in a gesture of independence, the American rebels had thrown the English taxed tea into Boston Harbour. Now the American Revolutionary War was expanding. In February France had joined the Americans and declared war on Britain. King George III travelled to Portsmouth to oversee military preparations against the French and made the decision to take the battle to the southern American states and the West Indies. In Britain, men were being pressed into naval service, though this was euphemistically called volunteering, made legal by the Recruiting Act of 1778. In spite of growing concerns for safe passage in the Channel and in the North Atlantic, and in spite of the difficulty of hiring good men for the trade, the Hudson's Bay Company (HBC) continued to send its ships to and from Rupert's Land every May and October. Generally there were enough Orkney men to hire on at Stromness. Who would not prefer to serve the fur trade in Rupert's Land rather than fight for half the pay and double the danger in the American war? Business remained good for the company, and plans were afoot to expand the fur trade farther inland from Fort Prince of Wales, York Fort, and Moose Fort, bringing the company into direct competition with the Montreal-based traders, who were commonly known as the Canadians or the Pedlars and later as the North West Company (NWC).[2] The HBC would have its own skirmishes to fight in Rupert's Land.

Ironmongers Hall with a View of Fenchurch Street.   L'Hotel des Ferronniers dans la Rue de Fenchurch a LONDRES

Figure 2. 1753 engraving of Fenchurch Street
where Hudson's Bay House was located.

Hudson's Bay House, *March 1778*

On 25 March 1778 Governor Bibye Lake, Deputy Governor Samuel Wegg, and members of the London Committee of the Hudson's Bay Company met in the offices at Culver Court, Fenchurch Street in London (Figure 2). As usual there was a full slate of business to discuss. February and March were the months to hire this year's provisioners for Rupert's Land—the butcher, draper, distiller, chandler, ironmonger, grain merchant, and gun manufacturer. Amounts of flour, peas, pork, beef, oatmeal, and even sauerkraut (disliked by the men but necessary to ward off scurvy) had to be determined, as did quantities of brandy, rum, Brazil tobacco, Virginia tobacco, and leaf tobacco for the servants' consumption as well as for the fur trade. Expenditures and arrangements for trading items, such as blankets from Whitney, cloth, kettles and pots, knives and chisels, trinkets and beads, were ongoing. The ships were in dry dock and the sailmakers had been hired to outfit and repair sails. Captain Fowler, sailing the

6

King George II to York Factory, and Captain Christopher, commanding the *Seahorse*, bound for Churchill, had been re-hired. All this was routine business—but crucial, as there was only one sailing to and from Rupert's Land each year.

On this day there was a more far-reaching policy to be officially discussed. For over six years, at the Royal Society of London, at the Thursday Club, at the coffee houses, and among his acquaintances, Wegg had worked hard persuading the Governor and Committee members of a change about which he felt strongly—expanding the company's trading posts into the interior of Rupert's Land to stop the flow of trade between the Cree and the Montreal traders.[3] The earliest accounts of their threat to the HBC trade had come from William Tomison, an Orkneyman, who had been sent to winter among the Cree at Lake Winnipeg and then Lake Manitoba in 1767 and 1769.[4] Andrew Graham, acting chief factor at York Fort, urged London to take action, but nothing was done. Trade continued to fall, and in 1772 Graham sent Matthew Cocking,[5] second in command at York Fort, to report on the state of affairs in the Saskatchewan River area where the Montreal traders were intercepting the Cree and trading with them before they made their annual trips to the company forts on Hudson Bay. Cocking noted about fifteen canoes and four masters with their men trading in this area.[6] Graham sent reports and a map to London, suggesting the establishment of a post at Basquia (The Pas), possibly headed by Samuel Hearne, the intrepid overland traveller who had reached the Coppermine River and the Arctic Ocean in July 1771. London approved sending Hearne, and in September 1774 a location was cleared for the first inland Hudson's Bay Company House at Pine Island Lake, sixty miles above Basquia, which Hearne had determined a better site.[7] There had been a considerable rise in the number of Montreal traders. Now there were at least sixty canoes belonging to them (although only thirty or forty affected the HBC trade), and Hearne identified ten of the most significant masters and their locations in his journal.[8] Hearne reported, "The Canadians having got to such a head and are distributed through the country in such numbers with so large a quantity of goods has enabled the natives of late years to supply themselves with goods at their own doors which they will do at a small disadvantage rather than have the trouble to frequent the forts on Hudson Bay."[9]

It was clear that to compete with these traders, the HBC had to take the trade to the "doors" of the inland bands, and that would require more men, more settlements, and accurate surveying and mapping of the territory. Since Cumberland House had been established the Committee had procrastinated, sending off explorations west and south, but without properly trained men. The men had tried their best, but were ill equipped to do this work. Hearne had told the London Committee bluntly that he did not have time for mapmaking on his journeys inland; "as my whole time were taken up in the management of one of the canoes both out and home, I had not an opportunity of making my remarks with any exactness relative to the plan of my track."[10] The only way forward was to hire a trained surveyor and cartographer who could accurately map the routes inland.

Two items of interest were on the agenda for 25 March: "Astronomers to be procured" and "Letter to Mr. Wales—Christ's Hospital."[11] William Wales, mathematics and astronomy teacher at Christ's Hospital School, would know some young men qualified to do the job. Wegg knew Wales personally as he had helped coordinate Wales's journey to Rupert's Land in 1769 to observe the transit of Venus. Observing this rare occurrence, the passing of the planet Venus between the Earth and the sun, provided astronomers with valuable information about the earth's distance from the sun.

The meeting adjourned and the members went off to dine at the Royal Society's Club in the Strand. At last it was settled—the best routes inland would be mapped, inland trading posts could be constructed in the most advantageous locations, and, with any luck, they would be able to counter the growing competition from the Montreal traders, who had already built a number of posts on the Saskatchewan River. The HBC would reinforce its claim to what had been granted to them by the Charter of 1670—exclusive rights to trade in all land drained by Hudson Bay. Maps were vital to this enterprise. They signified knowledge of the safest and most expedient routes, but, more importantly, they proclaimed the Hudson's Bay Company's exclusive right to trade in Rupert's Land. Wegg foresaw both the economic and geographic benefits of hiring a mapmaker.

The secretary, William Redknap, was instructed to write a letter to Wales and early next morning, standing before his long, slanted oak desk, the day's dim March light barely illuminating the paper before him, the secretary dipped his pen in the inkwell and wrote:

> Sir,
>
> The Committee of the Hudson's Bay Company intending to send out this year by their ships which sail the latter end of May next for their several settlements in Hudson Bay, three or more persons well skilled in mathematics and in making astronomical observations, under the direction of the chiefs at the respective factories, which persons are to travel inland with the title of inland surveyors, and to rise to higher stations in the company's service according to merit, & that each of the persons so employed shall have a fixed salary of fifty pounds a year, with the promise of a gratuity in proportion to services performed.
>
> The Committee therefore request you to use your best endeavors to procure persons answering the above description for the Company's service.
>
> I am,
>
>   Sir,
>
>   Your most honourable Servant,
>
>   W. R.
>
>   Secretary
>
> Hudson Bay House
> 26th March 1778.[12]

The young porter scurried up Lombard and Cheapside, past the magnificent St. Paul's Cathedral with its domed roof, to Christ's Hospital School, Newgate Street, and asked that the letter bearing the HBC seal be delivered into the hands of William Wales. Already the boys, in their long blue coats and yellow stockings, were gathering for Master Wales's class in navigational mathematics.

Wales had travelled the world. He had spent a year at Churchill in the bitterly cold stone fortress with temperatures at minus forty degrees Fahrenheit. Three years later, in 1772, he journeyed to the other end of the earth, joining Captain James Cook as assistant astronomer on his second voyage to the South Seas (1772–1775). When he returned to England in 1775 Wales was appointed Master of Mathematics at Christ's Hospital School and took on the task of revitalizing and professionalizing that 223-year-old school. Now, in 1778, at age forty-four, Wales had deservedly earned a reputation as not only an intelligent, respected scientist and adventurer, but as a humane teacher with a gentle and humorous bent, a man with a flair for storytelling. He had frequently entertained Governor Lake, Deputy Governor Wegg, and other members of the Royal Society with tales of his travels to exotic places.

A few years later, in the 1780s, Wales would teach three notable students who would eclipse him in fame: Charles Lamb, the essayist and poet; Leigh Hunt, poet, essayist, and theatre critic; and, most significantly, the poet Samuel Taylor Coleridge. Wales was well liked and certainly one of the more genial masters at Christ's Hospital School, not chucking books at his students, or rapping their knuckles, or flogging them, as was the custom with the Head Master himself. Wales could make navigational studies vivid to all his students. It is likely that Coleridge recalled Wales's tales of Hudson Bay and of the Antarctic when he came to write *Rime of the Ancient Mariner* in 1798. No doubt Wales entertained the boys, as he did the Royal Society in his talk of 1770, with descriptions of his first sighting of an iceberg: "a very large island of ice or rather frozen snow...It was as high out of the water as our main-top, and adorned both on its top and sides with spires indented in the most romantic manner...we weathered one island...three or four times the ship's length, and though so very near, we could not see its top for the fog."[13] That description is echoed in Coleridge's lines, "And now there came both mist and snow, / And it grew wondrous cold: / And ice, mast-high, came floating by, / As green as emerald....The ice was here, the ice was there, / The ice was all around: / It cracked and growled, and roared and howled, / Like noises in a swound!"[14]

Mr. Wales responded to the London Committee's request five days later with recommendations of George Beck and Joseph Lindley, both apparently adept in mathematics. Beck, in fact, had been slated for a professorship in Mathematics at the Royal Military College at Woolwich. For whatever reason, lack of experience in mapmaking or lack of interest, their names were dropped and Wales continued his search for the right man: one who was literate, trained in surveying, mathematics, astronomy, navigation, and the use of instruments and lunar tables, and someone who could draft maps. The company looked for men of character, who were "sober, honest and diligent," who possessed "youthful vigor," and were intelligent and prudent as well—a "Proper Person" in their words.[15]

A Proper Person, *April 1778*

On 14 April Mr. Wales wrote recommending a third man: "Mr Philip Turnor of Laleham Middx. 27 yrs age not marry'd brot up in farming business."[16] And with that Philip Turnor stepped into history. Noted in the agenda book for April 22 was "Philip Turnor—Observer,"[17] and perhaps on that Wednesday, the Committee's meeting day, Turnor went to Fenchurch to talk to the honourable gentlemen. The committee was well pleased with his qualifications and demeanour, and he was hired as the first inland surveyor for the Hudson's Bay Company.[18]

The official letter outlining Turnor's conditions of hire was written by the London Committee on 13 May and went into the packet of letters and instructions to be read by Humphrey Marten, chief factor of York Factory, three and a half months later in Rupert's Land:

> Being very desirous to have the longitude and latitude of our several factories ascertained and also of our inland settlements, and their respective distances from one another and from the factory on which they are dependent in order to settle with certainty the shortest communication between them, we have engaged Mr. Philip Turnor under the title of Inland Surveyor for three years at £50 a year. He is to mess at your table and also at the tables of our other chiefs during his stay at each factory, and to be accommodated in the best manner possible for his several journeys.[19]

Turnor's wage, the tone of the letter, the stipulation that he was to be provided with the best advice, assistance, and provisions, and was to mess with the chiefs—all this indicated his status as one of the top-ranking officers in Rupert's Land.

Who was Philip Turnor, a man whose first twenty-seven years could be summarized in so few words, "brot up in farming business," but who paddled and mapped his way into the history of Rupert's Land? How did he come to the notice of an important astronomer like William Wales? How did he make the transition from farming to travelling, exploring, and surveying? The search for such answers is a journey of discovery in itself.

JOURNAL ONE

Peterborough, Ontario

A journal of the most remarkable transactions and occurrences in tracing the early life of Philip Turnor by his four-times-great-granddaughter

The main river of information for my story of Philip Turnor has been his handwritten journals "of the most remarkable transactions and occurrences," which I read on microfilm from the Hudson's Bay Company Archives. I took numerous other tributaries: the company's correspondence books, the minute books, the ships' logs, the post journals—items by him and about him. His history became documented in 1778 when he joined the Hudson's Bay Company. But I wanted to discover the spring of his life—what parenting, education, character, and ambition led him to mapmaking and to Rupert's Land?

I began with a search for his birthplace and birth year. I searched fruitlessly, on two trips to England, through baptism records from Laleham, Middlesex. It was a eureka moment when I came across a letter in the HBC Archives dated 4 February 1786, sent by the company, and addressed to Betty Turnor[20] in which Philip is specifically mentioned as her son. Impoverished, and either widowed or divorced, Betty Turnor had requested fifteen pounds from her son. The secretary of the committee wrote to inform her "that the Draught from Mr. Philip Turnor in favour of Exuperious Turnor for fifteen pounds was paid at this House the second of November 1784."[21] I had discovered an unmapped route; now I knew the name of his mother, and that of another relative, Exuperious—a curious name! I had come across that strange name before, in the papers of a distant relative, Madeline Turnor.

Madeline emigrated from Staffordshire, England, with her family in 1911 when she was twelve, arriving in Golden, BC, then taking a riverboat to the Windermere Valley. She was a spirited, energetic, adventurous woman. She, like Philip, had a love of the untamed country and became one of the first female big game guides in Canada. She worked on ranches in the Windermere valley, trekked by horseback through the mountains from Radium to Banff, hunted bear up the Alaska coast one summer, and guided hunting and fishing parties. Her father, a retired doctor when he came to Canada, was named Phillip [sic] Watson Turnor and her brother was Gerald Exuperious Turnor. When Madeline settled into an easier life in Windermere in 1980, she turned to a different sort of trekking, making her way through the collection of family papers she had discovered in her tool shed. Recognizing the bearing these would have on the history of her ancestor, Philip Turnor, she wrote to the Hudson's Bay Company in Winnipeg in 1980:

> I am in the process of going through masses of old Turnor letters, bills, and manuscripts. Find it interesting but rather exhausting—found all this had been packed away in a box in the tool shed! Some of it goes back to early 1700, when Michael and Experious [sic] were Keepers in Beechwood Forest and had to keep account of game killed for sale to their customers.[22]

These two-hundred-year-old papers had travelled over the ocean, up Canadian rivers, and into a little tool shed in the Windermere Valley. But all that remains is this one extracted fragment from her letter. The letter itself disappeared from the HBC Archives and, more sadly, the "masses" of papers were all burned to ashes in a fire in 1980 that consumed Madeline's house and her tool shed.

However, there is no question that Madeline believed she was related to Philip Turnor and that Michael and Exuperious Turnor were part of that history. With so little to go on, was it possible to reconstruct Philip's early years? These boxes of papers going back to the 1700s would surely have divulged Philip's lineage and his connection to Staffordshire. "Exuperious" and "Beechwood Forest" were strong clues, and through months of searching genealogical sites and then travelling to Staffordshire I unlocked a few, but not all, of the answers.

Exuperious has been a first or second name in the Turnor family since the medieval period, largely, though not entirely, associated with Turnors in Staffordshire and Derbyshire.[23] The names, Exuperious and Michael Turnor, appear frequently in County Court Sessions for Staffordshire. As gamekeepers in Needwood Forest (which Madeline must have mistaken as Beechwood), they were often called to testify against poachers—not just ordinary poachers, but poachers of royal deer, for Needwood was a royal hunting ground, and both Exuperious and Michael were keepers of Eland Lodge, the hunting lodge of King George III (1760–1820).[24] Now, so to speak, I had arrived at the source of the river: Philip's father or grandfather must have originated in Staffordshire.

Exuperious was Keeper by 1775 and Michael a deputy Keeper by 1777. This was a time of tremendous economic, geographic, and social change; it was the era of enclosures, "a process by which land farmed in common was divided into enclosed fields."[25] Although the King's Land (the Duchy of Lancaster) and Eland Lodge were protected, other land in the area was being enclosed. Looking out from Eland Lodge at the old Venison Oak on which many a fine stag had been hung for gralloching (dressing), Exuperious and Michael must have wondered how these changes would affect their livelihood.

In the past, open fields had been worked in strips by tenants of a manor, and the common lands had been used to graze cattle, sheep and geese that roamed freely. Exuperious and Michael probably farmed as well as tended to the King's Land. But now land was being cleared and hedged in. Surveys were called for, roads and footpaths were laid out, and farms were divided by hedgerows and walls. Many of the poor cottagers lost everything and became homeless, but some small farmers saw this as an opportunity to work for themselves. Large landowners could buy up land to expand their estates or make a claim for an award of land by Act of Parliament. Mr. Lane, in King's Bromley, acquired a large estate and, some time in the 1790s, Michael became his land agent, although he continued still at Eland Lodge. It is evident that Michael had surveying skills, for he was asked to redesign Mr. Lane's roadway. Old Michael's son, Michael (1792–1871), and his grandson, Exsuperius [sic] Weston Turnor (1831–1909) carried on the family tradition and became land agents and surveyors. Old Michael, according to one writer of the history of this county, was "the most picturesque figure" of the time in this area. Intelligent, literate, and skilled, he was described in his prime as "an old man of gentle manners, as became his birth."[26] Both surveying and farming ran in the family.

I travelled to Staffordshire in 2011 and took all the small roadways to King's Bromley, Abbot's Bromley, Bagot's Wood, Needwood Forest. I visited a ninety-five-year-old resident who remembered stories about Michael Turnor, and I heard about the Manor Houses, the gate house, the areas of land that Michael might have surveyed. I went to Eland Lodge, now an equestrian school, and saw there the original hunting lodge, a low red brick building with barns and stables around it (Figure 3). Entry to the lodge was through a courtyard where, I imagined, in King George's day, hunters would ride up with their dogs and their kill. Perhaps the venison oak once stood there. A rustic doorway, made from nine-inch-wide plain planks, entered

Figure 3. Eland Wood, Staffordshire, England, Estate of the Duchy of Lancaster, and formerly the hunting lodge of King George III.

straightway into a kitchen. On a doorjamb there, I was shown King George III's insignia, a crown and GR, stamped there with a hot iron. I looked out at the landscape—what a fine hunting ground it must have been. As I walked out into the fields, I imagined that Philip had one day been there, or at least his father had.

Information about Exuperious, the Keeper, peters out after 1776. He may have moved south, perhaps squeezed out by the enclosures. Perhaps he ended up in Lambeth, Surrey (a farming area in the 1770s) where I discovered the will of an Exuperious Turnor who died in 1836.[27] Lambeth, across the River Thames from the city of London, is not far from Laleham, where Philip farmed, or from St. Mary's Church in Battersea, where Philip later married, or from Rotherhithe, where he worked upon his return from Canada. Is it possible that Philip and Exuperious both left Staffordshire to work in the south? It would not have been difficult for Exuperious to collect the fifteen pounds for Philip's mother from the Hudson's Bay Company offices on Fenchurch, just across London Bridge.

At any rate, it would seem that Philip Turnor was related to these Turnors. He would have been of the same generation as Michael of Needwood and Exuperious of Lambeth, Surrey, but whether they were brothers or cousins is uncertain. A connection with this family would certainly explain Philip Turnor's mathematical and surveying interests and talents, not to mention his well-noted hunting and shooting skills, which may have been honed on visits to Needwood.

Nothing more is known about his mother Betty. However, finding her name in the HBCA records led me to Exuperious in Lambeth and then to the discovery of a christening record for Philip, not in Laleham, Middlesex, but in Battersea. Philip Turnor, born to John and Betty Turnor, was christened on 26 November 1752 in the parish of St. Mary, Battersea.[28]

That such a distinguished gentleman as William Wales should recommend Philip, and that the HBC Masters should praise Philip as "a man of education and character and of manners,"[29] strongly suggests he had been given a good schooling, particularly in mathematics and astronomy. Unfortunately, there is no record that he was taught by Wales himself. His expertise in farm management and his skilled marksmanship fit with the Staffordshire Turnors' occupations as gamekeepers and land agents. He could have been self-taught in mathematics and astronomy like many young men, including William Wales himself. Philip mentioned in his journals that he had "an intent to go to the South Seas."[30] Would this have been with William Wales and Captain Cook in 1772-1775? He may have attended lectures describing such travels in 1776 or read Wales's "General Observations Made at Hudson's Bay," which came out in 1772, and his "Observations on a Voyage with Captain Cook," published in 1777. Was Turnor bold enough to have introduced himself to William Wales at this time?

Whatever the specific facts might be, Philip must have been a relative of Michael and Exuperious, as Madeline Turnor believed, and, while Michael Turnor was just stepping into his role as deputy keeper at Eland Lodge in Needwood Forest in 1777, Philip Turnor was to sail for Rupert's Land the next year. Michael's Staffordshire world narrowed over the next fifty years. Trees were cut down, diminishing the forests, hedgerows were erected, and roads and canals were constructed, all dividing and parcelling the open land. Philip, across the ocean in Rupert's Land, was about to map an immense territory relatively unknown to Europeans. Both, in their separate places, played out their destinies at a pivotal period of the environmentally and economically changing worlds of eighteenth-century England and Rupert's Land. ✳

Setting Sail for Rupert's Land, *May 1778*

Turnor likely went to the Hudson Bay Company's offices to discuss matters with Wales and committee members before sailing. He would have been welcomed into the Board Room, dark with mahogany shelves, oak wainscoting, and central table, the windows heavily draped in brown. The first governor, Prince Rupert, in his ruffles and wig, looked placidly down from his portrait, 108 years after his issuing of the first charter. There were maps on the wall and, no doubt, a world globe, but recent maps were rolled up and secreted away. The post journals, in their green or grey or red marbled covers, with the private business and personal notes from the chiefs at York Factory, Moose Fort, Albany Fort, Churchill, Severn River, and Eastmain—names with which Turnor needed to familiarize himself—would not have been made available, for they were locked away in vaults, as was all the correspondence. A central bookcase displayed the company's library—Busching's *Geography* (1762), Carver's *Travels through the Interior Parts of North-America…1766, 1767, and 1768* (1778), Cook's *Voyages* (1771), three copies of those, and Atkinson's *Epitome of the Art of Navigation* (1686). Around all was an aura of enterprise and secrecy, although in four years, when Wegg became governor, he would usher in an era of openness and sharing of information.

Though the maps were not seen by the public in order to guard the company's trade, Turnor would have been shown Andrew Graham's map of the Nelson-Saskatchewan-Lake Winnipeg region drawn between 1773 and 1775.[31] This map was only three or four years old. Graham was back in London now, in retirement, and perhaps Turnor had an opportunity to talk with him. Graham had drawn the known southern track along the Hayes River-Cross Lake route, although the chart was flawed because of his inaccurate placement of Lakes Winnipeg and Manitoba. However, Graham's was the first map to designate the western Indigenous lands, such as those inhabited by the Northern Keskachewans (Beaver) and the Western Assenpoets (Assiniboine), which he sectioned off geometrically almost like provinces on contemporary maps. Though the appearance of the map was European in its organization, it clearly showed that this land was occupied by different Indigenous nations. Perhaps Turnor also read Moses Norton's map (circa 1760), with its more informal nomenclature: "Inds clod in marten skins" and "ye track to Henday's tent."[32] Finally, he would have taken down Samuel Hearne's 1775 map, for in 1774 Hearne had travelled to, established, and mapped Cumberland House, the very place Turnor had been hired to survey immediately upon his arrival.[33] He stared down at the notations, imagining himself, in just over three months, paddling up the huge North (Nelson) River, thrilling to the thought of being the first to meticulously, accurately chart this route.

He was advised of all company procedures—that he would ship out on the *King George*, and, given his prominent position, would mess with the Captain, just as he would dine with the chief factors and masters at the various forts or posts in Rupert's Land, that his title would be Inland Surveyor, the first ever for the Hudson's Bay Company, and that his pay would be fifty pounds per annum. He had signed on for "only" three years.[34] Originally there was talk of a five-year stint, but, after hearing Wales's tales of the North, Turnor may have hesitated. Wales had a way with words. He would have awed him with descriptions of the aurora borealis and the icebergs, but would have warned him about the extremes in climate. You will be greeted, he would advise, "by hoards of voracious mosquitoes and sandflies…millions of them…so that it is impossible either to speak or breathe."[35] Wales would have sent a shiver down his back with stories of the extreme cold temperatures, of rooms so cold that the bedding froze and the bedboards were slabs of ice. Ice had to be hacked off the walls of the rooms. Everything froze, from the whiskers on one's face to the ink used to write daily reports. "It was so cold," Wales remarked, "I carried a half-pint of brandy, perfectly fluid, into the open air, and in less than two minutes it was as thick as treacle."[36]

Turnor had five weeks to prepare. Perhaps he returned to Laleham to say his good-byes, stopping in at the Three Horseshoes for a farewell pint with friends. His mother, no doubt, was worried about his welfare so far away, and concerned, too, for herself, as her son had been generous in his support of her. Was there a woman he wanted to say goodbye to? Then he was off to London to organize his clothing and books for the journey. He ordered woollen trousers and an overcoat to be made, and, most importantly, he arranged for surveying instruments and books. Wales procured the astronomical books that Turnor would need in Rupert's Land, the *Nautical Almanac and Astronomical Ephemeris* as well the *Requisite Tables,* and they discussed other equipment. Turnor requested a sextant and a watch from the company and, for his surveying box, had ordered two bottles of quicksilver, used to establish the artificial horizon, and parallel glasses, which would protect the quicksilver from the weather when observations were being taken.[37] A watch was provided by Deputy Governor Wegg, under stipulation that it was to be returned to the company when Turnor returned to England.[38] A field compass, thermometer, a set of drafting instruments, ruler, pens, pencils, sticks of India ink, watercolour paints, rough paper, and the precious Whatman's cream-coloured wove paper. All this needed to be bought and packed away securely.[39]

The *King George II*, the *Prince Rupert*, and the *Seahorse*, the three ships commissioned by the Hudson's Bay Company, were set to sail on 29 May from Gravesend, below London (Figure 4). Turnor was on board the *King George II* early that morning when she made the

Figure 4. Three HBC ships, *King George II, Seahorse,*
and *Prince Rupert IV*, at Gravesend, 1769.

customary gun salute in recognition of the Governor and several
members of the committee who had come down from London to
see their ships off and to pay the one-month's advance to the crew.
All was ready when, as Captain Fowler wrote in his log, "about 10
Captain Christopher [of the *Seahorse*] came on board and reported
his Ship to be very leaky...and [he] was ordered to proceed with the
Seahorse into Mr. Randall's dock in order to stop the Leak."[40] Impa-
tiently, Turnor waited five days while the *Seahorse* was under repair.
Finally, on 3 June they were ready to sail.

With stiff winds blowing, Turnor watched as the city grew smaller,
the Tower and St. Paul's dome blurring to grey dots. They headed up
the coast toward Yarmouth where a hired armed merchant ship was
waiting to escort their fleet to the Orkney Islands and a further hundred leagues west. The ship's crew would be keeping a wary eye out for
attack. England's ships were vulnerable as they travelled the North Sea
and the Atlantic, not only to the usual pirates and press gangs, but to
enemy Dutch, French, and Spanish ships, as those countries, earlier
that year, had entered the war supporting the American colonies.

They reached the Orkney Islands on 11 June, their final stop en
route to Rupert's Land. Turnor could see the low-lying isles, seventy
in number, like prehistoric green whales mounding out of the grey
seas. Mainland, where they headed for harbour, looked lush from afar,

Figure 5. Login's Well, Stromness, Orkney.

but was stony and barren of trees, and curiously marked by the huge stone pinnacles erected by Neolithic peoples, older even than the Pyramids of Egypt.[41] They anchored in Stromness harbour. The grey and sand-coloured stone houses stood tall and austere, their gable ends towards the sea, offering the least exposure to the sea's onslaught.

Login's Well, the company's watering spot, was directly opposite the inn where Turnor stayed for these two weeks (Figure 5). The narrow cobbled streets coiled out and around the village. Two or three hundred families huddled together in these houses, but when the Hudson Bay ships came in, the people congregated from all over the island and there was a buzz of activity during the day and dances on the streets at night. Turnor and Captain Fowler were entertained at The Haven, the home of David Geddes, the Hudson's Bay agent. Possibly they were taken up to The Whitehouse, where Captain William Bligh dined two years later on his return in the *Resolution* from James Cook's fatal voyage in the Pacific.[42]

Orkney men were interviewed for positions in Rupert's Land, and five new sailors and fifteen labourers were hired on for the fur trade. The Orcadians were considered the best in the business—hardy, upright, dependable, and used to harsh conditions and meagre, unvaried food. At six pounds per annum, the company offered more than these men could scrape together if they stayed home. In five years they might have enough to buy a fishing boat for themselves. The Orkney men always said they were going "north" but, at 59° North, Orkney, in fact, was over half a degree farther north than Churchill and two degrees farther north of York Factory, though its climate was more temperate.

On 23 June, Captain Fowler entered in his log that the *King George* and her sister ships "went out into the Road," the established route of travel. The next day they hauled in the longboat and "made clear for sailing." There was not much to see except league after league of grey rolling ocean. Occasionally they saw the sails of their own sister ships, once a boat of Davis Strait fishermen and then the tip of Greenland—only these events broke the monotony. But on 19 July Turnor had his first view of the icebergs that Wales had so vividly described, and watched with amazement and fear as the *King George* came within one hundred feet of an iceberg higher than the mast of the ship (Figure 6). Fowler apprehensively noted in his log, "it is a little uncommon to see isles of ice at this distance from the land."[43] The next day, when the sun shone brilliantly, Turnor could not believe the monumental whiteness that surrounded them.

They sailed for three of the finest days the captain had ever seen in that part of the ocean. But on 23 July Captain Fowler found himself faced with "a body of ice from the NE to SW & no appearance of a safe passage between it to the Island of Resolution." The weather was bad, with lightning and winds, rain and fog; many times they had to grapple onto the ice to prevent damage to the ships. They searched for days for open water. Finally, on 30 July they were in the Hudson Straits, but still "passing great quantities of ice." In twenty-two years of sailing to Rupert's Land and back, this was the most difficult journey Fowler had encountered. Generally a steady, matter-of-fact log keeper, Fowler now found himself resorting to superlatives: on 9 August he exclaimed, "we have passed the greatest quantity [of ice] I ever saw in Hudson's Strait before"; on 15 August they were

Figure 6. "Ship Among the Icebergs."

in Hudson Bay and he commented, "These 24 hours have had the wildest weather I ever saw in Hudson's Bay"; on 16 August he wrote, "The greatest part of these 24 hours we have had hard gales & very dirty weather. The sea at times has been very steep & irregular, which occasioned our shipping a good deal of water. I hope we have had the height of the gales…I believe no man in the Service ever saw such weather as we have had for the last 60 hours."[44]

What a relief it was when, on 24 August, they anchored in Five Fathom Hole and saluted, with seven guns, York Fort, the overseas headquarters of the Hudson's Bay Company.

2.

First Assignments

York Fort (Kickewaskahikun), Rupert's Land, *Fall 1778*

Turnor disembarked from the *King George* on 25 August and, in the longboat, sailed the seven miles to York Factory (Figure 7). From this distance out, he could see clearly the tracks of two great rivers, the Nelson to the north and the Hayes to the south. As he approached, the factory took shape on the slip of land between the two rivers, facing the Hayes. Eighty-nine days ago he was watching the noisy, ship-crowded Thames recede, and now, here in Rupert's Land, he was looking straight ahead into the mouth of the Hayes River, with nothing to see but the river flowing to a vanishing point under a full arc of sky that stretched from west to east. No bridges, church spires, or coal spumes. Only grey scudding clouds, tawny grass swaying with the wind and, beyond that, stunted black spruce and yellowing tamarack. Turnor looked away from the mesmerizing river to the wharf coming into view and saw the welcoming group of Hudson's Bay men and Cree families standing atop the steep clay bank sixty feet above the river. To the west of the wharf he noted with curiosity the brown haphazard line of inverted v-shaped Cree tents, and then, farther back, protected by the stockades and battery, the unexpected orderliness and seeming solidness, the Britishness, of the factory itself. The effect on him was of a startling brightness, a yellow-white, punctuated by the brilliant red and white Hudson's Bay Company ensign flying sternly, authoritatively, straight out, set against the vastness of primordial green and grey landscape.

Figure 7. York Factory in the 1770s.

Sixty-six days at sea. He had quickly enough found his sea legs aboard the *King George*. Where now were his land legs? The ground beneath him rolled and heaved like waves. His drunken walk up the embankment to the factory was made more unsteady by the spongy permafrost that gave way under his every step.

He, along with the sloop master, John Turner,[1] had been invited to mess with the chief factor, Humphrey Marten. Marten was some twenty years older than Turnor and had been here at the Fort the year that Turnor was born and would stay, off and on depending on his gout, stomach disorder, and other illnesses, until 1786. Marten was well respected by the company, although he did not hesitate to speak his mind and there were tensions with some of the chiefs at other forts. This night Turnor no doubt heard plenty about the independent-minded Samuel Hearne, chief at Churchill, whom Marten accused of drawing trade away from York. Hearne had replied to the London Committee that the accusations were "of so peevish a nature as not to claim the notice of my pen."[2] Turnor would have to sort out the politics of power quickly. He was not surprised to see Marten's Cree wife in his quarters, as he was aware that the company, unofficially, allowed the factor and officers that privilege. This, too, was an issue that Turnor would mull over. Only nine years earlier, Ferdinand Jacobs, chief factor of York at the time, had commented, "the worst brothel house in London is not so common a stew as the men's house in this factory."[3] Jacobs had taken measures to improve the situation, but Marten was not so strict. He had taken country wives. Pawpitch, his first wife, had been well treated by him, and he had been greatly saddened by her death seven years ago, noting her passing in his journal—not a common practice among the officers, who usually did not mention or name their wives. Marten's older son, in fact, was being educated in England, and Marten had another country wife and two more children.[4]

The meal at the fort was a welcome feast after many days on board of oatmeal and boiled mutton. The Cree hunters brought in fresh venison. There were delicacies of caribou tongue and heart, of roast goose and fresh fish. Most of all Turnor savoured the greens, the turnips and the potatoes, so small they were the size of an egg, all fresh from the gardens at the fort. He would soon be craving this on his journey inland. A dram of spirits, a mug of factory-brewed beer, and certainly French brandy completed his first Rupert's Land meal. In the August warmth, surrounded by the congeniality of English and Scots company officers, it was not too different from society in London.

The next day Turnor began his work. Surveying the fort was his first assignment. For some time Marten had been concerned about its deterioration and had hoped that a new structure would be ordered by the Governors. Turnor's first task was to draw a plan of the fort, designating the buildings and the low land, and make recommendations to London. The factory had been established in 1684, but between 1686 and 1713 there had been a number of battles between France and England for control of the forts along Hudson Bay and James Bay. The French held Fort Nelson between 1697 and 1713. Finally, when England was victorious and awarded ownership with the Treaty of Utrecht in 1713, Captain James Knight was sent as governor to rebuild the factory. He was appalled at its condition and in 1715 he moved the site half a mile downstream. During the next few years he erected the buildings that Turnor was now asked to survey. While not in prime condition due to periodic flooding and a precarious foundation on permafrost, Turnor concluded that, with some repairs and one flanker of men's quarters rebuilt, the fort could last a few more years. When the packet of letters and journals from York Factory to the London Committee was sealed on 3 September, Turnor's survey and recommendations were included. Marten would not get his new buildings.

Turnor's survey (see Plate 1) showed a one-hundred-foot-square structure, called the factory, consisting of four walls, or curtains as they were called, with four bastions protruding from each corner. The men's quarters were situated in this area. The buildings were constructed of logs and plastered on the outside. An early etching by Samuel Hearne suggested a two-storey factory. The powder magazine was a dome-shaped stone structure built in the centre of the inner yard of the factory. Outside this compact complex were a number of garden areas where they grew what produce they could in the short summers (greens, turnips, potatoes). A log fence stockade surrounded this area. Protruding like arrowheads from the two front corners of the stockade were a group of work rooms: the blacksmith's shop, the cooperage, the shipwright's and the carpenter's shops, the Governor's cookroom, and another warehouse, of which there were three in the area for storing furs and trading items. There were more gardens, a cowshed, and probably a chicken coop, as well as pig and sheep pens. Though not noted on Turnor's survey, there was a horse kept at the fort, well loved by the men. However, with insufficient feed available, he died within the year.

Around all this was another protective stockade, bringing the dimensions to 312 by 288 feet (slightly shorter than a football field but one and a half times as wide). The battery, with thirteen heavy cannon, faced the wharf and the Hayes River from where the threat of an attack would most likely come, and come it did from the French just four years later. A trail along the fort's left was noted as "the trading path," leading past one of the warehouses, the carpenter's workshop, and the shipwright's building, up to the factory itself. The Home Guard Cree would be camped in this area, near the river.

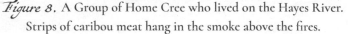

Figure 8. A Group of Home Cree who lived on the Hayes River.
Strips of caribou meat hang in the smoke above the fires.

The Home Guard, so called because they stayed near the fort,
supplied the HBC men with country provisions, primarily caribou,
geese, and fish, and with skins and furs for clothing (Figure 8). The
Cree men were essential guides, steersmen, and interpreters for the
inland travels. The women made and mended clothes, constructed
snowshoes, set traps and fishnets, and also accompanied the men
on some inland expeditions. It was not uncommon for the women
to develop relationships with the master and the officers, and often
these were political and social arrangements designed to promote
closer trade alliances with the company. The company officers sought
out women for sexual reasons, but also out of need for their skills in
everything from paddling, guiding, and translating to making clothes
and preparing food. Some relationships were based on genuine affection and lasted a lifetime; others were short-lived, particularly if
the HBC servant returned home.[5]

A few days before he was to leave on his journey inland, Turnor
was tested by an adventure that sharply reminded him of the diligence
he would need to survive in this country. On Saturday, 5 September,

Turnor offered, with five other men, to deliver venison and greens to the men anchored at Five Fathom Hole who were preparing to set sail for England the next day. After a good visit, the six men started back to York Factory at about 9:00 p.m. Edward Luitet[6] was the steersman, and the other men, thinking this was an easy journey of seven miles, fell asleep. A few hours elapsed before Turnor sensed something very wrong. The waves were rolling as they would on a large body of water; he dipped his finger into the water and tasted the salt of the Bay. Instantly he knew they were in danger. Ed Luitet, confused and chagrined, said he had not detected a shift in wind. They were now out in Hudson Bay, two hours away from land. They had no compass with them, but Turnor, using his knowledge of the stars and taking advantage of the flood tide, got them turned around and headed back to land. Several hours later, early morning light on the horizon behind them confirmed they were going towards the mainland. However, they had sailed north and were now headed around Marsh Point and into the North River (the Nelson) rather than the Hayes.

The next morning Marten was informed that the boat with Turnor and his men had not returned. He recorded in his journal, "This information gave me great uneasiness, as we have not the least intelligence of her." He immediately sent some of the Home Guard men out to the North River where he thought Turnor's group might have mistakenly gone and there they were found, all well, but cold and hungry. After some cheese and bread, they started back, but it was not until 8:00 p.m. on Sunday night, nearly 24 hours later, that the men arrived at the fort. As Marten summed it up in his notes to the London Committee, "Wind seems to be the occasion of their mistake, had it blowed strong at W, SW, or S, they must have been lost. Blessed be God it ended no worse."[7]

On 8 September Marten wrote in his journal, "got every thing ready for Mr. Turnor's departure."[8] The tailor had spent a number of days making clothes for the inland journey and, along with the woollen trousers, shirts, and overcoat with which he arrived, Turnor would take with him a moose-skin coat, a couple of pairs of caribou-skin trousers, and a beaver overcoat and mittens for the winter at Cumberland House. It would soon become apparent that he had neglected to request one particular item.

All "necessarys" had been stowed away in the canoes, including provisions (cheese, biscuits, a couple of cakes of gingerbread, brandy, a couple of loaves of sugar, some caribou tongues and flesh), gear (guns, gun powder, shot, hatchet, cooking pot, and blankets) and, most importantly, Turnor's instrument box with "the sextant, two thermometers, one bottle of quick silver (it being parted into two bottles), the parallel glasses," and his "box containing the books."[9]

Two canoes were readied. They were fragile looking to Turnor's eyes, much smaller and lighter than the voyageur canoes from Montreal that could carry a crew of ten or more men and could handle up to four tons of cargo. The Cree had by necessity designed a smaller canoe for use on their river systems of shallow, fast water with many portages. These canoes, about eighteen feet long, would each carry only three men. Constructed of cedar, covered with birch bark, or birch rind as it was called, and sealed with spruce gum, they were tougher than they looked and could be repaired along the way if necessary with extra birch rind and spruce gum that was kept under the bow. For the past thirty-five years of inland exploration the Europeans had employed Indigenous men and their canoes, never learning the craft of construction themselves. This was now a problem as finding dependable guides who would travel when the HBC men needed them was difficult. There had been various suggestions, one being Hearne's proposal of bringing prefabricated wooden boats from England. The company tried this in 1777, but the Cree refused to use them. Robert Longmoor,[10] the Hudson's Bay employee whom Turnor was soon to meet on his inland journey, was the first to learn the craft of canoe building, but he was unable to keep up with the demand, so Turnor's canoes had probably been provided by his Cree guides. Only a few company men had experience in canoes or on these rivers.

There were three tracks, or roads, to the interior: the Upper Track on the Nelson River, which Hearne had taken in 1775 and Turnor was now preparing to map, and the Middle and Lower Tracks along the Hayes River. The route commonly used by the Indigenous people to travel to and from the Saskatchewan River was the Middle Track, which went up the Hayes, through Cross River to the Summerberrry River, and into the Saskatchewan River.[11] It was shallow in places and, in fact, on his 1774 journey Hearne reported that his guides advised him to unload some of the heavy goods such as the bags of shot and

send them back.[12] The Lower Track, a deeper route, branched off
to the south, going through Oxford Lake and on to Lake Winnipeg,
but it was considered a more difficult and dangerous route than the
Middle Track. However, in the late 1700s it would become the most
travelled because it could accommodate the York boats,[13] and Turnor
would play a role in surveying that route.

On this, his first journey, Turnor was to chart the Upper Track,
the shortest of the three routes, it being the "general opinion of all
the natives in company that that will be the best way to get goods up
inland in large canoes, there being no obstructions except carrying
places."[14] Marten laid out Turnor's task:

> The Committee being very desirous to have the latitudes
> and longitudes of all their settlements properly ascertained,
> also their perspective distances from each regularly adjust-
> ed, you will be particularly careful to give them full satis-
> faction on those heads; and if time would permit, to make
> sketches of the rivers, lakes, etc you pass through, but by
> no means to retard your journey this fall on that account.[15]

The London Committee requested the earliest "intelligence" of
Turnor's work, and that "every transaction be executed with the
deepest secrecy." They further ordered that "for fear of accidents in
coming to the Fort duplicates should be taken of all material papers,
and transmitted to the Fort by different channels, each to be entrusted to Englishmen only."[16] The interior was a business battleground, a
Cold War in more ways than one. The Montreal-based traders were
the enemy, outnumbering the Hudson's Bay men about three hundred
to fifteen or twenty,[17] and they used any means they could to draw
out information about routes, trading goods, mapmaking, and new
settlements, and to entice the Bay men to their ranks.

Turnor, along with every employee, had been asked to swear
formally that he would not discuss company matters with outsiders.
Although the 1670 charter gave trading rights over this land to the
Hudson's Bay Company, the independent trading companies from
Montreal had made great inroads along the Saskatchewan River and
were threatening the Bay's supremacy. Both sides used trickery and
bribery to win over the Indigenous people to their trade, but the

Montreal traders were known to use fear tactics and force at times. Marten had written with frustration to the Governors that these traders "buy up [from the Cree] all the food they can," they falsely tell the Cree that the Hudson's Bay men have smallpox, they lead them to believe that there is no brandy or tobacco for trading, and that the ships are not coming. Marten finished: "Gentlemen, there is not a species of villainy except down right murdering your servants [that] they stick at."[18]

The next stage in the development of the Hudson's Bay Company's enterprise depended on Turnor's efforts and expertise. Since 1670 the company had paid little attention to the largest portion of the 1.5 million square miles of territory from Labrador to the Rockies (forty per cent of the land mass of Canada today) that had been granted them by King Charles II. Surveying the interior would lay down the most efficient routes, aid them in their selection of locations for inland settlements, and reinforce their presence in this land. Turnor worked in the best interests of the company, but he was equally attracted to the challenge and excitement of charting this unmapped territory.

JOURNAL TWO

York Fort National Historical Site

August 2005

The small eight-seater airplane flew low, following the grey Nelson River as if it were a highway, dipping over to the Hayes River as we approached York Factory (Figure 9). There was no runway. Incredibly, the plane just set down lightly on a small gravel spit across from the Fort. The clouds were grey and scudding, just as Turnor described them, and the wind was blowing up waves on the Hayes. Across the river I could see the clay bank furrowed from erosion. A skiff waited to take us across to the factory, but before I got in, I

Figure 9. York Factory on Hayes River.

leaned down at the river's edge to scoop up a handful of grey pebbles, mementos of my ancestor's presence in this landscape.

I was unprepared for the stunning white of the factory buildings standing so properly and pristinely against the green spruce, the fawn-green sedge grass, and the brown river. This would have been the site that my ancestor set foot on in 1789 when he returned from England for his second and last stay in Rupert's Land. When he arrived for the first time in 1778, the location would have been one-half mile farther downstream towards Hudson Bay, but erosion had forced the company to build anew farther upstream in 1788. Was he as surprised as I was to see a building so sturdily British, the land so green yet wild, the view so wide and unbroken? I looked at this silent, solitary, white edifice and imagined what Turnor might have seen and heard in 1778: a factory abuzz with activity—hammering and sawing in the carpenter's and the shipwright's shops; the metallic banging and the steaming of wooden slats in the cooperage; the smells of baking and roasting in the cookroom; and the rhythmic sounds of sawing firewood. Amidst the grunts of the men as they lifted and loaded goods at the wharf, he would have heard the unfamiliar language of the Cree in their camp near the trading trail and their bartering in the trading house.

After our guides checked the grounds for polar bears, we scrambled up the steep bank and onto a boardwalk laid across the spongy marsh land. We were mostly left on our own to prowl around a few of the main rooms of the factory that were opened to us, the remainder being deemed unsafe. The building is 174 years old, and there is no reason to dress it up as hardly anyone comes here. Though a National Historic Site, it is only accessible by plane or canoe.

The impressively large front door with black hinges no longer opened to let in the light and the travellers to the trading room: instead we entered at the back through a smaller door. The large room was almost bare, but as we looked up at the massive beams we could see their unusual construction: each main stud was bolted into the beam with an iron bar with a slit in it to allow for movement and shifting on the permafrost. We climbed to the second floor and saw a multitude of tables set out with all sorts of objects: tin dishes, animal skins stretched on frames, rusted traps, chains, axes, and other tools, cannon and cannon balls. Nothing was labeled; nothing was put away in glass cases. It was as it was. I climbed to the cupola from where I looked out on the Hayes and along the boardwalk, musing that this was the sight that Philip would have seen over 200 years ago: the river, grey-brown and strongly flowing into the Bay, the Hudson's Bay flagpole off to the right, the boreal forest to the back. It was a lonely, quiet scene now. I was glad that it was not tidy and organized, that there were no placards or tourist directions. Part of the thrill of being there was its remote, time-worn, unpretentious reality.

This is where Turnor's adventures began (or, at least, half a mile downstream). Fourteen years later he would reverse the direction and sail home from this exact spot. In between he mapped this country, west, south, and north, and he mapped himself as well in his journals and letters. I was soon to discover that his journals dealt mostly in distances, directions, portages, weather conditions, and the business of trade; they revealed, on the surface, disappointingly little of his personality. That, of course, was who he was: a man of science, a surveyor, fascinated with numbers, calculations and figures. There were moments, though, when I would catch glimpses of his inner territory. *

3.

"Near Being in The Wars"

Cumberland House, *September 1778 to March 1779*

1778

Septr 9th Wednesday at 8 AM Imbarked at York Fort for Cumberland House in Company with Geo. Hudson, Robt
Davey, Will Lutit and two Indians to steer our two
Canoes, was Saluted by 3 Guns from the Factory and
proceeded down Hayes's River to goe round the Point
of Marsh with intent to proceed by the way of Nel-
sons or North River. At 11 AM put on shore at the
Point of Marsh, the swell being so heavy was not able
to stand it, was joined by Sixteen Canoes of Indians
which are going from the Factory to their Familys by
the way of North River—wind variable Easterly clear
weather.[1]

Turnor's first day in a canoe on the Nelson River was unre-
markable. The journal entry exhibited his signature style—
the reporting of essential detail. That was his job. Ahead
of him he had 675 miles of river. He was thankful to have
with him men who had been inland. But he had not come here expecting any favours.

Robert Davey, an Orkneyman, had been inland three times and
could handle a canoe tolerably well. William Lutit had been in the
service for eight years,[2] so he too was experienced; a bulldog of a
man but a bit too careless, thought Turnor. George Hudson, three
years in the service, had been recruited from the Grey Coat Hospital

Figure 10. Eighteenth-century surveyor's field compass by George Adams, London, similar to a compass used by Turnor.

School in London, where he had learned the basics of reading, writing, mathematics, and navigation. He was just seventeen, a good, strong lad whom Turnor took to immediately, welcoming the opportunity to tutor him in practical astronomy along the way.

Metunekeshick and Nepinnoathink, their two Cree guides, were excellent steersmen, the best Marten could hire. Though the Bay men were becoming more canoe savvy, they still could not read the rapids, shoals, and turns or locate the portages the way the Cree guides could, nor could they repair so deftly the damaged canoes with the wattup (spruce roots), rolls of birch bark, and spruce gum. Turnor knew how to read maps and read the galaxies of stars, but he did not yet know how to get himself safely to Cumberland House, how to read the land and water.

His first day had been no test; they had put up after three hours, still in sight of the factory. But the next day they were on the Nelson River: "2 ½ miles wide very strong current," Turnor wrote in his notes that night.[3] It was a commanding river. As accustomed as he was to outdoor work, his body was not prepared for a day of sitting in a canoe, of paddling and portaging. His mind was overwrought with the multiple tasks he had to do and with the newness and danger that threatened at every curve and rapid in front of him. He was keenly aware that this river could claim lives.

The following day set the course for what was expected—nearly twelve hours of travel. Seated in the middle position in the canoe, Turnor took a track survey of the route as they paddled. He daily noted the time of departure, their location, direction, distances travelled and measurements of rivers, lakes, and falls, topography, latitude and longitude whenever he could, number and distances of carrying places or portages, depth of water when necessary, the weather, the character of the terrain through which they passed in terms of its ability to supply food and wood, and their putting-up time each day. Knowing the approximate speed of the paddlers and the time, he could estimate how far they had traveled. His magnetic compass (Figure 10) may have been difficult to use in the rocking canoe and he may simply have sighted from bow to stern. Periodically he would ascertain his latitude and longitude on land and make adjustments to his directions.[4] It was impossible, as Samuel Hearne had noted on an earlier trip, to manage a canoe, as well as map the track and record the statistics.[5]

1778

September 11th Friday at 7 AM got underway the Current strong
            against us, went 3 Miles and crossed to North side
            the river at 10 ½ AM began to track at Flamborough
            head, the river in this place about 1 ½ Mile wide, went
            4 Miles nearly SW, Latitude by observation 56°57'
            N°…then went 4 Miles nearly SW and 8 Miles WSW
            and passed a great number of small Islands went to
            N° of them all and put up at 6 ¾ PM on the N° side
            the River, the Land on both sides bold and cover'd
            with small Pines…wind SSW light breeze & Clear[6]

He took his first observation for latitude on this day, a straightfor-ward task. The sky was bright and clear and the sun nearly due south when they stopped for a break. He took his sextant out of its mahogany case, set up his artificial horizon, carefully pouring some quicksilver from one of his two bottles into the shallow pan. He placed the parallel glasses, like a two-sided teepee, over the quicksilver to protect it from any wind. He fitted a filter on his telescope and then, holding his sextant firmly in the vertical position, sighted the reflected image of the sun in the quicksilver. He brought the reflected image down to meet the direct image of the sun in the sextant's mirrors, clamped the index arm, and read the vernier scale. This measurement gave him the double meridian altitude of the sun. He had previously calculated the error of his sextant and would have to add that to his measurement. After correcting for refraction and consulting the *Nautical Almanac*

Figure 11. Eighteenth-century brass sextant made by Peter and John Dollond, England, similar to one used by Turnor on his 1790–1792 expedition.[8]

and the *Requisite Tables* he had brought with him, he was able to determine his first latitude by observation at 56°57′ North.[7]

For the next six days, from 11 to 17 September, as they passed from the Upper Limestone Rapids to Kettle Falls (near present-day Gillam, Manitoba), Turnor was initiated into tracking and handing the canoes. The current was strong, the river "crooked," and the banks "as steep as the roof of a house and full of loose rolling stones."[9] There was one falls after another. If he were on top viewing this vista, he might have called it sublime, but here he was in the middle of it and, indeed, diminished by it. He watched the men, who had experienced this before, roll up their trousers and remove their moccasins or rough leather shoes and woollen socks. They attached a line to the bow and the stern of the canoes, put the other end over their shoulders, and hauled against the current for up to seven miles at a stretch, walking along the bank when they could, but mostly wading in the shallow water. The second day was even worse, as they had to hand the canoes. Walking barefoot again in the strong current, the bottom sharp with stones, the rain heavy and cold, the men hung onto the gunwales of the canoes and dragged them against the current. Often they suffered bruised and cut feet that did not heal for days.

Turnor was no help. "For my own part," he wrote, "I wore two pair of English shoes entirely out in the tracking ground in walking a long the shore of which I could not perform above ¾ of the distance

TRACKING ON STEEL RIVER.

Figure 12. Tracking on Steel River.

not being able to stand on the face of the bank." He was unable to go barefoot, his feet not yet hardened to this work. He must have wondered why no one warned him about wearing his English boots. On 17 September he wrote with relief:

> Thursday this morning find we have passed all the tracking ground which is so exceeding bad that no person is able to track that cannot walk without shoes. The banks being exceeding steep in some places people will fall into the face of the bank two or three feet deep occasioned by the banks having given way at the top, being a kind of marl & clay, which appears to waste very fast. Other parts men are often obliged to go a great way into the river that the canoes may have room to pass the shoals.[10]

Chagrined by his own failure, though honest with himself, he put on the woollen socks and moccasins worn by the other men. Ahead

41

of him he knew he had a lot of toughening-up to do, both physically and mentally, if he was going to survive this "bold" land.

Just before reaching Split Lake on 22 September, their fourteenth day out, after paddling eleven miles they came to another falls. Will Lutit took off his moccasins and went a short way into the river to lead the canoe. The river was swift here, and suddenly he was "taken off his legs by the current and carried into the stream."[11] Desperately he held onto the canoe, but was carried farther into the river. The canoe overturned, he grabbed on, and was driven three hundred yards downstream before George Hudson, in the other canoe, could haul him and the overturned canoe to safety on shore. It was a close call.

Later that night, when he had recovered from the drama of the day, Turnor wrote the notes that would later go into his journal entry for the day: "It may be necessary to observe that it is not an unprecedented thing to lead up the falls as it is what must be done almost every hour in the rivers which we passed in this track."[12] Though sounding calm, he wanted the governors, sitting in their comfortable chairs around the board table, to understand the dangers these men faced every day. The many Orkney men, like Lutit, who signed on to serve at York Fort and Churchill Fort, were not afraid of the sea, but the river was a different beast and now that they were being sent inland to bolster the company's trade, they were unnerved. Lutit had braved the rivers a couple of times, but he and others who paddled inland felt that their pay, about six to eight pounds per annum, was poor return for putting their lives on the line. Already some were simply refusing to go.

Turnor matter-of-factly recorded the items lost in the overset canoe (gun, gun powder, shot, hatchet, pot, one pair of trousers, ten pounds of biscuit, two loaves of sugar, deer tongue) and those saved (three bags of clothes, all the blankets, one keg of brandy, a piece of cheese, and a trunk). But when he thought about the near loss of his own equipment and what it would have meant to his work here, he wrote, "my distress of mind on seeing the canoe overset may be much easier imagined than described as the loss of the instruments and books would have been irretrievable for two years at least."[13] To his great relief he still had his sextant, two thermometers, the parallel glasses, and his books, but he had lost one bottle of his precious quicksilver that, fortunately, he had divided into two bottles before they set off.

They continued to the mouth of the Grass River then through Stinking, Egg-gathering, Partridge Crop, and Paint Lakes, arriving on 29 September at Setting Lake, a long, relatively narrow lake with many islands, so named because it was a favoured spot for the Cree to set their fishnets. Here they met with the families of their guides, Metunekeshick and Nepinnoathink. After a grand feast of fish, the Cree men were ready to celebrate—and they began in the middle of the night. In their search for brandy they stumbled drunkenly into the HBC tents and tore them down. The next day they threatened to steal the HBC men's gear. Around noon, as Turnor wrote, "An Indian boy came to the tent and put the gun against it and shot into it, but being luckily loaded only with powder did no other damage than burning a hole in the tent."[14] Finally, about 3 p.m., all was quiet again and by the next day, the Cree guides being sober, they were prepared to carry on the journey.

Turnor had not expected such rowdiness, though the others told him it was common enough. This area was a favourite one for Cree summer camps and Hearne had documented a similar event, "a drunken frollick,"[15] on his 1775 journey. Requested by the governors "to give…his opinion on every matter that may occur" Turnor wrote: "The Honourable Hudson's Bay Company may think it imprudent to give the Indians liquor but without it, it is impossible to get them to do anything."[16] There seemed no way out of this dilemma. The company's competitors had been trading liquor to the inland Cree for the past thirty years, so much so that the Cree wanted to trade for brandy first, leaving some of their furs with the master to trade later for guns and ironworks.[17] Though the HBC was more reluctant than the Montreal traders to provide liquor, business was their priority as well and they could see no other way to compete.

Turnor had to accept this practice, and, consequently, he dealt with the results—undependable guides. The most derogatory word he used to describe the Cree on this occasion and on many others was "troublesome." Chief Factor Humphrey Marten was not so neutral. Concerning another incident, he noted in his journal how displeased he was with a "slothful" group of guides who had not done his bidding:

"God grant the time was come that we could do our own business without the assistance of these wavering, insolent, dilatory people."[18]

Turnor was now two-thirds through his journey to Cumberland House. The remaining twenty-five carrying places slowed them down and the weather turned miserably cold with snow and frost. The sixth of October was a particularly bad day. The river was full of shoals and the canoes had to be led twice by the men, barefoot in freezing water. Turnor had lashed his second and last bottle of quicksilver to the canoe, but, at the forty-ninth carrying place, Will Lutit had taken it out of the canoe, thinking the canoe leaky and in need of repair, intending, no doubt, to place it in the other canoe. At 5 p.m., eighteen miles on the other side of the Lake, Turnor discovered it missing. In spite of gales of freezing rain, Turnor desperately tried to convince the Cree guides to return for it, but they feared the lake would settle over with ice. Now he had no quicksilver for his observations. This was a serious loss. But he had learned two things—to respect the wisdom of the guides and to put small material losses in perspective. He toughened his mind, just as he had his soft English feet.

His guides, in fact, had read the weather accurately. Next morning they broke their way through the ice along the river edges with a pole. They pushed hard now to beat the freeze-up and on 9 October, their thirty-first day out, they reached Cranberry Portage, the height of land for this tract, which took them through Goose River and Goose Lake; on the other side of the watershed the current was now with them as it flowed towards the Saskatchewan River.

On 10 October they again cut through ice with poles and hatchets. Turnor's canoe was considerably damaged by the ice and he baled for an hour before they could stop to repair it. By the end of the day, however, they were at Pine Island Lake (Namew), passing by Sturgeon Landing where they saw Barthélemi Blondeau, a Montreal trader, and six of his men hard at work building a wintering house.[19]

The next day they saw Cumberland House bearing SSW and arrived at 4 p.m. It stirred Turnor when he caught sight of the Hudson's Bay Company flag flying high above the collection of log buildings. This was home for the winter; this was his new life.

With pine walls and plank roofs, the main building here was crude compared to York Factory, but it looked comfortable to Turnor and the men after thirty-three days on the river. Just four years ago, in

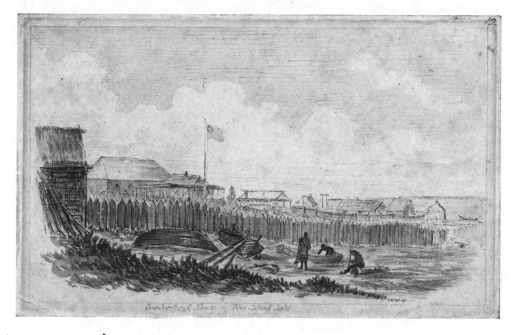

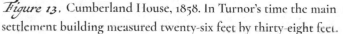

Figure 13. Cumberland House, 1858. In Turnor's time the main settlement building measured twenty-six feet by thirty-eight feet.

1774, Samuel Hearne had chosen this site at the crossroads of Cree territories and at the junction between travel east to the Bay and west to the Rockies. Here was the meeting place for the Swampy Cree whom Turnor had already met from around the Hudson Bay area, the Woodland Cree from farther up river (the Prince Albert area), and the Plains Cree from farther west. The Stone (Assiniboine) people, allies of the Cree, were also trading at Cumberland and Hudson Houses.[20] Cumberland House was the gateway to the west and a strong reminder to the Montreal traders that the company was claiming its monopoly on this territory.

In the main building there were several rooms or apartments, one that housed the master's quarters, another for the men's quarters, a trade room, and an upper-level warehouse. There was also a cook building, a storehouse, and a canoe storage shed. The stone fireplaces throughout were fired up at this time of the year and the parchment windows, made from stretched beaver skins, were shuttered against the cold.[21] Iron cannon balls had been heated and hung around the rooms for extra warmth. The travellers all looked forward to a wooden bed with a tick mattress and bedclothes warmed with hot bricks. First, though, a wash with hot water, and dinner.

William Tomison, an Orcadian who had recently been named inland master, greeted them warmly, unlike William Walker, an Englishman, whose nose was out of joint for having been overlooked for that position. Joseph Hansom, second to Tomison at Cumberland House, had quietly shaken their hands. Tomison was a man who took charge, and Turnor, at first sight, recognized the driving force of the man who was opening the west in the name of the company. Like all the Orkney men he was tough as nails, and had risen quickly from labourer to master at Severn to inland chief. He had travelled extensively on the rivers, could steer the rapids like a Cree guide, could speak their language, and knew their customs. His single-mindedness and his vision for the west would later prove personally perilous for Turnor but, at the present, Turnor thought that Tomison embodied the spirit of this inland venture.[22] Hansom, too, had experience inland on the Churchill and Sturgeon-Weir Rivers and one winter with the Montreal traders. He had been in charge of the house the previous year when Tomison was farther inland, and this year he had recently returned from a successful journey to trade with the Indigenous people in the Athabasca region.

At Cumberland House, the Cree hunters had just brought in fresh moose and geese. There would be a feast to welcome the travellers. As Turnor walked to the mess room the smell of home wafted over him—meat and fowl roasting, fresh potatoes and turnips from the settlement gardens. Bread. Perhaps a pudding with raisins. After a few glasses of wine, the conversation flowed.

"Why don't you outfit a man properly before he takes off on an inland journey?" Turnor asked with a laugh. "I wore out entirely my two pair of English shoes tracking through Limestone Rapids and Kettle Falls!"

Tomison smiled. "You English—you're soft! An Orcadian could teach you a few things. You'd better find moccasins and toughen your feet soon, or you'll not last here."

"I thought it might be the bear that would get me, but it's the river. Will Lutit narrowly escaped being drowned. Bad enough we lost biscuits and brandy, but to lose my quicksilver was hard. There won't be any until the next ship."

"Just a slip, a lapse of attention," mused the quiet Joe Hansom, "and a man can be gone. These waters are murderous."

"There's some bad water on the Saskatchewan, but, if we leave early in the spring, we'll go by snowshoe," Walker said. "We'll see how you do on those shoes, Turnor. Matters are stirring up there between the Cree and the Montreal traders. Those traders are a rough bunch, but they make an impressive wage. I could have had sixty pounds if I wanted to join them."

Soon they turned to political matters, the men wanting news from home that had come in the company's correspondence carried by Turnor. The war with France had spread to India, the West Indies, the British territory of Quebec, and the Thirteen Colonies.

"The American War continues very hot," Tomison relayed, "and we are advised to be on our guard. It is even more important now to have as little intercourse with the Montreal traders as possible. They are a menace, you know, keeping the Indians so drunk that they are easy prey. We have to build more settlements here to bring the trade to our company. Robert Longmoor, the best canoeman in our service, is up-river now and, you, Mr. Turnor, will map the locations of all our new houses. We *must* out-manoeuvre those traders."

Turnor nodded, taken aback by Tomison's passion.[23]

Between 15 October and 5 December Turnor "employed [himself] in making all the observations in [his] power for longitude, as likewise necessary observations for latitude."[24] Without his quicksilver he resorted to using water for his artificial horizon, but this soon became impossible as the water froze too quickly at these temperatures. Unable to make an observation for time and correct his watch, he could not conduct observations for longitude. It was frustrating. He fumed quietly about Will Lutit and the loss of his quicksilver, but he knew that there was a capsize quality to life in the North, and it would do him no good to complain. In this country there were far worse fates than the loss of quicksilver.

At the end of February the weather had warmed enough that he could resume his astronomical observations. Obtaining longitude by means of lunar distances required more work than determining latitude. Bright, clear nights were the best to measure the angular distance of the moon from a star, but he could also take distances of the moon from the sun during the day. To be accurate he should take more than one set of readings, each set comprising ten observations taken in succession, and from those a mean could be determined. Each session could take four to five hours. He first had to account for errors in his instruments (his sextant and his watch) and had to take a temperature reading. It was crucial to determine the local time, so he corrected his watch by ascertaining local time from two sets of altitudes of stars or the sun. Then he would determine with his sextant the angular distance between the moon and one star that was due east and one due west. He would check with the *Nautical Almanac* at what time this angle occurred at Greenwich. Since there are fifteen degrees of longitude for each hour of time, the difference in time could be translated into degrees west of the Greenwich meridian.[25] It was satisfying to fix a location, to know exactly where he was on this globe. He enjoyed this work with numbers, and, in spite of the cold, he was happy gazing at the heavenly clock. The skies were something of a connection with England, although, he had to admit, he was not homesick for any of it—yet.

Taking observations and computing were solitary activities, so he was happy for the conversation, dinners, cards, and music during the evenings when it was too cold and too cloudy to be doing his work. There were only about twenty Bay men inland at the time,[26] and various groups of them went farther west during the winter months to tent with the Plains Cree. Robert Longmoor had left Cumberland House with ten men in September, two weeks before Turnor's arrival, intending to go up the Saskatchewan River as far as Eagle Hills, the upper settlement established by the Montreal traders, but he had to stop and winter at a Montreal trader's house, later known as Upper Hudson House. Longmoor was a skilled servant and a fair and wise trader who knew both the ways and language of the Cree and the practices of the competition.[27]

The remaining eight to ten men at Cumberland House were kept busy during the winter months, cutting firewood, hunting, fishing, repairing their quarters, making sleds, snowshoes, and clothing, and mending fishnets. With few Cree coming to trade, they had little fresh meat and, had they not had great success with their own fishing and small game hunting, they would have been very poorly off. Turnor was an excellent shot and knew how to set rabbit snares and fishnets. Tomison was impressed enough to single him out in the post journals for snaring fifteen rabbits and shooting ten partridges in November. A good hunter like Turnor was a major asset at a wintering house.

Once the worst of winter was over and he could travel again, Turnor's orders were to take observations for the new settlement, Hudson House, established by Longmoor fourteen miles downstream from his wintering place. On 5 March, with three men, Robert Davey and George Hudson, who had been with him on the journey to Cumberland House, and William Walker, the "writer"[28] for Cumberland House, he set out on snowshoes on the frozen river. Turnor loaded his instruments and country provisions, some dried moose flesh, pemmican, and fat,[29] on a sled pulled by three dogs and they left at eight in the morning. Two days later, after heavy trudging, they met Charles Isham[30] and James Lisk with the packet from Longmoor. This had been the worst winter ever, they reported to Turnor. Their provisions were never enough and with competition from the Montreal traders increasing, they found it difficult to trade for food from the Cree.

Isham told him that tensions were running high. "There is great confusion between the Canadian Traders and the Indians. They are all striving against one another, and violence is sure to break out."[31] Isham, a Cree-English servant whose first language was Cree, had favourable relations with the Cree, and Turnor had heard he could be well trusted.

Turnor was apprehensive about this news of escalating friction, but at least he and his men would have an easier time walking in Lisk and Isham's trail. On 11 March it snowed and blew so strongly that the trail was covered and the snow so deep they had to take over from the dogs and pull their own sleds. Exhausted, they arrived at the ruins of James Finlay's House, one of the Montreal traders' houses built ten years earlier and abandoned. They were grateful for the shelter of the sagging and cracked walls. They had reached Nipawin Rapids, about 135 miles from Cumberland House, halfway through their journey to the new settlement. For the next eight days Turnor saw abundant evidence of the inroads the competition had made on the company's trading territory. They passed a house formerly occupied by the Montreal trader William Holmes, and the next day one built by John Cole,[32] two names Turnor would soon hear more about. On 17 March they came upon two houses at the confluence of the Sturgeon and the North Saskatchewan Rivers (near present-day

Prince Albert, Saskatchewan). Here two traders, Robert Grant and Barthélemi Blondeau, greeted him. Blondeau insisted that Turnor stay the night in his house. Next morning, Blondeau introduced Turnor to the conventions of inland hospitality.

"Where are my dogs?" Turnor turned to Blondeau accusingly.

"Oui, oui. Merci." Blondeau, who could speak no English, called Grant to translate for him. "We used them to fetch some meat for the camp. One good turn deserves another."

Blondeau spoke again in French, Grant translating: "We've heard from the Indians at Cumberland House that you were coming. What might be your particular business?"

"I'm travelling up river to help Longmoor." Turnor was uneasy about this questioning.

Blondeau continued with the utmost politeness. "What is this box of instruments you carry with you? The Indians say you are constantly staring at the heavens."

"Oh, I have had them some years since with the intent to go to the South Seas but being disappointed have always chosen to carry my instruments with me for my own amusement."

Blondeau smiled knowingly. "I suppose you believe the Charter gives the Company rights to this Saskatchewan River territory?"

"I know nothing about that. It doesn't concern me." After a slight pause, Turnor continued. "We'll be leaving as soon as the dogs return. Thank you for your kindness."[33]

The following day, 19 March 1779, they arrived at their destination, 280 miles from Cumberland House. Clustered together at this site were Longmoor's House, now called Hudson House, and within two or three hundred yards of each other, three Montreal traders' houses, one belonging to Jean-Étienne Waden and being looked after by the French Canadian, Gibosh,[34] one belonging to Holmes and Booty Graves, and another inhabited by Nicholas Montour in trust for Blondeau. Close by were ten small houses occupied by their men. Longmoor had wanted to be higher up river, but when he had arrived there last fall the river was already freezing and Blondeau had offered him this house, half-built.[35] It would have been foolish to continue on, so Longmoor and his men had accepted.

At times there was cooperation between the HBC and the Montreal traders. One good turn would be paid off with another. Also, given their fear of Cree hostility, the independent groups of Montreal traders welcomed the HBC men, believing there was safety in numbers. At other times, though, there was great rivalry; and in fact Turnor, in his capacity as surveyor, epitomized the reason for the heated struggles between the HBC and the Montreal traders, who did not want more competition than they already had among themselves. His mapping of the area would bring the Bay men inland. In response, and in an attempt to economize and organize, the Montreal traders began establishing partnerships. This was the beginning of nearly fifty years of strife that would eventually end when the two major opponents merged in 1821.

Hudson House, *April to May 1779*

For ten days since his arrival, Turnor had "met with nothing re-markable."[36] The carpenter was making him his own cabin and bed, and he would be glad to have some privacy for his writing and mapping. But matters were stirring here in their community of trading houses.

On 1 April he and Longmoor were invited to take breakfast with William Holmes, an Irish man with a reputation for a temper. Bold and more competitive than most of the Montreal traders, he was rising quickly as a leader and would become a partner in the various configurations of the NWC. But Turnor knew he was not to be trusted.[37]

In the course of their conversation Turnor learned that Holmes and a number of other Montreal traders in the area, Peter Pangman, Charles McCormick, Booty Graves, and Robert Grant,[38] had decided to form a general partnership to cut down on the ruinous competition among them. Though Turnor had heard unfavourable reports about some of these men, he congratulated Holmes on the consolidation, privately thinking this move would also advantage the HBC, for there would be fewer settlements and fewer Montreal traders.

A few days later, Turnor saw Holmes in action. A number of Assiniboine had come to trade with Longmoor but, as he had no liquor, they went to Holmes, who promptly locked them up until they traded all their skins with him. This was nothing new. Magnus Twatt, an HBC man, had dared to criticize Holmes earlier for the same actions, and Holmes, in a rage, had turned on Twatt, cursing and beating him.

Witnessing such ferocious political jousting for the first time, Turnor had much to write about in his journal entries. He was disturbed by Holmes's bullying and made it clear to the governors (although they would not read his report for six months) that the Bay men were having a rough time of it with the Montreal traders. To carry on the trade with spirit, he wrote, they would need to augment their numbers to fifty or sixty men. They were definitely at a disadvantage: the Montreal traders had nearly three hundred men, though, granted, they were not all working together. Furthermore, with their large canoes they were doubly efficient; five of their men in just one canoe could do as much as ten of the HBC servants with five canoes, and they had an easier track with the current coming before them into Sea Lake (Lake Winnipeg). Turnor concluded, "I am of the opinion that the Honourable Company have not lost less then 500 Made Beaver in wolves, beaver & foxes by this one gang of Indians for want of goods."[39]

Two weeks later, on 20 April, four Cree arrived at Longmoor's House to trade and, once again, because the HBC had no liquor, the Cree went to Holmes's House where they received both tobacco and liquor. One of Holmes's men travelled by horseback to their camp to ply them with liquor and, later that afternoon, a large group of Cree men, drunk on Holmes's liquor, arrived with thirty well-loaded horses. They claimed they came to trade with Longmoor, not with Holmes and his men, and "said the Englishmen were their country-men." They traded for everything Longmoor had that they wanted, but then went on to Holmes's House. Turnor and Longmoor watched despondently from their house, knowing that, for want of trading goods, the loss, "would amount to 1500 Made Beaver at least, mostly in beaver with a few wolves, foxes & martins."[40] More than that, they had lost future business, as the word would spread that the HBC had nothing to trade that the Cree wanted. Turnor wondered how long they would keep coming when the HBC disappointed them time and again.

Five days later, in the early morning as Turnor was preparing his canoe and pack to go up the river to Eagle Hills to determine its latitude and longitude, he heard great excitement down at the river. Two canoes of men working for Gibosh came in paddling furiously.

They had just escaped with their lives, leaving half their furs and all their goods and provisions back at the Eagle Hills settlement. One hundred and twenty Cree, they said, or perhaps more, had fallen on them and killed John Cole and one of Pangman's men.

Turnor had heard of John Cole, who had deserted the Montreal traders and joined the Hudson's Bay Company in 1772 and then deserted them to return to the Montreal traders in 1773. He was quick-tempered and as changeable as a weather vane. He took whatever advantaged him most—using any means at his disposal.

The next day Gibosh's men sent rumours flying around the settlement that the Hudson's Bay men had deliberately set the Cree upon the French Canadians. The French Canadians had lost respect for their Montreal employers, whom they referred to as Englishmen although many were Scots or Irish, and as a result had set themselves against all Englishmen. There were now four factions at each other's throats: the Cree, the French and the English Montreal traders, and the HBC men.

Later that day, Longmoor and Turnor were once again sent for by Holmes. It was not tea and pleasantries this time. There sat Holmes, alone in his house surrounded by a brace of pistols, powder and ball, and a cutlass.

"It is a bad situation," he said. "Now I have to defend myself against my own men. I want to warn you. They are against you and against every Englishman in this area. I am telling you that if any of our people are killed at the Upper Settlement, they will not let one Englishman pass the Setting River."[41]

"The French Canadians from the Upper Settlement say they have no such intention of attacking us," Turnor assured him.

But Holmes was crazy with fear and anger. "Even if all the Englishmen joined together," he said, "we would have the worst of it. There are only twenty-seven of us, including your company's fifteen men, and what arms do you have?"

"We have but four old guns, a pistol or two, a hatchet, but not a load of powder or ball."

"Graves will send you a keg of powder and a bag of ball. But that is hardly enough to defend us against 300 French Canadians or against the Indians."

"Half our men will stay under arms all night," conceded Turnor.

Who, thought Turnor, is the enemy here? I do not wish to stand with Holmes, but I trust the French Canadians less. Are the Cree stirred up so much they cannot be stopped?[42]

An hour later, six more canoes arrived from the Upper Settlement, and Turnor pieced together the events that had erupted in this crisis. It had begun the previous autumn when Kepouche and his band had gone to trade with the Montreal-based traders at their Upper Settlement in the Eagle Hills. According to McCormick and Gibosh, Kepouche had become very troublesome, no doubt from the liquor provided him. To calm him, they "gave him a glass of laudanum which put him into a lasting sleep."[43]

By now Turnor recognized all these names: Gibosh, McCormick, Holmes, and Cole. They had all been accused of various dishonourable deeds against the Cree traders—making them drunk, then locking them up; trading only in liquor and not in necessaries; cutting their tents in pieces. The traders' seductive liquor and tobacco were "keeping them [the Cree] very poor," Turnor wrote in his journal entry for that day—"the time they should be hunting they are running backwards and forwards to the traders and when they leave the traders they have no one single necessary."[44]

The confrontation on 22 April had arisen, as Gibosh told Turnor, when the band returned to seek revenge for Kepouche's death and to retaliate for the bad trading practices the Montreal traders had employed against them. They gathered in great numbers, with twenty-five tents encamped on the hill above the traders' settlement. The tinderbox situation ignited when Cole claimed that a Cree hunter had stolen his horse.

"I will shoot all your horses, if mine is not returned," Cole threatened.

"You are bold," retorted one of the young Cree hunters, "but you had better arm yourself, for I will shoot you tomorrow in your own house or at your own door. But if you will go now and hunt for your horse, I will not take advantage of you."

Cole, fearing for his life, stayed in his house.

Early in the morning of 22 April, after a tense night, an old Cree man came to McCormick. "Get up out of your beds and arm yourselves, for my people are coming to kill you," he warned them.

McCormick's Cree interpreter beseeched the old man, "Come in and smoke a pipe," but McCormick pushed aside the interpreter and blocked the old man's passage.

"Tell the Indian," McCormick ordered the interpreter, "to put on petticoats. Say to him, 'You are only an old woman and I will cut out your tongue'."

When the interpreter refused, McCormick sent for Cole, who could speak English, French, and Cree and was fond of executing such orders.

When he heard Cole's translation, the old man simply replied, "It is well."

The old man returned to his band, the Cree took down their tents, packed their things, and came down the hill to the settlement in small parties. They watched silently as the traders loaded their furs for departure. After a time, one of the young hunters, the only one armed at this time, picked out Cole, raised his gun, and shot him in the chest, killing him on the spot. Pangman's man ran after the hunter to shoot him, but the young Cree hunter reloaded, fired, and wounded him in the belly. He died twelve hours later.

Another Cree hunter had armed himself and gone to McCormick's house to kill him as soon as the first shot was fired outside, but the interpreter, expecting such a scheme, kept the Cree man talking, allowing McCormick to sneak away to safety.

With the first shot, both sides armed themselves and began firing. Three Cree men were wounded. Finally there was a cessation, flags were hoisted on each side and a peace was imposed, a peace that lasted as long as the five kegs of rum flowed.

"You are lucky today," spoke one of the hunters, "Ouraskis, our great war chief, is not with us or not one man would have escaped."[45]

Although the traders brought most of their furs down river, they gave up all their goods, including thirty kegs of rum, five cubic weight of black tobacco, nine cubic weight of gun powder, seven cubic weight of ball, three guns, and bale goods such as blankets, cloth, and ironwork.

The next day, 27 April, Turnor was informed that the Cree hunters were coming down river towards them "in the heat of blood." He and his men thought it best to return to Cumberland House. They got underway the following day, heavily loaded with furs, and dropped down the Saskatchewan easily. They arrived at Blondeau's at the mouth of the Setting River. There was no trouble there, in spite of Holmes's earlier warning, and they stayed for three days repairing their canoes. One day McCormick and Gibosh passed by, and they heard from them that, although all was quiet at Hudson House, the men were fearful and preparing to leave as fast as they could.

Turnor and Longmoor continued on their journey to Cumberland House and, in spite of blowing rain and cold, windy weather, they sped along, travelling between forty and seventy-five miles a day. On 9 May, after eight days' travel from Setting River, they arrived at Cumberland House and relayed the events of the Eagle Hills skirmish to Tomison and Hansom.

"I was near being in the wars," Turnor remarked to the London Committee when writing his year's report.[46] Turnor proved to be a competent reporter. His lengthy journal entry describing the Eagle Hills incident clarified for the London Committee not only the danger of the dissatisfied and angry Cree people, but the complicated and hostile relations between the French and the English Montreal traders and the HBC. The incident had tested Turnor's courage and his equanimity. Though remarkably calm about his own safety, deciding it was not "prudent" to go up river at this time, he defended the Cree, not only citing their reasons for revenge but adding, "the Indians did not behave as they ever have in other cases of the like nature." However, he did not hold back his criticisms of Cole, Holmes, and McCormick, and especially of the French Canadians, whom he described as "such a set of villains [he] did not choose to trust them."[47]

Because of the 'war,' he was unable to survey and map the area, but he had proven himself an astute reader of political territory. He believed that the Cree were not as opposed to the Hudson's Bay men as they were to the Montreal traders, and the next year Tomison and Longmoor went partway back upstream to rebuild Hudson House, although the Montreal traders were too afraid yet to venture back into that territory.

4.

First Journal and Map

At Cumberland House the men were building a stockade, preparing the garden, and repairing canoes. On 17 May, seven canoes of Montreal traders came down river and camped a quarter of a mile away. Wishing to hear how matters were along the Saskatchewan River, Turnor walked over to their camp.

He could not believe his eyes as he watched the unloading of one of the canoes. There was Nicholas, Blondeau's clerk, ordering the men to pitch his tent– a good one at that, Turnor noticed. Then a feather bed appeared out of the canoe. Turnor watched in amazement and disgust at these indulgences. He and his men often did without any tent, just rolled themselves in a blanket and slept under a tree. Nicholas and his girl were carried out of the canoe to their tent—carried so they would not muddy their shoes. Nicholas himself never touched a paddle, except for his own pleasure.[1]

Longmoor and Tomison told him later that Nicholas received £150 per year in wages, as well as apparel for both himself and whatever girl he had at the time. His pay was augmented to reflect his expertise in Indigenous languages, but even clerks who did not know any of the languages received £100 and clothing. Turnor must have muttered to himself that his salary was just half that of an apprentice clerk. Longmoor made just thirty pounds and was, without a doubt, one of the most able, hardy, valuable men in their ranks. No wonder there was the occasional HBC man who went over to the Montreal traders. They would certainly like to recruit Tomison and Longmoor, for those two had won the favour of the Cree and knew the territory well. But, from what Turnor had seen of these traders in the last month, he would not exchange his bedroll for a feather bed for any money.

Within the hour, the group of them, Graves, Grant, McCormick, Holmes, Blondeau, and Nicholas, came over to Cumberland House to inquire about the health of the Bay men. They warned Cumberland House that sixty canoes of Cree might well come down to them in the summer, still heated about the Eagle Hills incident. It would be necessary, thought Turnor, to leave more men here to guard the goods. He heard other news he did not like. Graves was going northward and Blondeau intended to winter along the North River. If so, as Turnor wrote in his journal, "I do not think that either York Fort or Churchill will get a skin from the North River Indians."[2] He also heard from them that Peter Pond had gone north into Lake Athabasca country last winter, "the first that ever has attempted to go far into that part of the Country."[3] There were a great many furs to be had, although these men wondered if Pond had survived, having heard nothing from him since his departure.[4] Turnor was intrigued. Perhaps he might undertake an expedition northward in the future, but now he had many rivers here and in the James Bay area to map.

On 24 May he set off to survey Pine Island Lake. He must have thought along the way of his predecessor, Samuel Hearne, who had chosen this spot for Cumberland House in the spring of 1774. He had never met Hearne, now chief factor at Fort Prince of Wales, but had heard of his adventures in travelling to the Coppermine River, the dreadful famines he endured, his story of the massacre of Inuit at Bloody Falls, and his fame as the first European to cross Great Slave Lake and reach the Arctic Ocean by overland travel—all these tales had made Hearne an heroic figure in the eyes of many Europeans.[5] On his return from the survey a few days later, Turnor discovered in Cumberland House a compass that had been left by Hearne. He picked it up, thinking no doubt of all the great distances it had travelled and of the daring explorations Hearne had undertaken. But what he noted in his journal, what interested him most, was that Hearne's compass was out by twelve degrees easterly. Turnor perhaps did not know at this time that Hearne's location of the mouth of the Coppermine River was 200 miles too far north, but he must have wondered about Hearne's accuracy, and knew for himself how important it was to account for all such errors in his instruments, especially his compass, watch, and sextant so his calculations would be correct. It was a reminder to him that he—the official surveyor—was here to make exact observations.

Holmes, Grant, and their men were still there when he returned. Once again they asked Turnor what work he was doing, believing he had been employed to reinforce the company's charter. They knew they were trespassers on HBC land, but they felt this was not a concern as long as the company quietly acquiesced.[6] With so few men there the HBC could not oppose them.

Turnor heard more stories that disturbed him about the treatment of the Indigenous people at the hands of the Montreal traders. Malchom Ross told him a gruesome story of a killing inland the previous winter. He and James Spence Sr. were tenting among the Cree when a French trader who joined them in their tent was attacked with hatchets and killed for no other reason than that he was French and worked for the despised McCormick. No harm came to Ross and his companion because of the respect the Cree had for the Bay men. Ross was an Orcadian, a man of integrity and many skills. He was as adept as any Cree guide in running the rivers and had learned their language. Seldom one to enthuse, Turnor described him as "a young man [though he was only two years younger than Turnor] of great veracity."[7] Whenever possible Turnor chose to travel with Ross, and Ross would be with him on his final expedition northward in 1790. For this immediate journey to York Factory, Turnor was allowed to choose his own steersman and, without hesitation, he asked for Malchom Ross.

The Lower Track, *June to July 1779*

On 9 June the men were ready to leave for York Factory. Once on the Saskatchewan they put up for the night at Fishing Creek, where they were joined by all the canoes—thirty-four—going from Cumberland House to York Factory. Such a number. Turnor noted, "Mr. William Tomison, Robert Longmoor, Charles Isham, Mitchell Oman, James Spence, Magnus Twatt & Malchom Ross steered their own canoes."[8] They passed the Middle Track, but their course was the Lower Track along the north end of Sea Lake (Lake Winnipeg).

They travelled relatively quickly with just a couple of days' interruptions, and on 16 June they arrived at the top of the Great Fall (Grand Rapids), where the Saskatchewan River empties into Lake Winnipeg. They carried the canoes for a quarter of a mile through a wooded area on the north side of the falls, where they put up for the night. Looking down the five miles of rapids, Turnor could see the Saskatchewan River surging through steep rock walls of white limestone on its way to Lake Winnipeg.

The following day they set off at 5:15 a.m., putting the canoes in a small creek that led into the falls. Some of their Cree companions thought it best to cross to the south side to shoot the falls. Cutabolinwan,[9] an old leader travelling with them, said no, that it was not customary to shoot on the south, only on the north side. Several Cree disagreed with him and crossed to the south. Joe Hansom, one of the HBC men, decided to follow them. He had been ten years in the service and four years travelling the inland rivers, including the fearful Churchill.

It was the wrong choice. Driven onto a boulder in the middle of the falls, Hansom's canoe smashed against the rocks and overturned. About three miles below, they dragged out his body but could not revive him. His Cree canoe-mate saved himself by clinging to the canoe for three miles before he could be rescued, but another Cree paddler suffered the same fate as Hansom, though his body was not found. About eight hours later that day, they buried Hansom upon a point on the north side of the river. This incident imprinted even more firmly in Turnor's mind the trust they must put in those who had been here before them: "in my opinion," he wrote in his notes, "the whole misfortune may be imputed to their not listening to Cutabolinwan."[10] Turnor could shade in the rapids on a map, provide a name, and leave a record of instruction for others, but old Cutabolinwan knew these rapids like the palm of his hand.

They were now into Lake Winnipeg, a shallow, unpredictable lake. The two drownings cast a pall over the group and, in the miserable rainy weather with the waves whipping up dangerously, they decided not to take any chances. Between 19 and 26 June they were weatherbound for three entire days, with limited travel on the remaining five days. Turnor took a latitude reading at 53°14' N at the bottom of Grand Rapids, only four minutes too far north by modern calculations, making his error about 4.6 miles.[11]

Finally, on 26 June they left Lake Winnipeg and entered the inlet to Buskescagnes Lake (now Playgreen Lake). More Indigenous names were appearing in his journal, although there were still places for which he had no name in either Cree or English, and he would refer to a lake vaguely as "kind of lake." He was easier with the Cree language, but not nearly as proficient as Ross yet. On the 29th they travelled twenty miles on a small part of the Nelson called Jack River, where Turnor pointed out that the Montreal traders had set up a House. Although Bay men had been through here as early as the 1750s, their settlement, called Norway House, was not established as a post until the 1800s. Leaving "kind of lake," they entered Sea River (the Nelson), went down the river another twenty-five miles, and put up for the night.

JOURNAL THREE

Norway House

August 2005

On 13 August 2005, I flew north (nervously) from Winnipeg in a twelve passenger Keystone Beech 99 airplane on an expedition to see where my ancestor Philip had travelled in the late 1770s. We flew serenely over Lake Winnipeg towards Norway House, voyageurs of a different era. Below us Lake Winnipeg spread out table-flat, like a shadow on the landscape. But it is not an innocent lake, as Philip discovered 226 years earlier. I, anxiously flying in a small propeller plane, could hardly imagine the courage it took to deal with the huge swells that he faced, particularly after witnessing the drowning of two of his men two days earlier at Grand Rapids. He had five days of start-and-stop travel hugging the north shore of the Lake. I had just an hour and a half of trepidation before we set down at Norway House, 450 miles north of Winnipeg.

In Philip's day the Hudson's Bay Company had not yet established a settlement here, though the Montreal traders had wintered on Jack River, the river that joins the Nelson to Lake Winnipeg through Playgreen Lake. But he had paddled through here, and on the very banks of the Jack River I had bannock and strong tea before touring the Hudson's Bay Company buildings that are still standing. The archway warehouse, erected in 1840, painted white with red roof and trim, is the oldest wooden building in the Canadian West. I walked through the archway down to the river, where the men in their canoes, or later in York Boats, would have pulled up to unload the cargo. The land, grey granite with green spruce, was low and flat. The warehouse was not in museum shape, the remnants inside just leaning against walls or hanging by nails. There was a large stretcher with a black bear pelt and a deer or elk hide, a pair of wooden snowshoes, saws, hoops, hay forks, and even an old wooden boat. The bell atop the warehouse had come from the *Seahorse*, the ship that took Philip home in 1792.

We tried our hands at rowing a York Boat before we went back for a lunch of wild mushroom soup, fresh fried pickerel, more bannock and tea. With mug in hand, I went to the river's edge, sat on a lichen covered rock, and looked down river, past the lush, reedy banks, to the route Philip would have taken. Perhaps he had stopped here too, for his own meal of freshly caught pickerel and bannock cooked on the hot rocks of a campfire. ✷

Echimamish River *June to July 1779*

On 30 June, after descending the Nelson for ten miles, Turnor and his men came to a small river that joined the main channel from the east. As they did not know the route north that continued on the Nelson River track,[12] they entered this small river to make their way to the Lower Track, the Hayes River. The Echimamish River, meaning "the water that flows both ways,"[13] was black from the swampy land around, and narrow—at times not more than four yards wide—but of a good depth. It is likely that Turnor was the first to survey this forty-mile route into the Hayes River system.[14] Soon this became the favoured track from York Factory to the interior, particularly when the York boats came into service. The current was easy against them as they made their way to a small bay. Here they carried the canoes about fifty yards over a low rock into another bay on "the other side of the Rock."[15] Portaging over this flat rock allowed them to move from the more difficult Nelson River route to the easier Hayes River route. Turnor took a latitude reading here, but otherwise registered no special interest in this curious river and advantageous rock portage on which, very likely, there were Cree pictographs.[16]

Now in the Hayes River, the men descended through a bold, rocky landscape, carried the canoes over the "white Fall" (Robinson Falls), carried again over the portage at what is now Hill Gates, passed through a myriad of lakes (now called Robinson, Logan, Max, Opiminagoka), shot three falls, and came into Pathepownippe Lake (Oxford Lake).

On 8 July they were underway in Knee Lake, a fifty-mile-long lake, so-called because it took a ninety-degree turn in the middle. At the turn Turnor noted that a strong magnetic attraction prevented his compass from moving. They camped that night at Jack Tent and stayed there two days while the guides hunted. Turnor took another latitude reading, his twelfth observation of the thirteen from this journey that he was to publish in an astronomical observations pamphlet in 1794. On 12 July they entered the portion of the Hayes River referred to as Hill River, which Turnor described as very crooked (so that they only made half the distance they paddled), full of islands and of so many falls that it seemed like one continuous fall. Turnor stopped counting them, but he recorded how impressed he was with the work of the steers- and bowsmen who "required little or no assistance from the Indians, only an Indian to lead the way."[17] How much paddling or carrying Turnor did is not clear, but he certainly knew the mechanics of shooting falls, portaging, and tracking, and he was always busy measuring distances, speeds, directions.

They were on the homeward stretch, travelling fifty miles the next day, camping a few miles beyond where the Pinnecutaway River enters the Hayes. On the 15th, after an easy run of thirty-nine miles, they arrived at York Factory. His first assignment, to map the route from York Factory to Cumberland House on the Nelson River and return on the Hayes River, was complete. He had travelled about

1500 miles in ten months. He had been as far west as the farthest HBC settlement, Hudson House, and he had surveyed the Echimamish connection between the Nelson and the Hayes Rivers.

Mapping and Writing, 15 July to 15 September 1779

His greatest pleasure over the next two months was spending his days mapping and writing up his year's travels. He felt invigorated by the challenges of this land. He had cleared his mind of the cobwebs of his old life, of limited opportunities, of family problems. He was mapping his own future, not just Rupert's Land. It was incredible to think what he had seen and learned in a single year.

He laid out his drawing paper, meticulously ruled his grid with the lines of latitude and longitude (the graticule), thinned his India ink, and applied the grey watercolour wash. He referred to his observation notes, and his mind filled with the memories of where he had been. His hand poised to place the first mark on the blank sheet. Between the three settlements, York Factory, Basquia (The Pas), and Cumberland House, was a huge expanse of territory for which he had few names. Some places had been given English names (Port Nelson, the Hayes, Hill, and Steel Rivers); others were noted by their Cree names (Tesqueau Lake, the Saskashawan and Pinnecutaway Rivers). He was a recorder, not a namer. Like a man of the Enlightenment, his markers were scientific: distance and landscape. He mapped the two routes he had taken as far west on the Saskatchewan River as Hudson House. Each squiggle, each bump, each twist represented much more than the line on his map—two deaths, loss of goods, his quicksilver gone, blisters, sore backs, mosquitoes, rain and sleet—but it was satisfying to see it marked out. In fact, he prepared two maps. One may have been a working draft as it listed the distances of the tracking and carrying places on the lower Nelson River where he had worn out his English shoes. He recorded only what he had personally observed on the Upper and Lower Tracks. Thus, there is a blank space between these two routes, and the network of rivers and lakes and the Middle Track itself are only noted, not traced out.[18] Proudly, at the end of August, he wrote in elegant lettering on both the maps, "A Chart of Rivers and Lakes Falling into Hudsons Bay According to a Survey taken in the Years 1778 & 9 By Philip Turnor" (see Plate 2).

They measured twenty-one and three-quarter inches by thirty inches. He folded them up and packed them in a chest, ready for transport back to the Hudson's Bay Company offices to be mounted on linen, then pondered by the committee men.[19]

Requested by the London Committee to comment in his journal on all matters, he began by offering his opinion on the men, expressing once again his admiration for the inland servants, specifically Tomison, Longmoor, Isham, and Ross, who were "little or none inferior to a good Indian," the Cree guides setting the highest standard of skill. Advising the committee that they would need sixty men inland, fifty of them assigned to go up the Saskatchewan, he encouraged them to begin training young apprentices to positions of leadership. George Hudson, an apprentice trained at the Grey Coat Hospital School, had proven his worth, as Turnor had predicted, and the following year he was promoted. Turnor was a natural teacher and supported young, hardy, talented men. Hudson, he wrote, did not complain about the hard work, or "having poor pike and no thing to eat with it," or of having "to roll him self in a blanket and lay under a tree." Turnor knew well that such things were not "allowed to be hardships" in this occupation.[20]

He had been a careful observer on his travels, not just of the landscape but of the trade as well. He noted that the NWC had taken about 17,640 furs out of the Saskatchewan area to the HBC's meagre 2,000.[21] This could be reversed, he suggested, if the HBC had more men, and if they employed flat-bottomed boats on the Saskatchewan River.[22] He offered specific instructions as to the hiring of a boat builder from the Orkney Islands and the construction of such a boat. He was not the first to urge the use of such boats, York boats as they came to be known, but he was another voice speaking from experience to the London Committee, who knew sums and figures and profits, but not practicalities. Although Turnor did not think these boats would work on the Hayes because of the rapids and portages, they were eventually adapted and used there by the early 1800s.

Turnor summed up his year's travel in a letter:

> I have the happiness of informing Your Honors I have had
> my health exceeding well and went through the inland
> journey with good spirits though with some difficulty as

expected. I cannot say I have a great aversion to the country at present though I was near being in the wars as will appear by my remarks in my Journal....Your Honors may possibly think I have given my opinion too freely but by my instructions I suppose my self conforming thereto...."[23]

He ended his journal with a few choice opinions—approbation for the new flanker and renovations to the factory, blunt criticism of some of the workmen who could neither build a set of steps nor lay a brick, and outright rage at the trading gun that he had bought "of Your Honors" which blew up, "but luckily did no damage." Overall, though, he expressed a positive and expansive vision for the company, a conscientious sense of duty, and a healthy ambition for himself.

JOURNAL FOUR

Hudson's Bay Company Archives, Winnipeg

May 14, 2008

I sat waiting at a table in the HBC Archives research room in Winnipeg for Turnor's first journal to be delivered to me. For the past two days I had been viewing his maps, but had not been allowed to touch them, even with gloved hands, so only my eyes could trace the lines he had drawn. He would never have imagined that a great-great-great-great granddaughter would be admiring his handsome work some 230 years later. I had first read Turnor's words, all neatly printed out, in J. B. Tyrrell's *The Journals of Samuel Hearne and Philip Turnor*. Then I had inched closer to the 'real' documents, reading his journeys on microfilm, struggling with his handwriting. Now, here it was in front of me, the very booklet in which he had written "A JOURNAL of the most remarkable Transactions and Occurrences

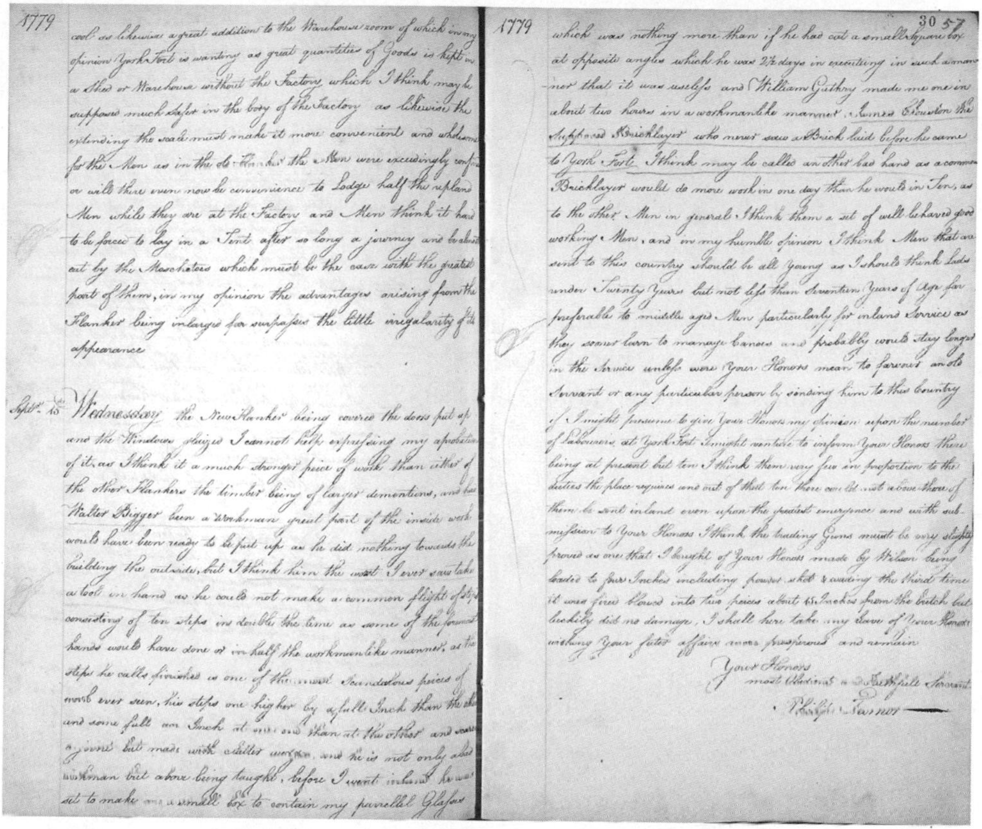

Figure 14. Final pages of Turnor's first journal
(September 1778 to September 1779).

from York Fort to Cumberland House, and from said House to York Fort from 9th Septr 1778 to 15th Septr 1779 / by Philip Turnor, Surveyor." Measuring seven and three-quarter inches wide and twelve and a quarter inches high, it has a hard board cover with a ripple-like red, grey, white, and ochre design. It is not leather, as I had imagined, but a common booklet that every journal-keeper would have been issued. I put on my white archive gloves and opened to the first page. This time I could run my gloved fingers over his words, the India ink letters darkening and lightening like shadows on a river. He wrote right-slanted, quite neatly, with not as many flourishes as I had seen in Chief Factor Tomison's journal. This was a good copy, which he must have made from his rough notes, for there was just one crossout.

Was I actually touching something of his, down all these years? Could I, like a graphologist, discern his character from these scratchings?

Knowing that it was common practice for the masters to have a writer or clerk to take dictation and transcribe pencilled notes, I inquired if we knew for sure that this journal had been written by Turnor. No, I was told, we did not. How disappointing. But he must have handled this booklet. He did sign it, I said hopefully, as I scrutinized his signature at the end: "Your Honors/most Obedient and Faithful Servant/Philip Turnor." Those distinctive flourishes on the P and the T must be his. But there is no sure answer—a simple reminder of the other currents of Turnor's life that can never be fully known. ✳

5.

Up the Albany River

Moose and Albany Forts, *September 1779 to February 1780*

Turnor was next assigned to Moose Fort, from where he was to map the rivers flowing into James Bay at the bottom of Hudson Bay—the Albany, Moose/Missinaibi, and Abitibi Rivers. The Montreal traders had established themselves at the head of the Albany River, southwards on Lake Superior, Lake Missinaibi, and at Michipicoten, and south and east in the Abitibi area towards Quebec. As with the Saskatchewan territory, the London Committee was determined to move inland from their coastal posts to counter this threat to their trade, and they required information on the navigability of the routes, the feasibility of the location of their few upland posts, and the adequacy of food supplies in order to facilitate the construction of more posts.

On 17 September Turnor and Matthew Cocking boarded the Severn sloop to begin the journey down the Bay to Severn House, where Cocking was master, and then onward to Moose Fort.

Turnor had met Cocking, a Yorkshire man nine years his senior, at York Factory the year before and knew his reputation as a courageous and competent inland traveller. During the eight-day voyage to Severn House they would have had much to discuss—the best track to take inland, the desperate need for experienced canoemen and canoe builders, and the tale of the uprising at Eagle Hills, which Cocking had visited in 1772. Cocking was happy to be heading back to Severn and his Cree wife and young daughter, and may well have spoken to Turnor about the advantages of having a wife.

Figure 15. Moose Fort, circa 1804.

They anchored on 25 September, spent a few days unloading the cargo in snow and gale winds, and then Turnor set sail for Moose Fort on the 29th. It was a trying journey in the small sloop, with the high winds, snow squalls, and sleet battering them. On a couple of days they shipped water. Quite fatigued by the weather and travel, Turnor arrived twenty-two days later at Moose Fort.

Moose Fort and London were almost at the same latitude, but that is where the similarities ended. Unlike his pleasant surprise when he saw York Fort for the first time, Turnor was shocked to see the ruinous condition of Moose Fort—a case, he thought, of bad hands hired for jobs for which they had not one ounce of training. He remembered that the bricklayer at York had never once laid a brick before coming to Rupert's Land.

To look at it, one would never know that Moose Fort was an important post. Established in 1672, it had suffered capture by the French in 1686, then destruction by fire twice. Built on wetlands and muskeg which were subject to tides, it had poor drainage and required constant maintenance. The whole place, thought Turnor, looked as though it was about to be abandoned.[1] The window frames were all askew, the windows themselves were broken and stuffed with rags and paper, the stairs to the chief factor's apartment and to the men's quarters were too dangerous to even walk on. When wood was needed to mend something, the labourers took what was handy. Someone had torn apart the gun chest so that the guns lay haphazardly on the warehouse floor.

Among company officials, it had the reputation of being one of the most corrupt of the HBC posts—too much alcohol, too little discipline, too much socializing with Indigenous women. There had been a number of weak chief factors who had let things go. To compensate, the company would send in a heavy-handed master who, in tightening the reins, destroyed rapport with the Cree. Edward Jarvis, who had just returned from a respite in England to take charge of the Fort, seemed moderate in his approach, but it would take a while to change things. He had been hired into the service as a surgeon at Albany Fort in 1771 and had quickly shown his worth, mastering the Cree language and willingly going out to survey water routes and territories between the Albany and Moose Rivers. He could draft a map, but he did not fare well on these expeditions. He had unfortunate luck with his Cree guides abandoning him, and he did not have the constitution for the hard life of a traveller. He came back so sick and thin from his 1776 journey that he required a strap tied over his shoulders to hold up his trousers. He decided that was enough, and refused to go inland again. Though he could not go himself, he approved of the policy of establishing inland posts to oppose the Montreal traders. He was also in a good position to advise Turnor on the difficulties, as well as the politics, of venturing into this territory at the bottom of the Bay, which would prove quite different from Turnor's inland journey from York Fort to the Saskatchewan River area. Though never a vigorous, healthy man, Jarvis could take command, and Turnor commented that by December the fort seemed "to wear a different face," with windows hung and glazed, stairs built, the men's quarters repaired, and a gun chest constructed.[2] With evident carpentry skills, Turnor may well have undertaken some of the repairs himself, as there was neither a carpenter nor sawyer on staff at the time. His surveying

Figure 16. Albany Factory, 1804–1811.

skills included building and repairing, as well as establishing location coordinates for the various houses.

Soon after Turnor's arrival at Moose Fort, Jarvis wrote to his colleague, Thomas Hutchins, chief factor at Albany Fort, about eighty miles north on the coast. Neither Jarvis nor Hutchins had been told that Turnor was being sent by the company to conduct more observations inland from their settlements, and they were miffed. It was no easy task to provision and manage a trip inland, as these masters were required to do for Turnor, and Jarvis bluntly told Hutchins that he could not outfit Turnor.

On 15 December Turnor set off on foot to Albany with Mr. John McNab,[3] the Albany Fort surgeon, and John Turner, master of the Severn sloop. He wished to consult with Hutchins on his next course of travels. Nine days snowshoeing in bitterly cold temperatures cannot have been easy, but Turnor made no mention of any hardships.

Albany pleased him: "A person could hardly suppose this place and Moose Fort has the same owners. Here everything seems in good repair. There is a sufficient stock of firewood and timber on the plantation and business seems to go on smooth & even."[4]

Thomas Hutchins, like Jarvis, had been hired on as a surgeon, and, with his scientific background, he took great interest in the natural sciences, sending home articles and notes on the wildlife of Rupert's Land. He also had some facility in taking astronomical observations. A few years earlier, in 1771, Hutchins had taken observations of the eclipse of the sun with the help of instructions sent from England by William Wales. Turnor and Hutchins must have enjoyed exchanging news about Wales—his rising reputation in England, his Royal Society work, his students at Christ's Hospital School, and the publications of his journey with Sir James Cook. Here at Albany, Hutchins was conducting tests on the congealing of mercury in the cold climate and, in fact, a few years later he would win the Royal Society award for his publication of the results of these tests. This, of course, would have interested Turnor, and he no doubt offered Hutchins what assistance he could.

Both the fort and the chief factor were more lively here than at Moose Fort, and Turnor felt more at ease. It was the Christmas season, when there was free time and enjoyment for all the men. The hog was slaughtered for the occasion, so there was fresh meat. Perhaps the cook brought in a flaming plum pudding to top it all off. Later on there was a game of "Foote Balle" in the snow, and ruddy with the cold, the men tramped in and warmed up with hot toddies of rum or brandy. The officers were given their allowances of European wines and brandy. New Year's Eve 1780 was celebrated as well, and Turnor, dark and tall, may well have started off the traditional first-footing with a gift of whiskey to the men. All that day and the next the men relaxed, amused themselves, played cards, and sat very near the fire, hoping this year would be a successful one with good weather, safe journeys, and bonuses for extra furs.

Henley House, *February to March 1780*

A decision was made: "Upon consulting with Mr. Thomas Hutchins he seems of opinion that it would be best for me to proceed inland from this place first, in which opinion I entirely acquiesce as Albany is most capable of giving me assistance, Moose Fort inland settlements being more nominal than real."[5] However, as he was to discover, Albany and Henley were also short of supplies. It was not until 19 February that Turnor was prepared to set out for Henley and for Gloucester House, the HBC settlement farthest west on the Albany River, a walking trip of over 350 miles—one-way. He had with him five men, including John Hodgson and George Donald, apprentices who had been educated at the Westminster Grey Coat Hospital and had joined the company in 1774 when they were only eleven or twelve years old. With their rudimentary knowledge of astronomy and mathematics, they were able to take observations and assist Turnor. Hodgson had already spent three years at Henley House, and in fact had drafted a chart of the Albany River to Henley House in 1775 and to Gloucester House in 1777. Donald had been inland, helping to establish a post at Lake Wapiscogamy on the Missinaibi River.

After eleven brutal days of trudging through snow for 150 miles, they arrived exhausted at Henley House. Although Turnor was not impressed by this post, it was, by this time, operational as a full trading house. In 1743, when it was established as the company's first inland post, it was simply a meeting place, designed to encourage the Cree people to visit Albany with their furs. After being abandoned twice, in 1755 and 1759, due to hostilities with both French traders and the local bands, it was rebuilt as a full trading post in 1774, five miles downstream from the conjunction of the Albany and Kenogami Rivers. John Favell[6] became the first master and Thomas Atkinson,[7] the surgeon, succeeded him in 1779. But, due to Atkinson's increased drinking, he proved incapable of managing affairs and Favell was recalled just before Turnor arrived.

The journey had taken its toll: "My own health is in so bad a state that I am not able to proceed but intend staying at Henley until the rivers open," Turnor wrote in his journal.[8] He was suffering from snow blindness, fever, and exhaustion. Thomas Atkinson tended to him. Several days' isolation in a darkened room helped the snow blindness, but his general run-down condition was a concern. It did not help that there were few provisions and mostly salted, not fresh, meat.

Generally, the Cree hunters would bring in fresh meat or geese, but in the middle of winter it was often rabbits or pemmican. This winter, however, had been especially hard, and few country provisions were to be found anywhere in the area. Hodgson recalled his 1777 journey when he had arrived back at Henley from Gloucester half starved, unable to do his surveying. Henley House was now so badly off that Favell could no longer feed Turnor and his companions and could not supply them for their journey to Gloucester, so Turnor, Hodgson, and four other men were forced to return to Albany on 17 March.

Turnor did not arrive to a feast this time. Hutchins had sent men out sixty miles to see what food they could find. Two weeks later they returned, unable to locate fish, fowl, or meat. Cree families were coming in starving. Hutchins supplied them with what oatmeal he could spare. The men were on short allowance and down to their last casks of salted geese. By the end of April, aside from his thirty-two men, Hutchins had over 100 starving Cree who were also depending on the house's supplies. The geese started coming in, but few were taken. Hutchins sent his men to Bond's Creek to collect the last seven casks of salted geese, putting the geese in a waterhole to freshen the meat. Though Hutchins presented an optimistic face to the men, in his journal he lamented the dreadful situation: "Is not this an alarming situation….oh that those who may read this may never feel the anxiety I do on this occasion and that they would hearken to these repeated representations I have made on this subject."[9] He hoped that London would listen and send more European provisions to last the winters. Thank goodness for the oatmeal and flour in their stores.

As soon as they could work the land, they prepared the gardens. At the end of June they were still short of supplies and Hutchins wrote to Jarvis at Moose Fort that for the last two days he had eaten only radishes, bread, and butter for dinner and supper.

Towards Gloucester House, *June to July 1780*

On 27 May Hutchins sent off the flat-bottomed boats with supplies for both Henley and Gloucester Houses. Ten days later, on 5 June, Turnor and John Hodgson set off in a canoe to catch up to the men in the boats. This time Turnor would survey the entire route, from Albany to Henley House to Gloucester House, and determine where the company could best establish posts to effectively cut off communication between the Cree and the Montreal traders.

The water on the Albany was the lowest the men had ever seen at this time of the year, only knee-deep. Every mile they had to get out and lead the canoe. Turnor thought it was almost impossible, but the boats were somewhere ahead of him, and if they had made it, so would he. The wind blew hard from the northeast and at night they had nothing to shelter them against the rain. It was "salt geese for breakfast, dinner, & supper and a short quantity of them."[10]

The third day they caught up with the boats, which were making painfully slow progress, and on 8 June, after nearly twelve hours, they had made only thirteen miles with immense effort, tracking and hauling the boats, sometimes with sixteen men on the tracking line up to their waists in the water. On 9 June, five days out, they arrived at Fishing Creek Fall, just forty-five miles above Albany.

Here the river flowed over flat limestone made treacherous this year because of the unprecedented low water level. The men had to unload the boats and lead and tow. They nearly lost two men when the clearing line flew from their hands and left them up to their waists without any support. Seventy-seven miles farther up they arrived at a creek called Chimahagan Seepe. There they met George Sutherland on his way to Albany. Seeing him, a young man of twenty-five, now crippled and walking with a stick, one leg quite useless, hauntingly reminded Turnor of the toll this land could take on a man. Sutherland had been sent inland to Sturgeon Lake for the winter to scout out the Montreal settlements and learn the Cree language. Conditions were so bad he had nearly starved, resorting to eating dogs, mice, and even his leather breeches, shoes and mittens. Turnor marvelled to see this man alive at all.[11]

On 21 June, after seventeen days on the river, they arrived at Henley House. On his trip up in February he had been ill and his eyesight had been damaged by snow blindness, so he had not conducted surveys or noted the condition and placement of the house. He now made comments in his journal for the benefit of the London Committee, and he did not mince words: "I think Henley House the worst building I have seen in the country both as to convenience and workmanship, the flankers [wings] all given way from the sheds and the sheds obliged to be shored, the platforms of the shed and tops of the flankers all rotten." Turnor knew a great deal about building, and his standards were high. In the case of Henley House, he not only advised a higher location and new timber, but specified the type of roof that should be added, made of strong London brown paper, tarred and made water tight with Smith's ashes strewn over it.[12]

They left for Gloucester House, 240 miles up river from Henley, on 26 June with five additional canoes, the flat-bottomed boats being unable to proceed farther. In the shallow water Turnor had such difficulty getting his large canoe up river that he had no time to take bearings and distances. He would have to do this on his return trip.

On 5 July they stopped at "the foot of Martins Fall" (now Marten Falls), near the junction of the Ogoki and Albany Rivers.[13] The next morning, starting at 6 a.m., they carried the canoes by the side of a falls, led over another falls, "carried over a large rock about 50 Yards," then carried over an island between two falls. There were no English names for this area and Turnor did not record the Cree names, but that particular "large rock" is probably where he took out his knife and inscribed "Philip Turnor July 1780."[14] What urge prompted him to leave his mark at this spot? Was it the difficulty of the journey, the beauty of the landscape, or perhaps his sense of accomplishment?

JOURNAL FIVE

Marten Falls: A Turning Point in Family History

Marten Falls. I recognized this name. Charlotte Turnor, Philip's granddaughter and my great-great-grandmother, was "married" there on 21 June 1841, an event that marked a turning point in the destiny of Charlotte's family line.

When Philip paddled through the area in 1780 he saw rocks, river, and falls, and perhaps a few Cree tents, for the foot of the falls was a customary camping place. A post was established there in 1784, and when Charlotte was "married" there sixty-one years later it had become a principal depot for the inland areas.

In 1840–1841 Joseph, Philip's son, fifty-eight years old and the father of twelve children, was working as an interpreter for the HBC on the Albany River. He generally worked in the Abitibi, Moose Fort, and Lake Superior areas, and this was likely the first time he

Figure 17. HBC post at Marten Falls, 1905.

had passed through Marten Falls on the Albany River. Though he had travelled many of the same routes as his father, he must have felt a special moment of closeness when he saw "Philip Turnor" etched on the granite rock.

On this trip or at the fort he met James Harper, a canoe middleman working out of Fort Albany, where his family resided. James, though 28, had not had time to look for a wife, for his father had died when he was seven, his Cree mother when he was fourteen, and he had to care for his siblings. James entered the service at eighteen and had spent the last ten years on the Albany River. But he wanted more for himself. His father William, an Orkney man, had been hired in 1808 by the HBC as the first white teacher to educate the Cree-Orkney children of the HBC traders and a few of the Cree children of the Home Guard. As a literate and religious man he also conducted the divine services, and would have begun James's education. William went on to become sloop master and was unfortunately drowned in 1820. Did Joseph, knowing of William Harper's reputation and observing

James at work, recognize this as a good match for his daughter? Or had James himself noticed young Charlotte, just twelve or thirteen, going about her work, setting traps, gathering wood, cooking, and sewing? Perhaps he had already spoken to Joseph about her.

The marriage was arranged by father and son-in-law, but Joseph wanted to give it special significance. In celebration of the union of Cree, Orkney, and English heritage, and to impart a blessing of sorts, Joseph must have determined it would take place at Marten Falls, where his father had inscribed his name.

I can imagine the young, anxious, dark-haired Charlotte standing beside her father as he addressed James. James may have told Joseph that he wanted to settle down rather than travel the dangerous rivers up north (thinking of his father's drowning), and that he planned to move to the Red River Settlement and farm. Charlotte's father would have told her she would be well looked after. Just three years later she and James would be settled on Lot 111, St. Andrew's Parish, deeded to him by the HBC.

But at Marten Falls on that June day, within sight of the grey granite rock bearing Philip's name, Joseph addressed James Harper:

> James Harper I this day consent to be your father in law and by the blessings of the ald mite god join you to my beloved Daughter Charlet Turner hoping that you will consider your self as well married to her as if you were joined by a minester.[15]

Charlotte's first child was born eight months later and named Philip. Their next child, my great-grandmother, Nancy Ann Harper, was born in 1845 at St. Andrew's. Life on their farm in the Red River Settlement brought stability and opportunities. Despite this, life was not easy. Charlotte bore fifteen children, seven dying before they were twenty-five years old, and although she lived until she was eighty-two, her young years must have been difficult away from her family, siblings, and community. One of the stories passed down from Charlotte's daughter was that it had been a hard life with so many children.

Ultimately this union and their decision to move south to the Red River shaped my history. Charlotte and James had most of their children, including my great-grandmother Nancy Ann, at St. Andrew's Parish. John Low Loutit, my great-grandfather, who, like James, was Orkney-Cree, arrived nearby at Lot 104 when he was just four. He became a blacksmith and a carpenter. So my great-grandparents were encultured by a community of retired HBC families. I do not know if they came under the influence of William Cochran, the founder of St. Andrew's Parish Anglican Church and a teacher of farming, but over a period of years they assimilated into St. Andrew's Parish society, largely populated by English-Cree and Scots/Orkney-Cree. ✳

Gloucester House, *July 1780*

On 8 July Turnor arrived at the narrows on Espashaway (Washi) Lake where Gloucester House was located. Only recently established in 1777 by John Kipling, the present master, it was a small house, suitable for about eight men. Turnor made no remarks on either the master or the appearance of the house. He and Hodgson stayed on for another three weeks, but found no guides to take them farther up country to Lake Nipigon and Lake Superior, so in that time he began writing his comments about the journey to pass on to the London Committee.

Travel inland from Albany was very different from travel inland from York Fort. Earlier he had told Hutchins that he preferred York, for at the bottom of the bay you starve in all seasons. "This Country," he wrote in his journal, "will not afford [country] provisions....I am of the opinion that should not Albany be better supplied with [English] provisions that it will be impossible to support Gloucester House."[16] Furthermore, he commented, the local Cree refused to travel with them, and rather than hunting for them, begged for food. In spite of this, Turnor felt that it was worthwhile to support Gloucester House as the furs that had been traded here would formerly have gone to the Montreal traders.

When five company canoes arrived at the house at the end of July he had reason for further concern: the lack of trading goods. They brought none of the goods that the Cree wanted—no cloth, blankets, knives, hatchets, ice chisels, guns, or shot. He noted that the York Fort standard of trade denied "all kind of trinkets," which he felt hurt their trade, for the Cree women loved items such as lace, rings, ribbons, paint and the like, and persuaded their husbands to trade for those items. The Montreal traders stocked these items, and furthermore, Turnor pointed out, their copper kettles were about half the price of the HBC brass kettles. But the chief difference in the trade between the York and Gloucester areas was the attitude to liquor. At Gloucester the Cree expected a brandy and some tobacco before they traded, but then, when sober, they wanted to trade for "cloth, blankets, powder, shot etc which they cannot do without." As animal skins for clothing were scarce in this area, they prized cloth and blankets. Inland from York Factory, at Cumberland House where the Cree had an easier life, "brandy is the chief trade," with the other items, "powder, shot, tobacco, knives, flints, steels" given as gifts.[17]

He had run on for over a thousand words on differing trading practices when, without a pause, he introduced another topic, one not often broached in official documents—the benefit of "keeping a woman":

> The masters of most of your Honors inland settlements particularly those belonging to York Fort would labour under many difficulties was they not to keep a woman as above half the Indians that came to the House would offer the master their wife, the refusal of which would give great offence to both the man and his wife. Though he was to make the Indian a present for his offer, the woman would think her self slighted and if the master was to accept the offer he would be expected to clothe her and by keeping a woman it makes one short ready answer (that he has a woman of his own and she would be offended) and very few Indians make that offer when they know the master keeps a woman, and those women are as useful as men upon the journeys.[18]

Clearly Turnor thought this practice was connected to trading customs. The kinship tie with the woman's family would promote good trading bonds. Though he differentiated between "wife" and "woman," suggesting a distinction between a Cree wife-husband relationship and a European-Cree union, he did not belittle the woman offered and was sensitive to her feelings. Women, he commented to the

London Committee, worked as hard as men on the journeys. Here at Gloucester he had observed the women bringing in rabbits and fish, cooking, sewing, and making snowshoes. Both John Kipling, the master at Gloucester, and John Favell, the master at Henley, had Cree wives and families.[19] Turnor may well have wished for the help of a woman, remembering how terribly he had suffered from snow blindness and ill health a few months earlier. And, more, a woman could teach him the Cree language.

It was common for a Cree man to offer his wife to a master. The Cree themselves had a flexible attitude towards relationships; multiple wives, exchange of wives, and separations were all considered normal. In their own relationships and in English- or Scots–Cree relationships, which could be temporary given that the men often returned to England and Scotland, it was the custom for the band to accept all children and wives back into the general community.[20] Turnor had heard of masters with two Cree women. However, contrary to the notion that multiple wives were not jealous, Turnor observed that in a relationship with a master, a woman "would be offended" if a second woman were offered to him. Had Turnor witnessed such an offering and was he sensitive to the woman's viewpoint, or was his British sensibility showing itself? It does not seem likely that he accepted or even that he was offered a woman by the Cree men who came to Gloucester House. Generally, only those officers who were masters were unofficially permitted by the company to keep a woman. However, it seems he had taken special notice of this practice and may have been thinking ahead to a time when he was more settled and could accept his own woman.

Albany and Moose Forts, *August to September 1780*

On 2 August Turnor started his return journey to Albany with the other canoes that were going back. The route to Henley was far less arduous this time, five days compared to thirteen going up, and he was able to focus on the surveying he had been unable to do on the journey upriver. He marked down on his rough map all the carrying places and the many small creeks falling northward and southward out of the Albany River. In four more days, by 11 August, they were at Albany Fort with little more adventure than a sunken canoe—no lives or furs lost. The East Main sloop was in, but, as no ship had yet arrived from England, provisions were scanty. There was one bladder of lard left, and one evening they had nothing but pancakes for supper. The next day they had a few plover, ducks, and geese brought in by the Cree hunters, who had heard the guns firing at the departure of the sloop. Living on the edge of starvation with the constant worry about provisions was a fact of wilderness life, but Turnor was not going to leave the matter unmentioned in his journal notes to the committee in London. He and Hutchins discussed the problem and took an account of what they had in the stores at Albany. The four bushels of barley, one hundred and twelve pounds of flour, ten pounds of butter, two pounds of cheese, a third of a cask of molasses, and twelve pounds of rice would not go far among fifty-nine men if the ship did not come in with the winter stores.

Turnor spent the month at Albany finishing his second map for the governors: "A Chart of Rivers and Lakes between Albany Fort and Gloucester House as taken in the year 1780 by Philip Turnor" (see Plate 3). It measured eighteen and three-quarters by twenty-nine and a half inches and, like his first map, was grey wash on rag paper with lines and lettering of thinned India ink. Mapping required a sturdy table, a steady hand, and sharp eyesight. He began by marking off the edges of his sheet with tiny precisely drawn rectangular boxes that alternated between shaded and plain, each rectangle indicating five degrees. Using the Mercator projection, he then drew in the fine lines of latitude and longitude across the page.[21] Now to transcribe the river to the map. He had taken latitude and longitude observations of both Henley House and Gloucester House, and they were precisely pinpointed on his map. Using his notes, he located the islands, the rivers and creeks coming into the Albany, the falls, and the twists and turns of its track. It was a simple, accurate view of the 400 miles of the Albany River he had travelled between Albany and Gloucester. Above and below the river line on the map was blank space. Although he had named, in either English or Cree, where other waterways entered the Albany, they were simply openings, for he had not travelled them. This map was like an aerial view of one roadway. How easy it looked on the map, he thought. But his journal would warn future travellers of its real nature. He was satisfied. This was the first survey of the Albany River that had been done with precision. Proudly he rolled it up for the 1780 packet to England.[22]

Nine days later, on 6 September, there was great relief when the East Main sloop arrived at Albany to inform the men that the company ship was anchored safely in the "Moose road."[23] They brought with them the packet of correspondence from England. Turnor set aside his personal mail while he scrutinized the inventory of provisions that England had sent out for the coming year. Comparing their needs here with the list of goods sent, he found them terribly wanting. It would be impossible to make up the difference with country provisions. Controlling his dismay, he wrote respectfully but firmly in his journal, "With submission to Your Honors I cannot help thinking the before mentioned provisions though so great a quantity will prove inadequate to the service required by Your Honors."[24]

That afternoon he could take time to read the news from home. Likely his mother, Betty, had written a letter wishing him good health. Perhaps there was news from a brother or sister. Philip's father was never mentioned and, as Betty would request money from Philip in a few years, it could be that he was deceased.

Newspapers were sent to York Factory first, but word would have spread down to the bottom of the Bay that Captain James Cook was on his third voyage, this one to discover the Northwest Passage. The American War was still raging. Spain had declared war on Britain this past June (1779), which had led to the unsuccessful siege by Spain and France of British-held Gibraltar. England was hard-pressed to find men to fight and the need to recruit had led to the repeal of the Popery Act, thus permitting Catholics to join the military. However, this produced widespread fears that there would be subversive attempts by Catholics to join with Catholic France and Spain against Britain. Lord Gordon and his supporters marched on Parliament on 2 June to protest the repeal, and the Gordon Riots became the most destructive battle in the streets of London during the eighteenth century. Though news of this riot may not have reached Turnor with the 1780 packet from London, he certainly would have heard news of the economic difficulties and the despair about the continuing war that contributed to these riots.

A few days later he took the East Main sloop to Moose Fort, arriving on 11 September. Chief Factor Jarvis requested that he take a survey of the buildings and report on repairs needed. Turnor and the house carpenter walked around the site, Turnor muttering the whole while about its dreadful condition. Not only did the west flanker require rebuilding, but the stockades, platforms, smith's shop, cookrooms, and saw house needed repairs, and the main girder of the chief's flanker needed to be taken up as it had settled. He knew more about construction than the carpenter himself. However, he felt that little could be done this fall, and on that gloomy note he concluded his second journal, dated from 17 September 1779 to 14 September 1780.

Turnor had been in the country for just over two years now. Unfortunately, due to ice, the *King George* had not been able to get to York the previous fall to pick up the York packet, so the governors had not yet received Turnor's maps, letters, and journals of 1778–1779. Writing his annual letter to them on 18 September 1780, he said, "It gives me some uneasiness not being able these two years past to answer my letters in due course." He hoped that his requests for quicksilver, the 1781 *Nautical Almanac*, and a telescope had been somehow foreseen and sent out, but he reiterated the urgency of obtaining those items.

His three-year contract was to expire next April, by which time he anticipated having surveyed the route to Lake Superior and Lake Abitibi. He was not unhappy with his life here in Canada, but he requested a change: "If your Honors choose to continue me in your service I shall submit my terms to your Honors generosity. I should be exceeding happy in being appointed to the charge of Henley House in case there should be a vacancy or any other appointment your Honors may think fit to confer on me."[25] Without a doubt, he wanted advancement, but did he request this trading position for health reasons or for monetary reasons?

If it had been frustrating not being in correspondence with the London offices, it was just as hard not being able to write home to his family. He was concerned about his ageing mother and would not alarm her with news of his snow blindness and his illness in March that left him quite debilitated. He would tell the others something of his strange existence here in the barrens. He could imagine them, in the late November winter light, reading his letters all the way from Rupert's Land. What would they think of the tales of drownings, of the killing cold of the winters, the insufferable mosquito swarms of the spring and summers, the near starvation, the peculiar taste of pemmican, his snowshoe expeditions, his scraggy appearance, and his wearing of leathers and furs from deer, bear, and moose?

JOURNAL SIX

In Touch with the Turners

September 2012

There are still Turners at Moose Factory—some 230 years after Philip Turnor left. They are descended in the male line from Philip to his son, Joseph Turner, to Joseph's third-born, Philip Turner. Joseph adopted the 'er' spelling of Turner although Philip Sr.'s name was almost always spelled with the 'or'. I imagine some clerk felt he was correcting an error, but to me, the 'or' of Philip's name gives him distinction.

When Dorothy Turner, a four-times-great-granddaughter of Philip, first contacted me, she was working at the hospital in Moose Factory. Her sister, Trudy, and their mother, Daisy, lived across the river in Moosonee. During my visit in 2012, two other sisters, Myrtle and Susan, arrived for a visit, and I met a brother who lives on the island. It was a family reunion for them—and, for me, an introduction to distant relations and to Moose Factory.

In some ways Daisy was a connection for me to the life that Philip's Cree wife must have led in the 1780s. Though Daisy had been born at Fort Albany in 1918, and not in a camp in the bush, she had spent time with her mother and father working a trapline along the Albany River. She remembered trapping marten, just as Philip's wife would have done in the 1780s. However, at age eight, Daisy's life changed when she was sent to the Anglican residential school in Moose Factory. She told me it was difficult, but not as bad as the Catholic school

Figure 18. Author with Turner sisters, Myrtle, Dorothy, Trudy,
and Sue, and their mother Daisy at Moose Factory.

where the nuns and priest were "hard." Daisy was quiet and mostly
listened to the rest of us discuss family connections, but she did tell
me she had unpleasant memories of having to scrub the residential
school's wooden floors when she was just a young child. She married
George William (Bill) Turner in 1938 and had eleven children. Bill had
also been sent to the residential school in Moose Factory, after which
he worked as an interpreter, much like his great-great-grandfather
Joseph. Daisy had been keen to encourage and maintain Cree culture
among the young, and she became involved in the Moose Factory
School, where she worked as a teacher's aide. In 1974 she wrote a book
on Cree syllabics, *Moose Factory Cree*, accompanied by an audio tape,
for use in the schools. She revised it over the years, and it has been
through nine reprints: nearly 7000 printed copies. At ninety-four
she was a small woman, but one who had been an influential "keis
kei noah ma kay skwao" (teacher).[26]

Philip Turnor was named a "National Historic Person," and a plaque was erected at Moose Factory to acknowledge the seven years (1780–1787) he spent exploring the Moose and Albany Rivers, and for producing "the first accurate maps of much of this part of northern Ontario."[27] While his longest stay at the fort itself was for seven months, from August 1781 to May 1782, it was his home base for those seven years. And it was here that his Cree wife and son Joseph settled in 1787.

It was grey, rainy, and just six degrees when we walked out to find the site of the old fort along Bank Road. Along the way we walked around Centennial Park noting the various HBC employee houses, including the oldest, a small, plain, wooden house facing the river that had belonged to Joseph Turner. These buildings had all been moved to the park from various sites on the island, except for the powder magazine built in 1865 that is in its original location. As tourist season was over, the houses were boarded up. Across the street was the attractive two-storey HBC Staff House. Though closed to the public as well, workmen were starting renovations and allowed us to wander through the rooms and look at the exhibits. It had been built in 1847, sixty years after Turnor's time, and had been through many transitions, being reused as apartments and then a museum. Turnor would have remarked that it was "in most ruinous condition," just as he had about Moose Fort when he first saw it. Buildings here were continuously under repair due to the climate and the lowland tidal and permafrost conditions.

We walked down a trail to the "mighty" Moose. In Turnor's day this bank would have been river, but it has silted in so that "mighty" is used ironically by the locals here who have seen many changes in their river. In the 1780s there would have been a launch here, just below all the HBC buildings, a launch that Turnor complained was too small to accommodate the sloops.

The next day we went out on the Moose River in one of the river taxis, a fibreglass boat with a tarp cover and a huge, 120-horsepower Mercury motor. I wanted to see the route that Philip would have taken to the Abitibi country. Our pilot was Willie Small, a kind, obliging man who suffered my naive questions with a smile. As the tide was coming in behind us and we were heading up the Moose River, with its currents running down to James Bay, the boat had to buck these competing flows. Willie told us that six or seven miles farther on up was the French River and fifteen miles on was the Abitibi, both rivers that Turnor had surveyed. This was his route to Frederick House.

Philip regularly joined the fall and spring goose hunts, and I asked Willie if he participated in them. "Harvests," he called them—a much better word. I asked if he knew of "Whayway Creek,"[28] where Turnor went to hunt. "That must be Wavey Creek where the wavies come in," he said. I checked this in Daisy's Cree book. Yes, "whay hay ow"[29] refers to the blue goose or wavey.

Willie took us back to Moosonee to catch the Polar Bear Express, and we retraced our route to Cochrane, 185 miles south. We passed the muddy, shallow Moose and then the trees crowded up against the tracks. It was as if we were passing through an open-roofed tunnel of black spruce, pines, aspens, poplars, and sky. Every so often it opened and we saw a river or a creek. Sometimes names were marked on white railway signs: Onakawana, or Wirtle, or East Jawbone Creek. We passed the Abitibi again and then slowed down for the Ontario Power generating plant established on Otter Rapids. Through the foggy train window I took numerous photos. I had wanted to see this place close up. I knew it was one of three very dangerous rapids on the Abitibi, and I knew it was here that Turnor had experienced one of his most difficult journeys. I could see why when I saw the huge slabs of granite at the foot of the dam that he would have had to navigate. ✳

6.

Three-Year Contract Fulfilled

Overland Journeys: Moose Fort, Albany, East Main, Mesakamy (Kesagami), *December 1780 to April 1781*

In October Chief Factor Jarvis wrote in the Moose Fort journal that they were ill prepared for the winter. They had only one cask of salted geese left and not enough firewood or hay gathered for the winter months. As a result of the poor diet, a number of men had scurvy. Their legs and thighs were swollen and black, their tendons so stiff they could only crawl.[1] They desperately needed fresh venison and geese. Turnor did not maintain his journal for the three months he was here, but, given the shortages and his disinclination to sit around, he no doubt went out hunting each day to contribute what he could.

His own work was held up. He needed the *Astronomical Ephemeris* to be sent from York Factory so he could do his computations of longitude.[2] However, he wanted to complete a chart of the Bay, and for that he needed more observations of the headlands between Moose and Albany Forts. When men from Albany arrived with trading goods for Moose Fort, Turnor took the opportunity to return to Albany with them, taking observations along the route. John Hodgson, who had been a good companion and useful assistant on last year's travels to Gloucester House, accompanied him. Though Turnor did not comment in any detail on this journey in his journal, six days trekking on snowshoes and sleeping in the bitter cold with wind whipping off James Bay must have been trying. The skies were clear for observations, but steadying his brass sextant, watch, and compass would take some patience. He was unable to complete computations from this journey without the *Nautical Almanac* and other mathematical tables, so he did not chart the area until he worked on his composite map in 1782–1783.[3]

They arrived at Albany on Christmas Eve. A fire and a few glasses of whiskey thawed his frozen bones. He stayed for the New Year's festivities to bring in 1781, then began his return journey to Moose Fort. Hutchins also sent a few of his men with three dogs to haul some trading blankets for Jarvis. It was "bad walking," Turnor wrote in his journal, and it took him nine days ploughing through the deep snow.[4] Though still a young man at thirty years, the harsh weather and laborious walking were taking a toll on his health. Ten days after they arrived at Moose Fort, barely enough time to restore himself, he left for East Main House to map the coastline around the bottom of the Bay. Once again on snowshoes, he and his three assistants trudged through the deep snow. One of the men, George Donald, had been with him on the journey to Gloucester the previous year and, having received training in practical astronomy at the Grey Coat Hospital School, was expected to help Turnor with his observations. Donald had done some mapping of the Albany River area, but his accuracy was affected not only by an episode with snow blindness, but because his instruments were damaged.

East Main House, on the east shore of James Bay on the East Main River, had been in operation since 1713. Like Moose Fort it was situated on a flat, lowland area, with James Bay on one side and a line of black spruce on the other. As they made their way around the bottom of the Bay and up to East Main, the snow was blinding in its brilliance. Turnor now knew how to protect his eyes with snow goggles, a carved piece of wood fitted to cover his eyes with the smallest slit to allow for sight.

Ten days after leaving Moose Fort, they arrived at Rupert's River. It was only a log tent[5] but a welcome reprieve from their own rough shelter. Two more days of walking and they arrived at East Main on 5 February, where Turnor was greeted by George Atkinson, the chief factor there for the past two years. Turnor kept his opinion of Atkinson in reserve, although he appeared friendly and competent on first meeting. Atkinson was about forty-five and had worked off and on for the HBC since 1751. He had a Cree family and a good relationship with the Indigenous people in the area that helped him develop a prosperous trade for East Main—five thousand Made Beaver in 1780. The Montreal traders were not far off on the Rupert River, and Atkinson had made a dent in their profits.[6] However, an inland trip in 1777 left Atkinson in ill health, and he often begged for the services of the surgeon from Albany. Both Hutchins at Albany and Jarvis at Moose found him difficult.

Turnor arrived back at Moose Fort on 1 March and spent the month putting down his observations of the two winter trips he had undertaken, all of which would be added to the map he would draw up in 1782. On 2 April, with George Donald and three other men, he started off for Mesakamy Lake, an area that had not been much explored. Walking south and east towards the lake, they managed only thirty-one miles in six days. Even though they travelled in the early morning, starting off at 3:00 a.m., the snow was too soft to support them and their snowshoes constantly broke through the crust. Deciding it was futile, they returned to Moose Fort on 7 April. They would leave this region south of Moose Fort for another year and head for Lake Superior.

Wapiscogamy, *Spring 1781*

On 11 May Turnor and Donald left in their canoe along with the bateau[7] for Wapiscogamy,[8] 150 miles up the Missinaibi River, the west branch of the Moose River. Because it was spring, the current was running heavily and the banks were covered in ice so they could not track. They had to follow the windings of the river near shore and that increased the mileage and made for twelve-hour days. However, there were no major problems on this section and they arrived at Wapiscogamy House on 23 May.

Donald had been master there in 1780, but John Thomas was in charge now. Thomas was critical of the condition of the House, which was nothing more than a log tent, and Turnor must have echoed those opinions. It had no proper foundation, no cellar to keep their salt geese cool in the summer, and the support for the girders and the chimney had been severely undermined by the dogs digging to get away from the mosquitoes in the summer.[9] Furthermore, it was not strategically located on a height of land where the men could see approaching travellers. Turnor had been asked by Jarvis to consult with Thomas on whether to repair the house or simply make it habitable until a better house could be built. The response, which did not arrive until spring 1782, indicated that Turnor had grander plans for Wapiscogamy than did the company: "The plan designed by Mr. Turnor seems to us too extended for our occasions; however as it may at the arrival of our ship be in great part completed we acquiesce therein, though we trust from the great plenty of timber you are furnished with, it will be attended with little additional expense."[10] It was Turnor's firm opinion that Wapiscogamy was a promising trading house and suited the local Cree band very well:

> I should suppose had this place been supplied with trading goods and properly managed at first it would have been a place of tolerable trade by this time as I think many Indians would come to this place which would not come to the Factory because at this place they can drink in peace which is more than they can do at the Factory. The home guard Indians both at Moose and Albany Fort constantly drink the brandy from them some times without giving them a part of it.[11]

As he had requested in his 1780 letter to the committee, Turnor hoped to be placed in charge of a house and earn a larger salary. He could see that John Thomas, with his Cree wife Margaret and two children, was content with that position. After all his travelling, Turnor thought he would like to settle, and, if all went well, he could finish his contracted work—surveying to Lake Superior and then Abitibi—by the end of this season.

John Thomas was a man who put his cards on the table. About the same age as Turnor, he was more experienced, having been in the service since 1769. He had travelled in this area for some years, going as far as Michipicoten on Lake Superior and Lake Abitibi to the south, and he made no bones about the fact that the company was not provisioning the men well enough to allow them to carry on their explorations or their trading. Due to "great fatigue, trouble & danger" in travelling this area, in 1777 he had demanded a contract for fifty pounds per year (a raise from his twenty pounds) plus a ten pound gratuity, and in the future he requested eighty pounds. He had actually signed a contract, inserting in his own hand the fifty pounds he expected. In May 1778 the governors angrily replied that he had no right to do that and they voided the contract, insisting he stay at his former salary. He felt unfairly treated and declined to go inland past Wapiscogamy. In spite of this boldness on his part, the governors thought he was a capable man and, in 1782, he succeeded Jarvis at Moose Fort at a salary of £130.[12]

Turnor had not met Thomas until now, but might well have heard through the grapevine of his displeasure with the committee. Perhaps Donald had heard about it and mentioned it while they were trudging their way through deep snow to East Main or Lake Mesakamy (now Kesagami) when conversation would be a welcome diversion. At any rate, when Turnor wrote asking for the promotion, he requested a raise to sixty pounds. He was granted the raise,[13] but, as the London Committee wrote, he would not receive a promotion as yet to master of a house:

> We are very ready to accept the continuance but cannot with propriety appoint you to the charge of Henley House; however you may depend upon our not being unmindful of you, and that we will take an early opportunity of promoting you. In the meantime, we wish you to proceed in going to and making observations to settle the longitude and latitude of Missinaibi and any other places which may be thought necessary and to make yourself master of the Indian language which will be necessary to qualify you for taking charge of any settlement.
>
> We have named you to be of the Council at Moose Fort whilst you shall be there which mark of our regard we hope will encourage you to be attentive and assistant to our Chief and to promote harmony in the factory without which no designs can be formed or executed for the extending our trade which ought to be the chief object both of our servants and ourselves.
>
> We remain
> Your loving friends[14]

Lake Superior, *Late Spring 1781*

On 7 June 1781, Turnor, George Donald, and three guides, including Abbicootch, Shenap, one of Sackawabisk's sons, and their
wives, left Wapiscogamy for Missinaibi Lake and Lake Superior. This
route had been well travelled by the Cree, Ojibwa, and Algonquin for
centuries. As for the Europeans, Radisson and Groseilliers had been
there over 100 years before Turnor, though not using the northern
river route, and by 1725 the French had a post on the Michipicoten
River from which they could make forays into the interior and establish trade. Alexander Henry, one of the Montreal traders, had
established a post there in 1767. Both Jarvis in 1776 and Thomas in
1777 had made exploratory journeys noting a couple of Montreal
houses, but Turnor's survey, his comments on the terrain, and his
map would enable the company to decide where to establish future
posts—all a part of their plan to intercept trade between the Montreal
traders and the Cree.

On their first two days of travel it rained heavily and they made
little progress. On 10 June the landscape changed dramatically. They
entered the Canadian Shield, "bold" land,[15] as Turnor referred to it.
Above this point on the Missinaibi, the route flowed through the
spectacular falls at Hell's Gate Canyon and the mighty Thunderhouse
Falls, and over more than seventy-five sets of rapids with a rise of
almost 330 metres. It required constant vigilance.[16] Turnor had no
time to admire the natural beauty, recorded no names for these falls,
and had eyes only for the dangers, for measuring the carrying places,
the height of the falls, the width of the river between the rocks, its
twists and turns, the mileage travelled each day. Above the broiling
waters of what is now known as Hell's Gate Canyon, he simply wrote
that the carrying place was "very level and good" and concluded, "I
should suppose the water falls about 100 yards in this fall which is
about 2 mile long between high perpendicular rocks."[17] The facts were
all he recorded—except for one interesting interlude with his Cree
guides, who experienced a strong spiritual presence in the area: "At
the carrying place was detained about 2 hours by one of the Indians
coming back and informing the others the Devil had taken a bundle
which he had carried partover the carrying place, upon which the
Indians wanted us to go with them in search of him."[18] Turnor, a man
of the Enlightenment, thought this was a trick of theirs to fright-

en the Englishmen so they could give them the slip and take off with the canoes. He refused to go searching with them, but agreed to let them go off on their own while he stayed watching the cargo and canoes. Two hours later they returned. They had met Cowesowescogee, an Upland Cree whom Turnor recognized from trading at Wapiscogamy. He, their devil, was in fact their benefactor. Coming upon the bundle, he had carried it across for them.

One mile farther south they came to Stone Falls and carried one thousand yards. Then they were at Thunderhouse Falls where the Missinaibi narrowed to forty feet or less, thrusting all its force between high grey granite rocks, the white foam spewing up, the rumbling felt in one's very core. Just before they ascended the portage for this falls, they saw at the base the fifty-foot tower of the Conjuring House Rock, the mystical pillar revered by the Cree. It was said to look like a shaman's tent or the shaman himself, the sunlight and shadow etching out a human face. The spiritual presence at Thunderhouse Falls may be Nebaunaubaequae, who is "a luring water spirit, tempting canoeists to run the rapids instead of taking the safe route along the portage."[19] Here the guides would ask for his protection and safe passage, perhaps offering a gift of tobacco or a medicine bundle. Turnor did not indicate any stop here, although they put up near a small island two miles on. Of this site he wrote only that they came to "the fall very high between two perpendicular rocks about 40 ft apart."[20]

Figure 19. Thunderhouse Falls on the Missinaibi River.

The next day, after travelling just seven miles, Turnor was "taken very ill" and they had to stop at noon, but he was able to get away early the next morning. Two days on they came to an area that had been ravaged by fire. Through the heavy rain they could see only burnt stumps and scarred woods. Abbicootch was concerned. He hardly recognized the land and found it difficult to determine his way.[21] Finally, on 17 June, they were in Mecawbawnish Lake (Brunswick Lake), having travelled about 105 miles from Wapiscogamy. They set out nets and were rewarded with twenty-five large tickameg (whitefish), which Turnor reported as being the next-best eating-fish to sturgeon. This lake might be a good place for a house, so he took an observation for latitude.

For the next week they worked hard leading and carrying over many falls as they continued to travel through the burnt landscape. On 23 June, in Missinaibi Lake, they came upon the ruins of Missinaibi House, built by John Thomas for the HBC in 1777. They took a short break here while Turnor took observations and investigated the burnt ruins of the house. He felt with certainty that the house had not been caught in a natural forest fire as they had been informed by the guides, but that it had been deliberately burned by one of the local bands.[22]

They were soon underway for Michipicoten. They passed a number of islands, the land "bold & rocky,"[23] and continued into Missinabeeasish Lake (Crooked Lake). Turnor made no mention of seeing the Ojibwa pictographs at the western end of Missinaibi Lake, including the frightening Mishipizhiw water spirit, who was associated with treacherous waters, and the Memegwaysiwuk, the hairy-faced little people who hid in the rock crevices. Surely he would have commented had he seen this granite rock face, over 100 feet in width, covered with ochre images of canoes, animals, and spiritual creatures. Was he fluent enough yet to know that the name of the river, Missinaibi, could be translated as "pictured waters"?[24]

They carried 500 yards over the height of land that divided the water flowing east into Hudson Bay and southwest into Lake Superior, and paddled into Wawakegummau (Dog Lake). The land was high and rocky; some woods were burnt, though some areas were covered with pine and aspen. They carried over Little Stoney and Big Stoney Portages, difficult treks over loose, rough stones. After Manitowik Lake they paddled past the Hawk River, by which they would return, and into the Michipicoten River, which they ran down to Cat Portage. On 26 June they portaged the two-mile Long Portage and High Portage "down two steep hills,"[25] passed the mouth of the Magpie River, and arrived at Michipicoten House, a journey of about 400 miles from Moose Fort undertaken in 33 days.

Michipicoten House was in the possession of a Montreal trader, J. B. Nolin, and four of his men. It was an "exceeding bad building," wrote Turnor, "and they have the pride to call it a Fort." It was roughly built of cedar and mud, just two rooms, and "the only fastening is a slight single bolt." However, it was a strategic post. The location on the south side of the Michipicoten River, a short distance from Magpie River, was well chosen, and in fact the Hudson's Bay Company would later put up their own house here. Turnor wrote a lengthy report for the London Committee, describing the fishing, the opportunities for maintaining cattle, chickens, and horses on the "fine Plantation," and noting the quantity of furs collected by Nolin. Nolin told him that if his partner came soon they might make a settlement at Mecawbawnish Lake. Turnor's advice was that "if your Honors should again settle a House near Missinaibi Lake it would entirely stop their progress."[26]

He seemed to have second thoughts about this advice, for at the close of his 1780–1781 journal he added a note: "It is out of my power to warmly recommend a settlement to be erected at Missinaibi Lake as I think the expense in supplying it will be very great in proportion to the trade that would be got at it as the country seems very thinly peopled and very scarce of provisions."[27] Rather he suggested sending some men from Wapiscogamy to trade at Missinaibi Lake or nearer Michipicoton for a month at a regular time each year.[28]

During the stop at Michipicoten Turnor climbed a nearby hill to get a view of the surrounding area and took his observations. The next two days were rainy and cloudy and, because he was eager to survey Abitibi this year and the weather was not clearing, they decided to get underway on 29 June, intending to stop near Michipicoten House if the weather cleared. It did not, and they carried on to the Magpie River, camping the first night at Wawa Lake, about eight miles from Michipicoten. The next day was drudgery: they carried the canoes almost half as much as they paddled them, lugging them through woods from one brackish swamp to another until they reached Manitowik

Lake. But it was the shorter route. Then they were back in the old track that they had taken for their journey going up, and arrived at Missinaibi Lake on 1 July and at the old Missinaibi House the next day.

On 5 July at the first fall, Turnor's canoe hit a rock and sank. They retrieved it, repaired it, and were on their way again by half past noon. He had lost his shoes, a tin pot, and his powder horn, but as he wrote, "[I] luckily saved everything else, my sextant getting wet, all the black came off the index glass and cracked the quicksilver. The black I think I can repair but do not know what to do to the quicksilver." Such accidents were commonplace to him now. In fact, when they arrived on 9 July at Wapiscogamy he wrote in his journal that they had "not met with anything remarkable."[29]

Turnor was also becoming comfortable with the Cree language and recorded Cree names of lakes and rivers in his journal more regularly. In doing so he recorded what he heard from his guides. Official English names, a stamp of ownership, were chosen by the London Committee (York Fort, Nelson River, Cumberland House), but the farther away from a HBC settlement, the more the naming was in the local language. On the final leg of the journey from Wapiscogamy (which was renamed Brunswick House in 1782) to Moose Fort, the many smaller rivers did not have English names. He wrote that they passed Showwesta Seepe[30] on the north side, Mesaquagamay on the south side, and the next day they came to Maatapuseswana-shish a Seepe or Rabbit River, where "the Devil was formerly caught roasting a Rabbit."[31] He continued to list the rivers: Menetaeskeek a Seepe, then Metockahagan Seepe, Jepass Seepe, Chimahagan Seepe, and Cutapewahagan Seepe. Perhaps he was thinking in Cree now. However, while the names appeared on his tongue and in his journal, they were not marked down on his map, except for "Je-pass Seepe." Noticeably, as they neared the fort, the names became anglicized, and he commented that a creek on the north side was "called by the English Hancocks Creek," and then there was French Creek and South Bluff Creek. The English preferred to name their places after themselves or after a location rather than, as the Cree did, tie the name metaphorically to the landscape or tell a story.

They pushed hard on the next two days, up at 3 a.m., paddling past the white limestone rock cliffs of the lowlands, through all the islands, by the small creeks, the wind hot in their faces. At 11:30 a.m.,

13 July, they were at Moose Fort. Turnor's notes and observations from this journey would be entered on his next map and would form the first accurate survey of the Missinaibi and Michipicoten Rivers.[32]

Towards Abitibi Lake, *July 1781*

Turnor was anxious to get underway to Abitibi Lake, but he had to wait for his guides to arrive. He conferred with them about the route to be taken, and they advised going up the Moose River to French Creek, then following a couple of branches of that river so he could see where Mesakamy House, the Montreal traders' settlement, was located. Since George Donald was needed by Jarvis at the Fort, David Laughton was to accompany him and three guides. On the first day, 27 July, it was impossible, as usual, to pull the guides away from the trading post, so they did not set off until 6 p.m. and put up three-quarters of an hour later. Calmly he wrote his entry for the day, "It may seem strange but Indians never travel any distance the first day." He provided them with a good drink the first night, and the second day, "being sleepy and the canoes leaky," the men stayed put. Turnor accepted this as the Cree custom and, when on 29 July they were ready to get seriously underway, he commented, "I have great hopes of making a quick journey, the Indians being well pleased."[33]

Little did he know what was ahead. They went into French Creek and in a few days were leading the canoes on a zigzag course through very shallow water in Nequagamashisktick Seepe and Keaskshasish a Seepe. He noted meticulously all the distances for the next five days—a sixth of a mile one direction, a quarter another, an eighth another. On 3 August he wrote in his journal that he "was not able to go in the canoe since the first day and a half but walked through the woods."[34] The canoes, even though being led, were battered in the shallow water. To make matters worse, on 30 July he recorded that the woods were on fire. They continued, but soon the canoes were so damaged by the rocks that the guides thought it best to return and take a different route up the Abitibi River. He could do nothing but agree, but he knew that it would be too late to take the Abitibi this year.

They put in a full day on the 5 August and, in the evening, a spectacular storm broke that Turnor felt compelled to write about: "The wind with rain came in the face of our tenting which was only birch rind put up to windward; upon which we turned our tent which we had no sooner done that the wind came about again with as heavy rain and thunder as ever I saw and the thunder so close that for ¼ hour there was not a second of time between the flash and the clap."[35] At the end of an hour, every piece of clothing was soaked. The best he could do was take off his shirt and lie in the wet blankets. At 4 a.m., when the rain abated, they lit a fire, dried themselves out, and started off again, arriving the following day, 7 August, at Moose Fort.

Another aborted trip. Twelve days out and only fifty-one miles each way. Next year he would not let the Abitibi defeat him.

Turnor was no complainer. The swarming mosquitoes and black flies that plagued most of the men, the long hours, the scanty and unvarying food, the weather—the cold, the damp, the heat, the humidity—these things were seldom mentioned by him. What was infinitely more important were his sextant and watch, which had been damaged, the black on his index glass having come entirely off. He would send the watch back for repairs and make do with the rest. He meekly asked the company for a tent. There had been no feather mattresses for him on his journeys, and in fact he had usually slept on the hard ground, but this time he wrote, "I hope your Honours will allow me a small light tent as it is rather uncomfortable laying under a tree all night after a hard days work."

Next year he promised the committee a map of the rivers and lakes he had travelled, and he listed the items he desperately needed for future exploration: a reliable watch, a new index glass, and more quicksilver. While asking that the watch the company had provided be repaired and sent back, he requested "a good Watch,"[36] for which he, himself, offered to pay twenty pounds, one-third of his yearly salary. It was important to him to be as accurate as possible. He concluded with the customary thanks for being allowed to continue in the service and expressed a wish for early promotion. In the meantime, he assured "their Honours" that he would travel to Abitibi Lake next year. He sealed his letter, closed his journal and observation booklets, and enclosed all in the packet—a year all neatly tied up in a bundle of measurements and directions, a small reflection of the real world he had navigated that year.

His three-year contract had been fulfilled as of May 1781. The company had been pleased with his work, and he had been renewed at sixty pounds per year for another three years. By canoe, foot, sloop, and snowshoes, and by his own calculations and astronomical measurements he had travelled nearly 5000 miles—as far north as York Factory (at 57°01'51" north latitude), as far south as Michipicoten on Lake Superior (at 47°56' north latitude), as far east as East Main (at 78°42' west longitude), and as far west as Hudson House (at 106°27'20" west longitude).[37] He had visited all the company posts, except for Fort Prince of Wales, surveyed them, and analyzed their future prospects. He had a more accurate, scientific overview of the company's inland settlements than any other man in the company's employ.[38] Of course, he still had the Abitibi country to finish surveying, but he was satisfied with what he had accomplished.

7.

Celebrations and Disasters

Moose Fort, *Fall 1781*

The ship arrived on 5 September. The unloading and loading of the ship was an event, and the Home Guard came around to trade for the newly arrived goods. The ship sailed on 21 September—and then began the goose hunt.[1]

Turnor went out almost daily to the hunting grounds at Whayway Creek, dealing out powder and shot, and joining the shoot himself. He may have camped out a few days with the Home Guard hunters. The hunt always stirred his blood, the men calling in the geese, the whooshing beat of wings, the sudden barrage of gunshots. A good hunt was crucial to their survival over the winter. One day he and five men harvested 220 geese, and another time John Thomas, the second in command at Moose Fort, went out to Bread River and came back with 1700 geese that the Home Guard Cree had got for the fort. The end of the fall hunt was always celebrated by the Cree people with a feast, the smoking of the calumet, and ritual dances of thanks.

Before winter took hold, the men had to gather the wood, harvest the garden, bring home the cattle, salt the geese, and put up the boats. Most of the work was done by 5 November when Jarvis, as usual, ordered a hog to be killed, and at night they made a "noble bonfire and rejoiced on the happy anniversary," the day in 1605 when Guy Fawkes and a number of English Catholics failed to blow up Parliament and assassinate the King.[2] Two cultures—two traditions of celebration.

With the celebrations over, Turnor returned to his mapping. It was disappointing that he had not been able to get to Mesakamy, but he would, come spring. And he had something else to think about in the spring. Sometime in September Turnor had accepted a Cree woman and she was pregnant with his child.

Mapping the Interior Man

For a man who set out to fill in the blanks of the vast north country of Rupert's Land, Philip Turnor left huge spaces concerning his own interior. He was especially silent on one matter—that of "keeping a woman," as he had described it earlier. Nothing is mentioned of her or their child (or children) in Turnor's journals or correspondence. This is not unusual. Officers generally kept their personal affairs out of their journals and letters, and Turnor was more business-like than most. Occasionally, however, mention was made in minutes or account books of payments made to a woman, or especially to children, but I found none for Turnor's family.

A son was born bearing the Turnor name some time in June 1782, according to the "Register of Births" in the family Bible passed down by Turner descendants. Philip could have accepted a woman from among the Home Guard at Moose Fort or from the inland Cree who came to the fort to trade during ship time and to join the hunt. Around this time, from 29 September until 11 October, Philip was at Whayway Creek hunting. He may have attended the goose hunt feast, been introduced to a Cree woman there, and joined in the ritual ceremonies. But wherever the meeting took place, I imagine it happened something like this:

A Cree captain and his lieutenants arrive to trade and hunt. Perhaps it is Captain Chichehennis,[3] the chief among the Home Guard Moose River Cree. He would have noticed Philip, who was an excellent marksman and always took his share in the goose hunt.

It would be an honour to establish a kinship with such a man. Perhaps the offer took place in a ceremonial tent at Whayway Creek or perhaps at the fort during a trading day. A calumet is smoked. There is no talk, just the cracking of the fire and the drawing of the pipe. Philip does not smoke, but, knowing the ceremonial significance, he may have taken a turn. After the pipe, Philip (with his limited Cree) and Captain Chichehennis talk of the comings and goings of the band, how much they harvested on the hunt, when they would leave for their winter quarters. In recognition of the chief's position, he would be offered a red captain's coat with a waistcoat and matching yarn stockings, and a hat with an ostrich feather. Other small items are given for the chief to share with his people. Brandy is offered all round.

Perhaps it is at this time, before the drinking and the serious trading begin, that the captain extends his gift. "You, Mr. Turnor, you are one of the chiefs here. A woman would help you. She will teach you to speak our language. Our people want to be your friends."

Philip may have been expecting an offer. Perhaps he has noticed this woman before. He does not refuse, for he knows that would offend both the chief and his daughter.[4] And he is ready to have the pleasure—and the help—of a woman. He promises to "cloath" her and provide for her, and offers a special gift to the chief—a gun or a blanket. And so he has a Cree wife who takes her small bundle of things to his quarters. She will warm his bed, cook for him, make his snowshoes, teach him the Cree language, interpret for him, paddle in his canoe—and bear him a son.

The chief and his men go to their tents with more brandy, gathering up the gifts of bread and prunes. When they are finished their feasting and are sober again, in a night or a day or two, they return to the fort and smoke another pipe together with the officers.

The serious business of trading begins with a speech from Chief Chichehennis, a plea for fair treatment in their negotiations.

"We need guns and powder. We bring you geese from the hunt, furs, and provisions. Treat us well. Give us good measure of the cloth,[5] which our women like. When you measure our powder, do not put your thumb within the brim. Treat us well."

"I am pleased you have come to trade with us," responds Chief Factor Jarvis. "You have brought many furs. We will treat you well. We have good blankets and kettles and guns."

The account book is taken out and the Standard of Trade (showing the values of trade objects in terms of Made Beaver—MB), is consulted—one gun for fourteen MB, one kettle for one and a half MB, seven to ten marten for one MB, one to two lynx for one MB, and so forth. The trade is written down—sometimes paid, sometimes a debt.

The trading done, the book closed, there are the final gifts to be presented. The chief is given more powder and shot, more tobacco, some oatmeal and prunes.

Judging from the single, short entry he wrote at Gloucester House about union with a Cree woman, Turnor would have respected her and found her assistance indispensable. She would teach him the Cree language, which he had been instructed to learn, and she would help him forge ties with Cree leaders. At the very least, this was a political union, not unlike many European aristocratic unions, for purposes of power, status, and financial benefit. But, I believe, given the man he was, that he had affection for her.[6]

She, my great-great-great-great grandmother, may not have had a choice in the transaction, but she certainly would have understood her role in such an alliance with this important white trader and surveyor.[7] She had seen among other officers that these liaisons were often temporary, for the men returned to their homeland when their contracts were up. She would have been prepared for that, knowing that her people would always welcome her and her child back.

Did Philip use her Cree name or give her a British name? Perhaps she sat with him during the dull afternoons, watching him at work on his maps, giving him lessons in her language. She, in turn, would learn English. She would have cared for him through the winter when he suffered his muscle spasms and pains, giving him teas and rubbing his joints with salves. When Philip snowshoed to Albany in March and when he set off to survey Lake Abitibi in May, did she return to her family who were settled around the fort, or did she accompany him into Abitibi country? It is difficult imagining her in the last month of her pregnancy in a canoe swept along by the dangerous Sextant Rapids.

Most likely Joseph was born at Moose Fort, where her own family were camped. She would have constructed for herself a small brush hut in which to give birth in privacy.[8] There she stayed alone with her baby Joseph for a few days, wrapping him in moss she had gathered earlier in the year and swaddling him in the tikinagan, the wooden cradleboard.

There are so few coordinates to mark on the map of Philip's personal life; but I take this "Register of Births" to be the most accurate notation we have that connects Philip and his son, Joseph. Unlike the map locations determined so precisely by Philip, there are several versions of Joseph's birth: Dorothy Turner, a four-times-great-granddaughter of Philip Turnor who was born at Moose Fort, as was her father, wrote that "Philip Turnor fathered Joseph (whose mother was from Wapiscogamy [Brunswick] House) in 1782."[9] Pearl Weston, also a four-times-great-granddaughter of Philip Turnor, stated that "Joseph was born about 1784, therefore his birth likely took place in the Moose Fort or Abitibi country."[10] The HBCA Biographical Sheets indicate his birth date as "ca 1783."

Figure 20. Tikinagan or cradleboard.

Wherever my great-great-great grandfather Joseph Turner Sr. was born, he would have travelled with his father and his mother on the Moose River and the Abitibi River. When Philip returned to England in 1787, he would have been five, old enough to remember a face, a story, the English language. He and his mother would have gone back to her people, among whom he would be raised in the traditional Cree ways. But his mother proudly told him about his father. He continued to learn English from the men at the fort. From his earliest days, his mother encouraged him to be enterprising. In 1799 when he was about seventeen, he took a position with the Hudson's Bay Company as a labourer and canoe man, moved up the ladder to become master of Frederick House like his father, and fulfilled the last forty-two years of his service as an interpreter in the Moose River, Albany River, and Lake Superior regions. For his long and dedicated service he was given a house in Moose Fort[11] to live out his final two years, dying in March 1865. ✳

"Doleful Tidings," 1782

The child born in the spring was the only happy news for a year. Late winter 1781 through 1782 ushered in the worst few years for the company in nearly a century. The smallpox epidemic was the first crisis to strike. It had decimated the upper Missouri River bands in 1780 and moved up to Cumberland and Hudson Houses on the Saskatchewan River in December 1781. The Cree brought news to the inland houses of camps with tents standing silent, no human or animal sound echoing in the white winter air. Turnor, tucked away at the bottom of the Bay at Moose Fort, was unaffected by the disease and did not even hear the terrible news until the epidemic was over.

At Cumberland House and Hudson House, where the stricken Cree came for help, William Tomison and William Walker dealt as best they could with the desperate scene. Men, women, and chil-

Figure 21. Joseph Turner's 1863 house, at left, at Moose Factory Centennial Park Museum.

dren dragged themselves into the forts, begging for help. They were violently ill with fevers, vomiting, and severe weakness. Some of the men, fiery hot with the fever, threw themselves onto the snow to cool off, which only worsened the symptoms. Many died within four days, even before the lesions appeared. These two HBC houses turned themselves into hospitals. They enforced quarantines, isolated the sick, imposed airings in the sunshine and fumigations with sulphur, and tended to the immediate and proper burial of the dead, thereby lessening the spread as much as possible, though digging graves in the frozen earth was no small feat. Because of their exposure to the disease in England, the English themselves were relatively immune and only one man of mixed ancestry at York Fort came down with smallpox. Rumours flew that ninety per cent of the northern peoples had died and that fifty to sixty per cent of the plains nations were gone. None of their traditional medicines provided any relief, and the disease devastated many bands. Though smallpox had appeared before, in epidemic proportions from 1737–1738, this time it was more pervasive and destructive.

It was not until 26 August 1782, four or five months after the crisis, that the shallop from the north brought a letter from Matthew Cocking, interim chief at York Fort. "Dear Sir," he wrote to Jarvis, chief at Moose Fort:

> I believe never letter in Hudson Bay conveyed more doleful tidings than this; much the greatest part of the Indians whose furs have been formerly & hitherto brought to this place are now no more, having been carried off by that cruel distemper, the small pox....
>
> On the 2nd of July Mr. William Tomison with 22 English assisted by only two Indian lads and a few women arrived. Mr. Tomison informed me that the small pox had destroyed most of the Indians inland. The whole tribe of U'Basquiou Indians (their former Assistants) are extinct, except one child, and that of the several tribes of Assinnee, Poet, Pegogomew and others bordering on Saskatchewan River, he really believed not one in fifty had survived. He said that some of the Indians who went to war last year having met with a tent of Snake Indians who were ill of

the small pox they killed & scalped them, by this means they received the disorder themselves and most of them died on their return.[12]

Cocking managed to save his Home Guard by keeping them away from the travelling families.

The disease continued to attack the Cree in the hinterland areas of Gloucester House, Henley House, and Brunswick House until 1783, but did not reach the houses themselves.[13] Nor did it reach Albany Fort or Moose Fort. Some bands were spared; some were devastated. At Brunswick House, a year later in 1783, Turnor noticed an increase in trade because the Cree arriving at that House had not been affected by the epidemic. Overall, however, the disease took its toll. Bands suffering great losses amalgamated with other bands, which altered trading patterns. Some bands relocated. The devastation caused low morale among Indigenous people as well as the HBC men. In some areas, with fewer Cree hunters, there was a continual worry about starvation. In areas hardest hit there were fewer skins to trade, and fewer guides, hunters, and food suppliers to aid the company men. The impact was felt by Churchill and York Factories and reverberated across the ocean as well, for no dividends were paid out by the company from 1783–1786.[14]

At the same time that smallpox was ravaging the camps on the Saskatchewan, Henley House on the Albany River was destroyed by fire. Turnor, at Moose Fort, did not receive the news until 4 March when Hutchins, in great sorrow, wrote from Albany to Jarvis:

> …Henley House was burn'd down to its very foundation, on the 12th of January [1782] about midnight. In it every thing consumed, and what is a great aggravation of the distress 3 poor men J Luitet, R Cromaritie & James Rowlands perished in the flames. Mr. McNab [the master] and two men escaped naked to an Indian tent, but were much froze before they got there. This catastrophe was occasioned by a lamp accidently catching hold of some birch rind with which the men had lined their bedplaces to keep out the wind and rain, as the place was in a ruinous condition and being so very small & the fire beginning so winded the

conflagration soon became general so that it is almost a wonder any lives were saved at all.[15]

John McNab, surgeon and master at Henley, came to Albany, where he stayed for nearly two months before he could face once again the ruins of Henley House.

Turnor, deeply affected by the news, helped in the best way he could by drawing up plans for a new house at Henley. He took great pains to see that it was right. On 25 March he walked to Albany, perhaps hoping to consult with both McNab and Hutchins about the final draft for the new Henley House. However, McNab had just left for Henley, but Hutchins thought Turnor's plan was "very judicious."[16] It was a long journey for a short meeting, but, as Jarvis wanted Turnor back at Moose, he returned as soon as the thawing weather and rain allowed him to set off.

Abitibi Lake, *Spring 1782*

Turnor prepared for his journey to Abitibi Lake, this time choosing to go up the Abitibi River. His first two unsuccessful attempts the previous year had been on French Creek towards Mesakamy Lake. Jarvis had finally rounded up three long canoes, and, thankfully, a tent had been made for Turnor so he and his equipment would stay dry. Accompanying him on this journey were the reliable George Donald, who had been with him on two previous journeys, David Laughton, who had been on the aborted journey to Abitibi last summer, and John Leask, alongside six Cree guides and steersmen. Jarvis, however, in his letter of instructions to Turnor, ominously wondered if the guides might be "insufficient" on this trip.

Turnor set off on 23 May. In this, his fourth year of work for the company, Turnor had earned genuine admiration from Jarvis, who commended Turnor's "usual accuracy" in astronomical observations as "far above all praise." Turnor's assignment was to take observations of the Montreal traders' house on Lake Abitibi, map the route, determine if a settlement was desired by the Cree, and trade in the area for twenty days. Jarvis signed off his letter of instruction saying, "I cannot conclude without expressing my satisfaction in having so few directions to give a gentleman whose abilities & diligence leaves me little further to add than my wishes for your health."[17]

On 3 June, ninety miles up the Abitibi River, Turnor began passing through a series of three rapids that, in spite of nearly 5,000 miles of wilderness experience behind him, shook him to his core. The area was primordial, 300 million years old, with towering banks, and sills of lamprophyre spread like sheets across the river, creating devilish rapids:

> 90 miles very good river…but the last 10 pray God defend me from seeing worse provided I preserve my life and eye sight. Almost all falls the banks twice as high as the top of the flagstaff and so steep we cannot stand in the face of them, the woods all burnt and not an Indian knows the road. Had I known as much as I do now of the river I should not have been easily persuaded to have come this way.[18]

These dangerous rapids brought forth from Turnor the unusual plea to God to prevent him from seeing worse, an invocation seldom seen in his journals or correspondence.[19] A man of the Enlightenment, he depended more on science and rationality than on God's intervention.[20]

How did they get up these rapids? They could not line the canoes from the bank, and they did not portage. Just as John Thomas did on his 1774 journey to Abitibi Lake through similar terrain, they must have gotten out of the canoes and, standing on the slabs of rock, hauled them across,[21] or they might have poled through the water if that was possible.

The second set of rapids was particularly fierce, and David Laughton and Shenap's canoe was swamped. Laughton lost all his personal gear, not to mention trade goods, guns, twine, and blankets, about which Turnor said nothing to Laughton, who was shaken enough by the accident. But Turnor's loss was the greatest. He wrote to Jarvis,

> With great uneasiness I at present address you to inform you with the irreparable accident which happened this day which is the loss of my sextant by the swamping of the canoe in which it was, and what is aggravating I could hardly get it into the stern of the canoe that I thought it impossible

for it to get out. Would be obliged to you to send George Donald's quadrant & the quadrant belonging to the stand as between the two I hope in a great degree to supply the loss but not to my satisfaction as I shall entirely depend upon Jupiter, and doubt too much upon my watch as I fear I shall not be able to take the altitude of stars exact.[22]

The success of his mission depended on the sextant. Waiting an entire year, until the ship next May, was intolerable for him. However, gathering himself together, he finished off in a steady voice, "I hope to fight thro' it."

He marked on his map "first bad fall," now called Coral Rapids. The second falls, where he lost his sextant, has been named "Sextant Rapids."[23] The naming immortalized the challenge of these rapids and Turnor's tale. He again left his mark on the northern waters as he had two years earlier when he had carved his name on the hard northern granite at Marten Falls in July 1780.

Turnor dug out a new blanket from the trading bundle to give David Laughton. The guns were damaged and he was not comfortable trading them, so he returned them with George Donald, who was taking his letter containing the list of items they needed replaced. In the meantime, he planned to drop down the river to a fishing hole, hoping to find food rather than eat up the trip provisions.

Undoubtedly he maintained a journal for the trip, but only his map and two letters exist to show the route he took. From Moose Fort he had ascended the Abitibi, locating the following places on his map: "South bluf creek," "French Creek," "Ceader River," "Ceader little River," the "Abbitibbe Little River," then "first bad fall." Once he left these rapids (Coral, Sextant, and Otter), the clay-brown waters of the Abitibi quietened, and he had a peaceful journey to Abitibi Lake. At the southeastern end of the lake Turnor noted on his map a Montreal traders' settlement, "Abbitibbe House." His route home to Moose Fort was from the northeastern end of the lake into La Reine River and across the height of land to Bread River (Patten River). Then he travelled up Burntbush River and made his way over territory that had not yet been mapped.[24] He canoed across Mesakamy Lake, taking French Creek down to where it meets the Abitibi, and then headed home to Moose Fort.

With the sextant he had taken observations at Plum Island, where the Little Abitibi and the Abitibi River meet, but had to resort to the quadrant to record observations at the mouth of the Abitibi Lake, at the Montreal traders' settlement, and at Mesakamy Lake. Back at Moose Fort he would do the calculations for latitude and longitude to be sent home to the London Committee and, later, noted in his pamphlet, *Result of Astronomical Observations made in the Interior Parts of North America*, published in 1794. Turnor's map was the first scientific survey taken of this route.[25]

JOURNAL EIGHT

Transactions and Occurrences Regarding Sextant Rapids with Mr. Rick Isaacson, Canoeist

7 NOVEMBER 2011: Hello Mr. Isaacson, I am researching the journeys undertaken by my ancestor Philip Turnor. I came across your website today, and see that you run a number of canoe trips in the area. Would you have any photos of Sextant Rapids? I believe that set of rapids was named after Turnor's accident there when one of his canoes was swamped and he lost his precious sextant. Thank you, Barbara Mitchell

14 NOVEMBER 2011: Hello Barbara, Was very interested to see your email. After Otter Rapids (Power Dam now) Sextant is the first set of rapids moving down the Abitibi River. It's a very technical rapid that almost everyone in the canoe scene avoids. It is followed by Coral Rapids, then 9 Miles rapid. It's a section of river I do not run with clientele. I do not have pictures of it….Rick

Figure 22. Rick Isaacson canoeing Sextant Rapids (April 2012).

16 NOVEMBER 2011: Hello Rick, I'm sorry you don't have photos, but I assume you have seen them. This is what my ancestor, Philip Turnor, wrote about the falls: "90 miles very good river...but the last 10 pray God defend me from seeing worse..." (3 June 1782).

16 NOVEMBER 2011: Actually I haven't seen them, but I do know they have high cliffs on both sides. (Native friends have told me). I will run them one day with another skilled paddler in a skirted canoe. There is no room for error. But I will do it. When I do, yes, I will take pictures for you. I loved reading what Philip wrote about the falls (Thank you).

* * *

20 APRIL 2012: Here you go, Barbara. Thought you would enjoy these photos. The mean looking Rapids you see in the pics are Sextant Rapids. My partner for this run is a good friend—Mark Long (highly skilled). Not too many people venture in this section of river....We pulled out at Onakawanna River at my native buddy's camp 70 km down river as planned. Just beat the snowstorm on the water....Thought about your ancestors when we were running it. Best Regards, Rick.

21 APRIL 2012: Hello Rick: I hope you will allow me to write your story into my biography of Philip Turnor. I will need some more details....

22 APRIL 2012: Here they are:

SATURDAY, APRIL 14: put in at 11:00 AM. Paddled Sextant Rapids, Coral Rapids, Nine Mile Rapids that day. Arrived at our tent site around seven that evening (about 35 km down river). As far as Sextant Rapids it's a technical Class 4 Rapid...consisting of seven ledges...some holes big enough to spill a raft...finishes with about a 8 foot drop on the last ledge...almost 2 km in length. Deep enough channel due to the high banks...the volume of water being pushed through it. That makes it very difficult to line a canoe...or walk the shore. A class 4 rapid is maximum you can run with a canoe...which needs to be completely covered by a skirt...and run by professional paddlers. So it's a serious run and easy to understand why people have drowned in it...especially in cold water conditions.

SUNDAY, APRIL 15: this morning moved down river about another 30 km paddling through Black Smith Rapids arriving late afternoon at William Tozer's Camp at the mouth of Onakawanna where it drains into the Abitibi River (William is a professional guide, a legend throughout the area and very good friend of mine). Stayed the night.

MONDAY, APRIL 16: this morning pulled canoe and gear to railroad track 3 km away with ski-doo where we flagged down Polar Bear Express. Just beat the snowstorm on the water. Take care, Rick. ✳

Moose Fort, *Fall 1782*

On 2 August, as Turnor and his men paddled down the Moose River on the homeward stretch to the factory, 800 miles north three French warships commanded by Jean-François de Galaup, comte de La Pérouse, were making their way through the fog and ice into Hudson Bay. The French, who had joined the American states against Britain in 1778, had recently lost to the British fleet in the Caribbean and had been ordered to exact their revenge at Hudson Bay with the capture of Prince of Wales and York Forts.[26]

On 8 August the seventy-four-gun ship and two frigates anchored five miles off Fort Prince of Wales, beyond range of the cannon. Samuel Hearne, chief factor, realized immediately that his thirty-nine men could not oppose their three hundred or more armed men, and on 9 August he capitulated without a shot being fired. The French spent the next two days ransacking the fort and burning what they could. They took any goods of value they found, including furs and quills, estimated at £14,580,[27] but they left some food and guns for the Cree. Hearne, John Turner, the sloop master, and other officers were taken prisoner and put aboard the French ships, but were treated with civility.

On 15 August Captain Fowler arrived farther south at York Fort in the *King George*. He sighted the three French ships and realized he must save his men and the company's goods from the French. Humphrey Marten, who had just come back to Rupert's Land with him, disembarked to take charge of York Fort, and Matthew Cocking boarded to return to England. They quickly loaded what furs and packets they could. Fowler knew the waters, which the French did not, and as the French tried to manoeuvre in the Nelson River mouth he sailed by on the Hayes River in the night. In fact, the French had nine days of difficult navigation in this tidal river that was shoal and rocky at low tide. None of those taken prisoner would provide advice, and the French had to constantly take their soundings. After finally landing, they marched to the fort where, on 24 August, Major Rostaing and his French troops were at the gates demanding the keys to York Factory. Marten described the surrender in his journal:

> At 11 this morning observed the French troops in motion. Soon after about 3 or 400 of the Regiments of Armagnac

Auxerrois with artillery & seamen in all about 700 men
came to the Fort and demanded entrance. Before this I had
hailed them and told them to halt. At first they took no
notice but on my acquainting them that if they did not halt
I should be obliged to fire at them they halted. I demanded
a parley which was granted. They delivered a letter signed
La Perouse and Rostaing offering us our lives and private
property but threatening the utmost fury should we resist.
On which I delivered terms of capitulation which being in
the main agreed to, upon Honor I delivered up the Fort.[28]

Though Marten and Hearne were criticized for surrendering so quickly, they knew that lives would be wasted if they attempted to take
a stand against a far larger force. Marten and Hearne were both
allowed to sail home in the sloop, the *Severn*, arriving at Stromness
on 18 October 1782.[29]

Philip Turnor knew nothing of this. Farther south at Moose Fort
all was completely normal. It was late summer, the mosquitoes and
black flies had become tolerable, and the late summer sun soothed
his aching joints. He had with him now his Cree wife and his child,
Joseph, who likely had been born at or near the factory in June while
Turnor was on his Abitibi journey. Turnor's wife lived in his quarters and looked after him, mending and sewing his clothes, cooking,
tending to the child, going out on her trap line, and dressing skins.

Turnor began to chart his Abitibi trip, but as the ship was due
to arrive in a few weeks, he soon turned to the more immediate task
of writing his letters and journal, and preparing a list of the observations he had taken on the Abitibi trip to send via the autumn ship to
England. If his appointment came through, the map could be worked
on during the long winter days at Wapiscogamy House.

The *Seahorse* anchored on 23 August, and the men began unloading supplies and loading her with the homeward-bound cargo of furs.
Captain Richards came ashore on 26 August, and he and Turnor
and Jarvis spent an afternoon walking around the area to determine
a new site for the factory. Business had been steady for a number
of years and with the expansion of inland settlements going ahead,
expectations of even greater prosperity were in the air. As the three
men contemplated the site of the new building, they were oblivious

that the two key forts of the fur industry in Rupert's Land were being destroyed, and it was just this day that Jarvis first received news, perhaps still unread as they walked around, of the smallpox decimation. In fact, though the company carried on with its plans, it incurred considerable expense for the next three years in re-building its forts and increasing the complement of men.

In the correspondence from the governors Jarvis received a note indicating that Turnor was to be promoted if he could be spared from the building of the new fort. Turnor was pleased and, in his letter to the governors, he thanked them: "I am exceedingly obliged to Your Honors for the honor you have conferred on me by appointing me Second of the Factory and Master at Wapiscogamy or Brunswick House."[30] It was a shorter-than-usual letter. He submitted the journal of his Abitibi trip, offered no opinion about the potential for an HBC settlement, and concluded requesting a new thermometer, a *Nautical Almanac,* and that repairs be made once again on his watch and on a sextant that required quicksilvering. Though he had lost his sextant in June on the Abitibi and was unhappy about using a quadrant, he had apparently located another sextant. On 21 September Captain Richards took the salute and sailed for England.

The crises of the past year, the smallpox epidemic and the destruction of Prince of Wales and York Forts, underlined the great difficulties in communication between the forts and posts. News was undelivered for four or five months. On 23 September, a month after the destruction of York, Peter Willridge, in charge of Severn House, had been the first to hear. He composed a frantic plea for help to Jarvis at Albany, nearly 500 miles away:

> I have taken this opportunity to let you know the melancholy situation we are in. Prince of Wales Fort and York Fort is taken by 4 French ships and is destroyed and all carried off the goods & men; now there are only 6 men of us, except you find us men and power we cannot keep this place, without we be supplied by the 1st of March we shall be obliged to set out for Albany. Pray Sir, if possible send a man that can take the charge of this place....York Fort & Churchill struck without firing a gun, for God's Sake assist us...."[31]

Jarvis likely did not receive this until 24 February 1783, for on that date he wrote John Thomas, chief at Moose Fort. Severn House was not challenged, nor were any other posts, because La Pérouse's men were so fatigued, so hungry, and so ill from scurvy and other diseases that they were forced to sail for home. Turnor did not hear the news of the raids on Churchill and York until March 1783, seven months later, when he was at Brunswick House.

The inland posts had difficulty surviving that winter of 1782, as did the Cree who were dependent upon the two key forts. The next summer, Tomison and some men from Hudson House canoed down to York, arriving at the ruins on 1 August 1783. They put up a log tent and another tent inside that one to house the 6,000 Made Beaver they had brought down. By 8 September there was still no sign of the ship from England, so they were forced to return inland, where they had to buy provisions from the Montreal traders. Humphrey Marten, arriving from England, missed them by just one week. Hearne also returned in August and put up the frame house he had brought out from England, but there had been no time to insulate it. They had a cold winter of it, provisions frozen so solid that they could not thaw them except by putting a whole barrel into warmed water. Many of the Indigenous people trading with Churchill had starved to death during the absence of this fort, and Matonabbee, the great leader of the northern peoples, had hanged himself in despair. The war and the smallpox epidemic, occurring at the same time, disrupted drastically the trading traditions, and it took a number of years to re-establish them. In the meantime, the interior posts gained in prominence.

8.

From Surveyor to Trader

Brunswick House, *1782 to 1784*

Travelling with canoes and the flat-bottomed bateau they had constructed in June, Turnor left Moose Fort on 30 September for Brunswick House, where he had been appointed master. John Thomas, now chief at Moose Fort, recognized Turnor's "known experience," and did not go into detail with his instructions.[1] Turnor was assigned four men (the joiner and three labourers) who were to build the new house. On this journey though, now that he would be settled at a house, he was accompanied by his Cree wife carrying baby Joseph, now three months, in the cradleboard.[2]

A bed place was quickly built for Turnor's use, then the men all set to work building the new house—sawing wood, framing, building doors. There was little variation in the work except for some hunting or some brewing. From October to February the Cree were away in their wintering places, so there was no trading. One of the men became ill with vomiting and Turnor, perhaps with advice from his wife, made him bark tea, which relieved his condition. Turnor himself was not well. With the damp, cold November weather, his rheumatism set in, inflaming his knees, shoulders, and wrists. He could barely hold the pen. Maintaining his journal, charting his surveys, and even hunting were out of the question.[3] His wife would have prepared teas and salves for him. Though he kept a daily journal, as he had on his travels, days went by when there was nothing to write but a simple line: "Wind north, clear weather, the people as before [that is working at their jobs]."[4] During the Christmas "holyday" he allowed the men a week off work, not the usual one or two days. Perhaps there was an extra drink offered, a game of cards, some music if they were lucky enough to have a fiddler amongst them. Unlike Hutchins, Jarvis, or Atkinson, Turnor made no mention of any divine service held on Sundays. Even during the Christmas season he did not conduct religious observances. He must have been too much a man of the Enlightenment to offer up prayers. The men could observe as they wished.

In March Muscaco, with Captain Chichehennis and four other factory Indians, came for help to haul six sledges of deer flesh. Later in the month Captain Pequetoosahaw sent in some furs and provisions in return for a supply of cloth and powder, and a few days later Nemaycoose and Aquanabon came in with furs and provisions. Names of the hunters and traders were now remembered and recorded, perhaps with help from his wife.

Ordered Back, *March to June 1783*

Turnor had been suffering silently with his swollen limbs. On 5 March he hired a Cree lad to accompany one of his men to Moose Fort for medicine. He wrote in his journal that "for some time past [have] been <u>violently</u> afflicted with the rheumatism."[5]

Three days later George Donald, Anthony King, and John Laughton stumbled through a winter storm, arriving at Brunswick House from Moose Fort with the news of the destruction of Prince of Wales and York Forts. There was still fear that the French would return in the spring and take the rest of the forts, and Turnor was ordered to return immediately to Albany for a council meeting to discuss security measures. That, however, was impossible. He could not travel. Turnor sent a letter to John Thomas at Moose Fort saying, "I cannot walk or lay in one position fifteen minutes together."[6] However, he submitted his suggestions for their strategy of defence and promised to come as soon as he was able.[7]

After the council meeting at Albany, Chief Thomas wrote a note to Atkinson at East Main and to Turnor at Brunswick outlining the action agreed upon. They were to relinquish the inland settlements for the time being and concentrate all their forces on opposing the enemy, expected to return through Hudson Bay and James Bay. They were ordered to pack up their respective houses, burying the non-perishables (the trading goods and tools) to keep for their return. Thomas requested that they quickly complete the spring trading and inform the bands that they would return for fall trade. He expected them at Moose Fort by July or August. The Cree around Moose, Albany, and East Main were forming a league of their own to fight the French alongside the British. Chichehennis was going to Albany and Nappish to East Main to enlist their comrades.[8]

As spring weather arrived Turnor noted an improvement in his ailments. The return of activity helped. By 30 April he told Thomas that he was perfectly recovered.[9] Perhaps he began mapping again. The ice on the river was breaking up and the bands were bringing in their furs. He had made progress with the Cree language and had been able to determine who were the leaders, the captains and the lieutenants, as they were referred to by the British. Lieutenant Shawpawtick and his people and Cowesowescogee, all well stocked with beaver and other furs, arrived in May. A few weeks later Captain Sackawabisk came in with 6 canoes and brought 177 Made Beaver and a twenty-five-foot canoe that Turnor needed for the Abitibi trip. Turnor cultivated these trading alliances with special gifts. The captains received coats, worthy of their rank. In June he was particularly pleased to welcome Captain Stemma, one of the most important leaders at Michipicoten. He will "prove of consequence,"[10] thought Turnor, and treated him well with brandy and tobacco. The hunters went away pleased with their trades, and Turnor was "of the opinion this House will soon be worthy of the Honourable Company's notice."[11]

Finally, on 10 June, after the last band had come in and sobered up from their spring celebrations, and after taking an inventory of the goods at the post, he turned the management over to George Donald and left for Moose Fort, arriving three days later. He had had a rough winter, being incapacitated for at least four months with his rheumatism, but the spring trade had cheered him.

Moose Fort, *Summer 1783*

The threat of invasion from France was on everyone's mind, and Turnor's opinion was sought by Thomas at Moose Fort and by Jarvis at Albany. Given the concern of another French attack, should the inland men return to the main posts? There were various opinions, and George Donald agreed to go to Michipicoten to discover for himself.

Atkinson, chief at East Main, was brewing trouble. In a public letter that the London Committee would read, he accused the Moose Fort council of injustice and bias against him and East Main. He did not want to withdraw his men from East Main to defend Moose Fort, and Jarvis was enraged that Atkinson was the one dissenting voice regarding the defence plans. Writing to Thomas, Jarvis fumed that the officer of East Main had descended into illiterate language that was beneath the character of the Hudson's Bay Company.[12]

The men were working on safeguarding Moose Fort, repairing the gun ports and the muskets, and servicing the sloop. On 28 July the men were mustered. Turnor was requested to read them a "paper" compiled by Thomas on the company's policy of bounties payable to the men in case of injury or death in times of war. As they had not experienced a threat of war since 1763[13] and the original documents had been mislaid, Turnor simply read them the general promise of payment, and then Thomas asked the men "to declare whether or no they would fight if necessity required it…upon which they unanimously held up their hands and declared they would fight and gave three cheers."[14]

Thomas was one of a few fiery men in the company who criticized the "calm surrender of York and Churchill." As he wrote to his colleague Jarvis at Albany, he "could almost wish to meet an enemy that we might have an opportunity to vindicate the glorious name of Englishmen."[15] Though Turnor, who prized loyalty and honour, followed all instructions from Thomas, his superior, he likely did not share his militaristic fervour.

They continued preparations for war, clearing the land around the fort and loading the guns. Tension was palpable and imaginations ran high. In fact, the men were sure they saw a ship out in the bay and sent the shallop off to determine whether she was friend or foe, but they found nothing. When Donald returned from Michipicoten on 23 August, he reported that peace was concluded between Great Britain and America.[16] He heard that Michilimackinac had surrendered to the Americans on 26 July last and that the Americans were now an independent state, but that Quebec and Montreal were still held by the English. This was some assurance, but still rumour. The men continued to report vessels approaching Moose Fort, but, by the end of the month, Thomas indicated that "we now begin to doubt the reality of [these sightings] and suppose [them] to be nothing but what the shallop's crew have formed in their imaginations."[17]

Still, the men and Thomas himself remained anxious. The rainy weather did not help. Was the ship from England going to come with the much-needed supplies for the winter months? They were short on powder, on salt, on everything. Was England, in fact, still in control of Rupert's Land? Thomas contemplated sending the *Beaver* sloop to England with the news that there were still men here on the Bay, that all had not been taken by the French.

On 17 September at 2:20 p.m.—exactly recorded by Thomas—two Cree came running up from the bottom of the island. They had heard thirteen guns. Was this another false alarm? One of the Cree messengers was prepared to proceed to Albany with a warning if the ship should be an enemy.

Mr. Falconer was sent out into the roads in the shallop, but heard and saw nothing. Strange that the Cree should hear guns and they could not. The weather continued very thick. On Friday, 19 September, the day broke with fine weather. A vessel could be seen in Ship Hole, and the men nervously watched her approach. About five miles from the fort she hoisted St. George's Ensign. A cheer went up from all the men. It was the *Seahorse*, safely anchored in the roads. They were secure for another year.

Turnor's third map, "Chart of part of Hudsons Bay and Rivers & Lakes falling into it by Philip Turnor," was completed between 1782 and 1783 and probably went to England on this ship (see Plate 4). If he had begun it at Brunswick House he would have had ample time to finish it in his two months at Moose Fort. It included the route shown on his Albany River map of 1780, as well as his more recent journeys to East Main, Lake Superior, and Abitibi Lake. It was nineteen and three-quarter inches by twenty-eight and three-quarter inches, about the size of his previous two maps. The graticule was neatly lined out for every five minutes of a degree. It was confidently drawn and labelled in India ink. Everything about the map was clear, clean, and spare.[18]

Another Winter at Brunswick House, 1783 to 1784

The company was determined to establish a settlement at Abitibi Lake. In their May 1783 general correspondence they requested Turnor, "in whom we place the fullest confidence as a man of education and character and of manners,"[19] to lead the expedition. George Donald was to be his assistant and Edward Clouston, his writer.[20] They also sent Mr. Germain Maugenest, previously an independent trader, "whose former intimacy with the Natives may be of service to us on this occasion."[21] The company suggested abandoning Brunswick House, believing the Cree would either go to Moose Fort or to the inland settlements of Henley or Gloucester on the Albany River. In their opinion, a settlement at Abitibi would bring them a great advantage in trade, and it appeared, as well, that they viewed this as a pivotal move for Turnor:

> We recommend the Abitibi establishment to your particular attention, as it will give us great pleasure to have it take effect, and afford you an opportunity of distinguishing yourself in a most acceptable manner and entitle you to the esteem of / Your loving friends.[22]

However, given the state of war and uncertainty during the summer and fall of 1783, it was impossible to proceed to Abitibi. In September, Turnor wrote to the governors that he would undertake the journey in the spring of 1784. As always, he did not hesitate to express his candid opinion, and in this instance it was a grave reservation about Mr. Maugenest:

> I am sorry to inform Your Honors that I promise myself very little assistance from Mr. Maugenest, as he is entirely unacquainted with the Abitibi country and consequently with the Indians and their connections, and I am convinced he can but illy shift in the winter as he cannot use snow shoes and am apprehensive he is very little acquainted with the difficulties in travelling as it is necessary in your Honour's service for the persons in the superior stations to share some difficulties with the men or they soon loose their spirits.

Nevertheless, Turnor agreed to follow company orders and receive any assistance from Maugenest "that is founded upon reason." He likewise, respectfully, refuted the company's intention of closing down Brunswick House. It is "in an infant state," he responded, but he believed it would flourish in the coming year, though he had to admit that the murder of Shawpawtick and two of his nephews at Henley by hostile bands had been a great loss and would upset the delicate balance of power among the Cree in that area. If Brunswick had stayed open longer in the spring, the men would not have travelled to Henley and such a tragedy might have been averted.

In the same letter he argued for an increase in salary with his next contract:

> I hope Your Honors will think me deserving of £80 pr annum and flatter myself you will not think it unreasonable when Your Honors consider the extra expense that I shall be at in living at a place deprived of most comfortable necessaries which the Factory affords except those procured by myself and undertaking new hardships which I did not expect to be put to.[23]

But that was for Abitibi. For this winter Turnor had to return to Brunswick House. On 9 October he left Moose Fort with eleven men and three Cree, most of whom were sent to get the upland boat and bateau up river. Only Turnor and four men were to reside at Brunswick, but likely he had with him his Cree wife and Joseph, who now would be over a year old.

Thomas sent along the usual instructions, though he made a point of questioning Turnor's trading practices from the previous year. Last winter Turnor had presented "some particular Indians with cloth, a thing unprecedented... & though no doubt intended for the best it is contrary to the Company's orders & intentions."[24] Although Turnor was not to withdraw this gift for fear of affronting them, Thomas ordered Turnor, in general, to "confine [his] gifts (setting aside the above exceptions) to articles of less value as beads, brandy, and tobacco." In the five years he had been in this country Turnor had treated the Cree fairly. He had raised questions about trading damaged guns; he was concerned about the flow of liquor; he noted their trading habits and was eager to supply their needs. Cloth and blankets were necessities for the Cree of this area, for, unlike trade at Cumberland House, leather from large animals was not readily available for clothing.[25] Turnor's wife may well have influenced his trading decisions, and it is notable from his letters and journal that Turnor now knew the Cree traders and hunters by name: Weenewagon, Cooconap and Chichehennis, Shashemisawow, Mistoose, Messescape, Wappicrew and Muscaco.

On 23 October, three days after they arrived at the post, the cargo had been unloaded and stowed and the returning men had departed, leaving Brunswick House quiet with just five men. They dug up the buried provisions and trading goods from last spring and began preparations for the long, cold winter. There was little to report and Turnor's entries were again sparse and repetitive: "the people as before," his usual refrain. The fact that the company was not interested in continuing Brunswick House may have daunted his spirits. He had tried hard last year to bring in the trade to Brunswick House and, though he did not know it right now, the company letter dated May 1785 complimented him on the business and had approved another year of trading for Brunswick.

The winter passed uneventfully. Apparently there had been no recurrence of his rheumatism, or perhaps his wife had controlled the symptoms with her knowledge of natural remedies from local plants and trees. On 24 March 1784 he left Brunswick House, arriving on 3 April at Moose Fort to prepare for his Abitibi trip.

In the midst of normal activity around the fort, an unusual incident occurred which implicated Turnor and unsettled Thomas, the master. On 24 April Thomas recorded in his private journal, "This day Richard Small behaved in a very disorderly manner refusing to go to work when ordered and offering to fight with Mr. Turnor but as the man by some means had got intoxicated I ordered some of the men to put him in his cabin and deferred resenting his insolence till he became sober."[26] A couple of days later, when Small had sobered up, Thomas attempted to talk to him and get an apology. Apparently Small, emboldened by the brandy, had objected to being ordered to work by Turnor. He refused to apologize and Thomas felt he had to make an example of him: "I observed to him that had Mr. Turnor even been his equal and had he insulted him in England in the manner he had now done here the laws of our country would have brought him to account for it and therefore as he persisted in his error I told him I'd make an example of him lest he should corrupt others." Thomas mustered the men in the courtyard, ordered two men to strip off Small's shirt, which they did reluctantly, with one of them protesting that the flogging was unlawful. Thomas delivered the ten lashings himself. Thomas was clearly unsettled by this business and wanted the company's approbation of his actions. Someone, presumably on the governors' suggestion, had written in the margin of Thomas's journal, "approved cautiously." Turnor may well have wished that this incident had not gone as far as it did. Although he was aware of the hierarchical structure of the company, and he certainly disapproved of laziness and complaining, he had a more egalitarian view of how to achieve and maintain harmony with the regular servants—and that was to share work with them, as he had recently expressed to the governors regarding their hiring of Maugenest.

In May there were more delays to Turnor's Abitibi trip. Men could not be freed to assist him until a foundation was begun for the new Moose Fort and until Brunswick House was supplied. The large bateau started off for Brunswick House on 21 May, heavily loaded with ten men and cargo. Turnor had encouraged the building of and use of bateaux for inland travel, but in shallow water there were often problems. Thomas got word that the large bateau had run aground, and Turnor was called into duty to go up river with two small bateaux to free it.

9.

Establishes First HBC House at Abitibi

Temporary House, *1784 to 1785*

Finally, on 14 June they were ready to set off for Abitibi. Turnor was concerned that the rivers would be low and difficult as it was late in the season. They had two loaded bateaux to go up river as far as they could—to Plum Island he hoped. He had tackle to help them over the carrying places. There were also four small and four large canoes, unfortunately not in good shape, as a couple of them had made the journey before, so their bottoms were badly scraped. This, in fact, was why they were turning to the bateaux, which could withstand the damage incurred by rocks, but they were heavy brutes to take over the carrying places.

Turnor was in charge of nine company men, seven Cree men, and six Cree women. Likely his wife and child were with him. As specified in his previous general instructions, he had with him George Donald, Edward Clouston, and Mr. Maugenest. Last year, the company had been "wholly disappointed" with Maugenest's efforts at Gloucester House,[1] and they were hoping he would redeem himself on the Abitibi venture under Turnor's leadership. It would have rankled Turnor if he knew that Maugenest had been offered a contract for £100 per annum, compared to his own at £80.

This assignment was Turnor's opportunity to make his mark. The Abitibi country was unsurveyed as yet, although others, including John Thomas, had been this way before in 1774. The settlement he was asked to establish would be the first Hudson's Bay Company post in the area.[2] The men would receive compensation for breaking new ground: forty shillings for setting up their residence there and ten shillings for their travel. Turnor had been granted the terms he requested, eighty pounds per year, and better provisions for his table to compensate for the rough living conditions. He was also to receive one shilling per score of Made Beaver he received from the Cree, and the men would receive three pence. Even with this increase, though, he was making less than Maugenest.

They were just twenty to twenty-five miles up river on 17 June when Turnor was forced to stop. He wrote Thomas:

> I now sit down with a heavy heart to inform you of our misfortunes; in the first place the other bateau lost her passage between the Bushy Islands and I was forced to send Mr. Donald for her in the night; afterwards, tho' I carried my bateau up Hancocks Creek [Hancock River] and had been left a long time waiting for them, I was forced to return and steer the other....My boat has either been badly caulked or slightly put together. We lost the day yesterday in drying goods which got wet by the leakiness of the boat when there was no visible signs of her having received any damage, but E Clouston can best inform you concerning her. She works well but is overloaded. This day at the ripple above (or rather opposite) the mouth of Cuttopohagen [Kuetabohigan River] I had the misfortune to break my boat and before I could get any canoe to me the water was over all the bundles of trading goods. It was a sharp stone that had cut her & I do not know when she got it. The water is very shoal.[3]

Turnor sent back five bags of powder that were so sodden they were mere pudding. He returned most of the twine, now useless for trade, and he asked for a few provisions, some salt, oil, sugar, and hard bread, to replace what was lost. "Believe me distressed," he wrote to Thomas, "but not spirit fallen. You may judge my confusion when 2/3 of the cargo is opening about me and the wind blowing my paper away."

Mr. Clouston, in a small canoe, returned to Moose Fort with Turnor's letter and requests. The reply from Thomas was reassuring:

"I was much concerned to hear of your misfortune but as fretting will little help us, don't let it give you uneasiness. A few beaver or marten skins will repay the loss."[4]

Turnor and the men left the next morning, the wind blowing so hard they could not hear themselves speak. It was not until 8 July that they arrived at Plum Island, only 4 miles up river from where the Little Abitibi comes into the Abitibi, and 140 miles from Moose Fort. As he told Thomas in a letter of that date, had they been able to leave earlier, the river would have been less shallow and they would have had an easier trip of it. He doubted very much that there would be time for a second trip this season with supplies.

They left the bateau here at Plum Island, and Abbicootch, Coco-michiman, and another Cree man built him a large canoe, twenty-four feet long, four feet wide and twenty-two inches deep: "It is not so good as I could wish but it was a bold offer and attempt of them."[5] While some of the Cree worked at the canoe, he, his men, and Mekis, Mistoose, and Pewetacon worked on damming the Little Abitibi to catch much needed fish. They laboured intensely for twenty-eight hours, moving stones and timber into a horizontal v-shape, then hanging nets at the point to catch the fish funnelled there. To their dismay, the dam flooded out in a couple of hours. The nets they put down produced only a few fish, the water being too shallow for even the fish.

Turnor was now faced with a succession of rapids, including the dreaded Sextant Rapids where, two summers ago, he prayed to God to prevent him from seeing worse. Was the water shallow enough to pole up in the canoes? Although there were a few days of easy pad-dling on this river, the current was swifter and trickier than on the Missinaibi, the granite sills on the river's bottom creating unpredict-able currents. "This river," he wrote, "is a very bad river, the water is so exceeding thick that you cannot see stone which soon ruins an old canoe. We were forced to give new bottoms to two new ones."[6] They carried a dozen times. After two long portages he reported that they had lost one of the old large canoes, "but no lives and little damage except the loss of the canoe."[7] Their stopping to repair and to build canoes was seriously depleting their provisions.

On 8 August, eighty miles from their intended destination on Abitibi Lake, he stopped at the confluence of the Abitibi and the

Frederick House Rivers (near what is now Cochrane, Ontario) and decided to set up a temporary house. He paid heed to the pleas of his own men, who said they "would not go inland to eat beaver skins and...the netting of snow shoes.[8] It was late in the season and clearly the men were frightened they would starve. Too many times they had seen the consequences of little food—the walking skeletons coming home from wintering inland, or the men plagued with scurvy, their gums bleeding and their limbs black and sore with ulcers.

The local Upland Cree also urged him to settle here and not go to Abitibi Lake. They advised him that there were more fish available here than at the lake, and in fact Turnor had seen for himself two summers before that the band at Abitibi were in great want of provisions. Mommockquatch assured him there was good hunting here, that his people hunted bear in the fall, beaver in the late fall, and deer and rabbit throughout the winter.

Furthermore, Turnor was told it was wiser to settle here than on Abitibi Lake, for if they did go to the lake that would establish two competing houses within easy range of each other, and that would lead to jealousy among the bands. The Upland Cree told Turnor that at the lake, "when they are drunk [they] may go from one house to the other and quarrel with each other which they should not do [until] they have time to sober again and [they] would rather trade with us at a little distance from the Lake." Turnor wondered if this was a ploy, commenting to Thomas, "how reasonable that may be I do not pretend to judge."[9]

However, having considered all the arguments, he felt he had made the best decision and wrote to John Thomas at Moose Fort, "I am sorry to inform you we have not reached Abitibi Lake but find if I continue such an unsuccessful journey we shall be in great danger of want of provisions, therefore have stopped at the mouth of Piscoutagamy River [Frederick House River]....It seems a likely place for provisions."[10]

Turnor sent all but six men back to Moose Fort for the winter. He and four others began building a log tent for their winter house while Maugenest went with another servant and one of the Upland Cree to find the best fishing areas for their winter stores. Likely Turnor's wife stayed with him here, and she would fish, set snares for rabbits, and cook for him.

Master at Frederick House, *1784 to 1787*

Though John Thomas commended Turnor for his decision and thought that the temporary place sounded good for provisions and trade, he warned him that Mommockquatch "for his own convenience might be led to give the place a better character than it deserves."[11] He was correct. By the time Turnor had spent a month there, he too realized that he had misjudged the location: "I rather begin to be fearful I have been a little mislead as I do not find this place affords so much provisions as represented, but hope the winter will prove favourable to us. I would be glad of an order next year to remove to Abitibi Lake in case it should be thought better than remaining here which information and experience only can determine."[12]

In this same packet of letters, Thomas had included personal letters for Turnor from England that had arrived on the September ship. These were not happy reading. Turnor had known by last year's mail that affairs were not going well with his mother, Betty, who had requested money from him. It is unclear whether her husband had died or abandoned her, but she had been left on her own with few resources. On the ship's sailing last September, Turnor had sent instructions to the London office to provide his mother with six pounds on his account to be paid through Exuperious Turnor.[13] This was handled in January 1784. Now the letters just received indicated that she needed more money. By last month's sailing he had sent orders for fifteen pounds to be paid to Exuperious Turnor for his mother. He had much on his mind with these family difficulties in England.

However, his immediate concern was this site. They were not finding venison and fish and would have to move in the spring. About one thing he had been correct: Mr. Maugenest was not working out, and Turnor wrote in his 13 October letter to Thomas that he was sending Mr. Maugenest back to Moose Fort since Maugenest was "of opinion that his attendance here can be of no service."[14] He also sent back three other men who would be needed to bring supplies to the temporary post in the spring.

In spite of his worries about the location, he wrote Thomas in March, "We have enjoyed a good state of health and spirits."[15] He complained only about the tailor, who did not manage to make the blanket coats they needed for the trade, and the poorer-than-expected

FREDERICK HOUSE

A Hudson's Bay Company post named after a son of George
III, Frederick House was established here in 1785 to prevent
Canadian fur traders in the Abitibi region from intercepting
the passage of furs to Moose Fort (Moose Factory) on James
Bay. Throughout its operation it encountered intense, occasionally violent competition, particularly from a rival concern on nearby Devil's Island. As a result it never flour-
ished. After its manager, two labourers and a number of native people were murdered during the winter of 1812-13,
Frederick House declined further and was no longer permanently staffed. The post was finally abandoned in 1821 when
the merger of the Hudson's Bay and North West companies effectively ended the struggle for control of trade in the area.

Erected by the Ontario Heritage Foundation,
Ministry of Citizenship and Culture

Figure 23. Frederick House Plaque, Barbers Bay near Connaught, Ontario.

hunting. Perhaps the company of his wife and young child kept his
spirits high over the cold winter days.

In June 1785 Turnor and his small contingent of three men moved
fifty-two miles south to Lake Waratowaha (now Barbers Bay, about
two miles east of present-day Connaught). Though he was still uncertain that there would be provisions enough around this area, they
were situated where the company wanted him to be—in the midst of
the three Montreal trading settlements, one at Lake Abitibi, one at
Soweawamenica on Mistinikon Lake about seventy to eighty miles
away, and the third, south at Upatchawanaw, at the narrows of Lake
Timiskaming. He named the new post Frederick House, as instructed,

after the second son of George III. It was the first post he had personally established and the first post in this area for the HBC.

In the meantime, Thomas outfitted men to carry supplies to Frederick House. On 4 June guns and other trading goods were sent, amounting in value to over 2,500 Made Beaver. Considering that Moose Fort trade was about 3,000 Made Beaver, Thomas and the company obviously had high hopes for profitable trade at Abitibi.[16] Thomas did not want to send a fall trip, so he hoped that he had sent enough provisions for the six men who would be stationed there for the winter. Aside from six casks of flour and six months of meat, Thomas added that he had sent items for Turnor's own use, including "9 gallons of foreign spirits, some coffee, tea, chocolate and sugars."[17] It was a gruelling trip for the men, hauling the loaded bateau and canoes up the shallow river, and transferring everything to canoes for the last part of the journey.

Edward Clouston brought more supplies, arriving about 16 July. He and Turnor started the men on building a house for the winter; then Turnor turned the post over to Clouston for the summer, bid him good luck, and left for Moose Fort on 19 July. His wife and child would be happy to see relatives at the fort. Six days later he arrived at Moose. He sadly reported that he had only 800 Made Beaver from the spring trade, far short of the number of furs for which they had hoped.

It was good to be in company again; it seemed like a throng to be among twenty-five men here at Moose Fort, always coming and going. Of course, he had his maps and journals to work on, but over meals Turnor would hear the news from home and from the other houses and factories—the rebuilding of York and Prince of Wales, the numbers of the trade. Perhaps he had on occasion a few too many glasses of rum, but it helped with his rheumatism.[18]

They were here for two months and, if his wife's family was from among the Home Guard, she would have reunited with them or, if not, her family might have travelled here for the summer. Little Joseph, three years old, would be quickly learning both Cree and English.

When Turnor saw the sails of the *King George* in the roads on 8 September he hoped that she was bringing him happier news from home. There was a letter of praise from the committee: "We received your letter dated 8th August 1784 and are well pleased with your proceedings toward Abitibi as that is a service which requires to be carried on with the greatest spirit and vigour. We are more than ordinarily interested in its success: your knowledge & good conduct will, we doubt not, greatly contribute to it."[19]

However, the news from his mother was disturbing. He received copies of the letters between her and the company. She was now living in Birmingham and had requested twenty pounds, which had been paid out to her in May.[20] Turnor also received a letter from the company asking him to approve further payments to his mother. On 20 September he signed approval for a further fifteen pounds withdrawal. He was puzzled about whether or not she had received his first fifteen pounds, payable in 1784 through Exuperious Turnor. Was there a problem here that required his attention? He had a few personal payments to make from his salary for books and instruments he had ordered and perhaps a few things for his family, not to mention the rum, but the balance of his wages were paid out to Thomas Hutchins, now the corresponding secretary for the Hudson's Bay Company in London, presumably for use by his mother.[21]

He had not yet signed his third contract, but with his child and wife here he felt committed to stay, and, furthermore, he wanted to prove himself at Frederick House and rise further in the company. Before the ship sailed, he signed on again until 1787.

He set off for Frederick House on 26 September 1785, arriving on 18 October. After the obligatory inventory check Turnor took over from Edward Clouston, who returned to Moose Fort. Five of the men who had accompanied Turnor on the trip up stayed on with him for the winter.[22] Life went on as usual at this small establishment, broken only by occasional visits from the Cree hunters who would show them fishing and hunting places, and by the Montreal traders. On 28 December, the master of Soweawamenica and three of his men arrived from their settlement on Mistinikon Lake, up the west branch of the Montreal River. Turnor noted only that the master and his clerk were Scots, born in Montreal, and that they could speak good English.[23] They stayed four nights and were well treated, no doubt with rum or brandy being passed around with the evening meal. Turnor provisioned them before they left. This kindness was paid for with information, for Turnor learned that they intended to make a settlement nearby in the summer, in hopes of obtaining better access to Abitibi furs and routes—all the more reason for Frederick House to survive.

In the dark days of the new year, 1786, he worked on the accounts and was alarmed at the trading debts. In February he wrote uneasily to Thomas:

> The few Indians that I have seen has behaved very well both in respect to provisions and furs, and I remain in hopes of a good trade. The only doubt I have is in the unprecedented debts keeping some of them away. I now send you a list of debts that will surprise you as it has done me, and not a beaver of my debts paid last summer, though most, indeed all, the Indian debtors worth notice came in with many more furs than would have paid their debts.[24]

This worry was taking a toll on his health. It was not just the debts but so much else—the men were ill with scurvy, their mouths and gums so sore they ate only by small spoonfuls; the quickly diminishing provisions; his fears of starvation; the mice ravaging their food, eating away at the trading cloth and blankets. He requested medication for the men and himself from Mr. Cluney, the surgeon at Moose Fort.[25] The diet they had to subsist on here did not help—salt geese, salt meat, nothing fresh. Though Turnor spoke of his own poor health, he did not mention having scurvy and perhaps his biggest concern was his rheumatic condition of aching, swollen limbs. Possibly his wife prepared for him a tea made from the leaves and twigs of the cedar or spruce tree which were known to combat scurvy. Fresh meat and greens were the ideal treatment, but these were not available in the middle of winter. With his men so ill, he pleaded with Thomas to send someone to help.

Thomas replied as soon as he could, but could not send a man until the river was open. He could not oblige Turnor with a cat to control the mice, but he suggested chests, which he would supply. The debt was a problem, and he gave Turnor a short lesson about trusting the Cree:

> Your list of debts are beyond doubt enormous, but if the Indians that have been trusted so largely should visit you again, and not be able to pay you in furs, you must put them in a method to discharge part by working for you

in fetching up goods and building large canoes. Trusting or not trusting Indians must be left to the discretion of the Master of the several settlements, as some Indians may be trusted very largely with the greatest safety, some again cannot be trusted so largely, and there are others that it would be neither prudent or political to trust at all, but from the manner that the debts have been trusted at Waratawaca [Waratowaha] should judge that you have not been sufficiently explicit with Mr. Maugenest and Edward Clouston or that they have been very inattentive to your instructions.[26]

Although Thomas, in a letter to Jarvis, exonerated Turnor, acknowledging that the debts were "trusted by the persons in charge during [Turnor's] absence,"[27] namely Maugenest and Clouston, he appeared to believe that Turnor had not managed the House as frugally as he should have with regard to trading goods and provisions. Thomas warned Turnor that he would not be able to help him in the future as much as he had this year. It was almost impossible to find Cree canoeists who would take supplies to Frederick House. Nothing would persuade them to do this exhausting trip, except, as he wrote, the "fear of disobliging me." He reminded Turnor that all "depends on the precarious disposition of a people we can't command."[28] The truth of the matter was that the route was difficult, the hunt and fisheries sparse, and the upland bands were poor and had to hunt for themselves. This was not an easily sustainable post.

Around the end of June lightning strikes set the woods ablaze for miles around them. The men had to be vigilant and clear the land around their house every day. The smoke drifted in on westerly winds. They were fatigued from having to be on constant watch, and Turnor's nerves were raw with worry. On 6 July two Cree men arrived at Frederick House to tell him that the log tent, stocked and staffed for the summer at his previous site on Piscoutagamy River in order to prevent the Montreal traders from locating there, had been destroyed by fire. Thankfully, his men survived unharmed.

John Leask arrived from Moose Fort on 20 July with three canoes and trading goods. Turnor took an inventory of the goods and turned the house over to Leask for the rest of the summer. He hoped that Mr. Cloney, the surgeon, was still at Moose Fort and wrote in his journal, "My state of health being so very precarious, I thought it best to get advice."[29]

On 27 July with four canoes and eighteen Cree, likely his wife and son among those, Turnor headed back to Moose Fort through a blackened landscape. A few miles off he could see that the fires were still alive, with leaves flaring, fire snapping and leaping from tree to tree, ash falling like snowflakes through the air, sifting over all their belongings. It was an eerie trip back to the factory, and he was glad when he arrived on 2 August. He was soon doing odd jobs, including looking after the cattle. As his health improved he began his mapping and calculating. He had observations for both his log tent and Frederick House, and his next map would show those sites. The ship came in around 27 August and with it the letters from home.

There was a packet of letters from his mother and also one from the company regarding her, a troubling letter questioning whether she had received the money from Exuperious Turnor, paid out in November 1784. She had written the company four times between January and April, so was obviously in dire straits. They had replied on 4 February with a reminder: "The Directors recommend it to you to draw as little of your son's money as possible, but if you cannot do without it you may draw upon them for fifteen pounds in May next [1786]."[30] He could not take the ship home this year as he had signed his contract, but knew that he would have to return to England next year.

The company was pleased with Turnor's efforts the past year and instructed him to do more surveying in the coming year.

> We should like to see a chart of the communication of your new settlement with the three places you mention most, Abbitibi, Soweawamenica and Timiscaming or Up-astinanow [Upatchawanaw] & if you have time before the arrival of the ship next year we should be glad to have a general chart including all the places both on the coast and inland which you have visited, with their true situation from your own observations.[31]

Another letter had arrived on the ship from the company to Edward Jarvis at Albany Fort. Marked "most secret," Turnor probably never knew about it. He and some other men had caused concern with at least one factor, and rumours had floated home to the company:

> We have received intimation that some of our servants at Moose (particularly Mr. Turnor) are greatly addicted to drinking: we apply therefore to you in confidence as a person who will not deceive us to learn the real characters of Mr. Turnor, Mr. Cloney, George Donald & Anthony King: you may give us this information in a distinct letter, and we depend upon receiving from you a true account of their several characters.[32]

Who had complained? Was it Thomas? He was a reasonable man who admired Turnor, although of late he had grown concerned about Turnor's trust of the Cree people and his worry about provisions and poor trading goods. Turnor had become particularly anxious about trading inferior guns after his own company gun blew up. In fact, the company had written Turnor directly, insisting that they always sent the best guns for trading, and they hoped that he would have "no further occasion of complaint."[33] Perhaps it was Turnor's request for a cat to deal with the mouse problem that made Thomas think Turnor was becoming difficult. Whether it was company direction or Thomas himself, the orders in this year's letter of instructions for Turnor were more pointed than usual. Thomas specifically indicated that the religious tracts the company was sending out to Frederick House were to "discountenance immoderate drinking…and every other vice." He ended by stating that the master should "encourage the sober, diligent, and enterprising among [his] men" (although some version of this directive usually appeared in the instructions). It may also have come to the attention of Thomas that Turnor did not regularly, or perhaps ever, provide divine services. The stipulation that masters should perform a divine service was more specifically worded this year: "That the public service of Almighty God may be duly performed on Sundays and all other proper occasions, you are furnished with a Bible and common prayer books which are to be kept at the house."[34]

The complaint about Turnor's immoderate drinking specifically referred to his time at Moose Fort from July to September 1785, although Thomas may have felt that a request for nine gallons of spirits for the fall and winter of the coming year was excessive. Turnor's over-imbibing may have been directly related to his health problems, both physical and mental. Fatigue and aching joints were his chief complaints, possibly related to his rheumatic condition. But he also had worries about the Cree debts, the management and situation of Frederick House, and his mother's financial situation. Frederick House did not have the most congenial social environment and a few extra nips of the rum and brandy that the company allowed for his table alleviated some of his aches and pains.

Turnor departed Moose Fort on 13 September, arriving at Frederick House on 18 October after 36 days travelling. Once again it was not an easy trip: "I had the misfortune of nearly making a total loss of my canoe, and had not the other canoes been at hand we should most likely have lost our lives." He discovered that not only had the summer trade been unsuccessful, but the Cree were all complaining of hunger. Turnor, in spite of his reputation as an excellent hunter, got no fish, venison, or rabbits on the journey to Frederick House. They would have to depend on English provisions, but, as he wrote Thomas, "six pounds of flour each per week made into dumplings is but bare allowance, especially to Indians who have children with them." Was he thinking of his own family? He would not just stand by. He changed the order to one pound each every day, an extra pound per week, but still they suffered from hunger. Turnor had become more forward in his complaints that the company was not outfitting the men with the best resources, whether it was food, trading goods, or equipment. As a postscript, he added that the canvas that Moose Fort wrapped the flour in was so bad that much of the flour was lost. This canvas, he wrote, might be called sailcloth, but it would be "impossible for any vessel to go to sea with such stuff, being not so good in comparison as brown paper."[35]

On a positive note, he discovered a well-built house on the new site: "I found everything in good order, and a house for my reception which does Edward Clouston credit; 'tis built in a very pretty manner according to the plan I left; it is both comfortable and convenient." That brightened the prospects for the winter.

Christmas came and went without much notice. No mention was made of the use of the religious tracts that had been sent. The men "spent the day as usual," although on 28 and 29 December they were allowed to amuse themselves.[36]

In January and February 1787, the Cree hunters came in with scanty provisions, just a few fish and rabbits. In February, Turnor sent a couple of his men with two of the Cree hunters to Pasqua-hagamy Lake to try to learn how to net more fish. In March they were so anxious for supplies that two men offered to go to Moose Fort. Turnor sent a letter to Thomas along with them: "I believe the season has combined against us, seldom two days settled weather, so that we cannot get a snare to stand, and rabbits are exceeding scarce, one day's fish per week, and a person might walk a week and not see the track of a bird." One cask of flour had not been enough, he complained: "I have not tasted bread three times for a month past....It is hard denying an Indian a piece of bread when they come in. The Canadians supply them with Indian corn & fat."[37]

March and April were better trading months for both furs and provisions, and Turnor tried his best to win over the Upland Cree to the company. He went so far as to trade the moccasins right off his feet for a prime beaver pelt. He gave out a captain's coat to a promising young hunter, and he sent tobacco and brandy to a Timiskaming Cree, in an effort to entice him to trade furs with the HBC rather than the Montreal traders.

Because of the unfavourable weather Thomas was unable to send anything until nearly the end of May. He had not been entirely pleased with Turnor's request. He was "surprised," he wrote on 28 May 1787, that Turnor found it necessary to send men down early for additional supplies. Speaking from experience, Thomas wrote that he believed one cask of flour per man was "<u>fully sufficient.</u>" Furthermore, he remarked, "Your pieces of bread or the Canadians' Indian corn and fat does not induce the Indians to visit either you or them." Turnor had also pointed out in his letter that it had been useless to send men to waylay the Cree for trade when the men could not speak the language, and, finally, he requested two of the Home Guard to accompany him on his spring surveying mission to the three Montreal traders' settlements. Thomas replied, adding a testy postscript telling him that he had overstepped the bounds of his position:

P.S. 'Tis to be regretted that you did not find out the impracticability of sending two parties to waylay the Indians sooner and send your two men down by the canoe in the Fall by which means you would have avoided driving yourselves to such great straits and miserable conditions; twill I find be totally unnecessary for us jointly to plan any operations for the Company's service, as you always find it necessary to deviate from what may be determined here. All the Home Guard Indians seem disinclined to accompany you further inland, so that if the proposed expedition cannot be executed by Englishmen, and any upland guides you may procure, it must be dropped for the present.[38]

Thomas was obviously not pleased with Turnor and with the drain of Frederick House on supplies at Moose Fort. As customary, though, he wished Turnor a good journey. The men with supplies and the letter from Thomas arrived on 29 June, and Turnor penned a curt reply to Thomas three days later: "Sir, I shall comply with your instructions as far as seems conducive to the Honourable Company's interest. I have engaged such Indians as I think necessary to accompany me on my journey to the Canadians' settlements. I shall return to the Factory as soon as convenient."[39]

Turnor, who was supposed to receive full support from all posts to enable him to do his surveying, must have felt let down by Thomas. Perhaps the flogging scene with Richard Small flashed through his mind, for Thomas did not like to be challenged. Turnor might have recalled as well the letter from Thomas a year ago, expressing dismay that the Cree canoeists would not cooperate, writing that they were "a people we can't command."[40] Now Turnor was not complying, and not complying because he had some sympathy for the Cree people. He may not have proved to be the master that Thomas wanted.

The greatest offense, in Thomas's mind, was Turnor's drinking. Turnor had been under observation for the last two years, and in Thomas's letter to the governor and committee to be sent home with the ship in September, he wrote: "I am sorry to find that drinking more than is consistent with sobriety should have been so prevalent a custom at Frederick House," and "Mr. Turnor himself has been very faulty in this respect."[41] Other men at the house, William Bolland,

George Beckwith, and George Donald, were cited as well in the List of Servants' Characters. Donald had acknowledged his fault and therefore was back in good standing. As a final transgression of protocol, Turnor did not examine the arriving inventory of trading goods and provisions, although he counted and signed an invoice for it. Donald, reporting this to Thomas, also stated that only eight bundles of furs had been collected. Establishing Frederick House had been a more difficult task than any of them had foreseen.

Turnor was not to know that Frederick House was ill-fated. Because the rivers were difficult to navigate, supplying it was always a challenge. Rabbits and fish—that was all they could get for country provisions during the winter. The difficulty with Frederick House was not simply Turnor's management. The masters that came after him likewise demanded at least six months' European provisions and more men to staff the HBC houses. Competition with the Montreal traders' settlements made for a dismal trade. After 1794, in order to improve trade, Frederick House became a warehouse for two new settlements, one southwest on Lake Kenogamissi and the other, Abitibi Fort. Philip's son, Joseph, became master at Frederick House in 1805, when he was just twenty-three, and then took charge at Abitibi, Kenogamissi, and Wyakash Lake until 1821. Joseph was not at Frederick House in the winter of 1812–1813 when the occupants and some neighbouring Ojibwa were killed by an Abitibi man, Capascoos. The number of dead reached twelve or fifteen. Frederick House was never permanently staffed after these events and was finally closed when the two rival companies merged in 1821.

But at the present time there was optimism, on the company's part at any rate, that a successful house could be established somewhere in this region. On 8 July 1787, a windy, rainy day, Turnor set off with three canoes to survey the Montreal traders' settlements. He had with him one Orkneyman, William Sinclair, and nine Cree. Though there are no existing notes of this journey, the route he undertook from Frederick House to Lake Timiskaming and back was incorporated into his large map completed in 1794. This was the farthest south he was to travel.

Perhaps his wife and Joseph, now five, accompanied him on the survey. There is another possibility. John Thomas noted in the Moose Fort journal that on 9 July "John Leask, 3 Indian men, and a boy and three women returned with 4 canoes from Frederick House."[42] This boy might have been Joseph and, perhaps, Turnor sent his wife and son up to Moose Fort to reintegrate with her family, knowing that he was leaving in September for England.

On his surveying journey Turnor went up the Frederick House River to Nighthawk Lake and then by portage and small rivers to Soweawaminica Settlement on Mistinikon Lake, where he took some observations. Here his group crossed the Arctic watershed and the streams began flowing south to the Ottawa and St. Lawrence Rivers. They set off for the next settlement, descending the Montreal River through Matchewan Lake to what is now the town of Latchford. He made three portages before entering Lake Timiskaming, then, turning south, he arrived at Upatchawanaw at the narrows of the lake on 27 July. At Upatchawanaw he met James Grant, who had been trading in the Timiskaming area since 1777.[43] On his return, Turnor reported to John Thomas that Grant had offered him £150 per year plus eight per cent on the trade to leave the HBC and join the Canadians.[44] It is unlikely that Turnor was tempted—he was on his way home to deal with personal problems, he was concerned about his health, and he was loyal to the company.

Having noted the latitude of both Montreal trading settlements, he returned by the same route. It was obvious to him that it was not an easy route between the Montreal and Ottawa Rivers and James Bay, so there was little danger that the Canadians would move farther north.

He arrived at Frederick House on 10 August and two days later he explored a possible overland carrying place between Frederick House Lake and the Abitibi River, but found that it would be impossible to transport goods by this route. Having completed his task of locating the settlements and mapping potential routes, he packed for his return trip to Moose Fort and left on 14 August, arriving at Moose Fort six days later.

Though Turnor likely thought he would never return to Rupert's Land, he may not have known of John Thomas's overall opinion of him, sent to the committee:

> If you should think gentlemen of employing Mr. Turnor again as master of a settlement I hope it will not be at a place that belongs to this establishment, for to do him and

the Honourable Company justice I think I may with truth aver he's somewhat deficient in the necessary qualifications for serving them to their interest. To travel and survey the country would best suit with his disposition and in that line he might be serviceable.[45]

On 9 September Turnor boarded the *King George III*, commanded by William Christopher, to sail for England. The *Beaver* sloop, captained by John Turner, sailed with her through to Hudson Strait and parted company from her when they sighted Resolution Island. Five weeks later, having sailed the western route to the Scilly Islands and the Downs off the coast of Kent, rather than the northern route via the Orkney Islands, the *King George* anchored in the Thames and was boarded by the customs officers. It had been a clear sailing.

JOURNAL NINE

Separation

1787

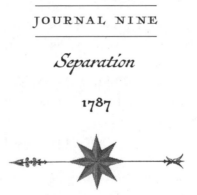

My four-times-great-grandmother and her son, Joseph, settled again among the Home Guard Cree at Moose Fort or with one of the Upland bands—wherever her home had been. Joseph was five years old and would easily adapt. But his mother made sure he continued to learn English from the men at Moose Fort. She may have stayed with her family or she may have taken another husband.

She told young Joseph that his father travelled many, many rivers in this country "with only the stars to guide him."[46] She would describe to Joseph how his father would take his instruments from the wooden box, set up his sextant, observe the heavens, then mark down figures in his journal. But it was her people who knew the rivers and lakes like the backs of their hands and would guide him to the inland posts. Young Joseph remembered this and told his son, Joseph Jr., who passed those words down the line to my fourth cousin, Pearl Weston—such a faint echo of Joseph's voice and a personal glimpse of Philip. Another cousin, John MacDonald, was told a story about Philip arriving at a Post exhausted and nearly frozen, his leather garments stiff as boards against him. The Cree people told him that leather must be thawed on the person before a strong fire, or his clothes would have been hard and useless.[47] Was this at Brunswick House or Abitibi? Perhaps Joseph's mother laughed as she told young Joseph about his English father who did not know the Cree ways.

Did Philip feel sadness or guilt when he left his wife? Did he think that, in his child, he was leaving a part of himself in this northern country? It is unlikely that he saw them again. Although he would have heard of a few children who had been educated in England, such as Charles Isham, it was unusual, and Turnor had little money to provide for this. There is no indication that he left funds for them, but perhaps he knew, or even expressed a wish, that the company would hire his son as soon as he reached an age. In fact, Joseph was readily accepted into the service of the Hudson's Bay Company in 1799, at about seventeen. In England in that year, Philip was barely surviving. A son would have been a blessing, had Philip been in Rupert's Land.

Joseph was literate and did well for himself, rising to the highest positions open to an English-Cree servant. Within six years he became master at various houses in the Abitibi area, and ended his career as an interpreter and a guide. Like his father, he was a good carpenter, a good bateau steersman, and a much better canoe steersman.

In about 1804 Joseph married Emma, probably a Cree or Orkney-Cree woman, and they had thirteen children, spreading out like the streams and creeks from the main river. Joseph's wife, Emma, was called "Mrs. Turner" in the journals. Unlike Philip's wife, who was never mentioned in documents, Mrs. Turner entered the written history and is acknowledged for her hard work. She was good with nets and snares and looked after the traps. She traded alongside her husband. She tended to the ill. Philip was their first son; Joseph, the second son; and Charlotte, their ninth child, was my great-great-grandmother. ✳

10.

Decisions to Make

Approaching England on the *King George*, Turnor witnessed, as he had often in Rupert's Land, a spectacular display of aurora borealis. Dancing spirits—that is what the Cree called them. "A dreadful and near fire" is what some Londoners thought, more frightened than awed by the aurora and questioning whether it was a sign of invasion or war.[1] A letter writer to the *St. James's Chronicle* postulated that it was caused by the influence of the moon, but requested the celebrated astronomer Mr. William Herschel, who had recently discovered the planet Uranus in 1781, to provide his opinion.[2] The skies were particularly active in 1787, producing volcanoes on the moon, as Herschel described them in a paper presented to the Royal Society in April. He also observed that auroras were visible as far south as Padua, Italy—a rare occurrence. Though Herschel did not know that auroras were energized by sunspots and solar wind, and not the moon, he was at the forefront of investigating the luminous phenomena in the skies, and the public was fascinated with these discoveries.

Whether it was the stars, navigation, travel, or inventions, this was an age of intellectual curiosity, the Age of Enlightenment. The public wanted to know about the newest and most exotic discoveries. There were daily announcements in newspapers of lectures, talks, and books published. Advertised just before Turnor's arrival in England was "A New Royal Authentic and Complete System of Universal Geography," which contained the "whole of Capt Cook's Voyage Round the World," a book Turnor would be eager to see.[3] This momentum of discovery and curiosity had taken Turnor to Rupert's Land. Although his first three maps, and the one he was working on now, were intended for the company, would the public, he wondered, be interested in seeing the extent of the company's territories?

The *King George* moored near the HBC warehouses and unloaded her cargo of furs and the packets with letters, journals, and maps from Rupert's Land. The crew were given credit slips to cash in at the HBC offices and set off down the cobbled streets to get their pay and stop in at a pub.

With a population of nearly 900,000, London, Europe's largest city and a world centre of commerce, was throbbing with activity.[4] It had been over nine years since Turnor had set foot in England. The noise, the throngs of people, the pace of life—he had forgotten all this. Coaches and carts clattered past him towards the centre of the city, and the buildings crowded in on him. He looked down at the River Thames—thick and brown, stinking of sewage and garbage—nothing like the Nelson River flowing pure over grey granite. The constant bumping of strangers put him on edge. A chorus of vendors assaulted his ears: fresh eel pie, ripe apples, custard, a glass of gin. Red and white marbled legs of mutton and beef, and plucked, yellow chickens hung in the butchers' shambles, but the stench from the discarded intestines overwhelmed him. Moose Fort, population thirty, salt goose, and moose meat, was another world.

He wanted to get back to the countryside at Laleham. But, first, he had to stop at Hudson's Bay House to collect the balance of his pay, sixty-one pounds, get instructions for his map work, and see who might be home from Rupert's Land. He was looking forward to a visit with his mentor, William Wales. Turnor had returned for health reasons, but also to look into his mother's affairs. Her last withdrawal from his account had been March of this year. Was she still living in Birmingham, or had she moved to Lambeth, Surrey, where Exuperious Turnor lived? He would visit her as soon as he could and make her comfortable.[5]

Settling down in Laleham, he began courting Elizabeth Hallett, a woman of his own age, thirty-five, who had been born in Battersea, very near Lambeth. In fact, she and Turnor may have known, or known of, each other since childhood, for she had been christened on 2 April 1752 and Philip on 26 November of the same year at the same church, St. Mary's of Battersea.[6] She also had connections with Uxbridge, just ten miles from Laleham, where Turnor had been farming before going to Rupert's Land and to where he had now returned.

As he adjusted once again to English life, he went into the city more frequently. William Wales may have introduced him at this time to Nevil Maskelyne, the Astronomer Royal, who resided at Greenwich and who was responsible for the publication of the *Nautical Almanac.* Turnor may already have thought of asking Maskelyne for a position doing computations and observations.[7]

Spending time at the HBC offices in Fenchurch, reading the newspapers in Lloyd's coffee house, or taking a pint at the nearby King's Head with a friend, Turnor slowly got caught up on the news of the world. Earlier this year the Society for the Abolition of Slavery had been formed, and there were petitions to the government, announcements of protests and rallies, and women were wearing the newly created Wedgwood medallion with the motto below a chained black man, "Am I Not a Man and a Brother?" He had sympathy for that movement. Pitt, the prime minister, spoke eloquently on behalf of the abolition of the slave trade in 1787 (and again in 1791 and 1792), and, although the motion was defeated in Parliament, there was an aggressive anti-slavery movement afoot.[8]

Turnor set about drafting his map, and he may have been instructed by the company secretary to confer with Samuel Hearne, chief factor at Churchill, who had arrived in the autumn on the *Seahorse.*[9] The company had just received Malchom Ross's journal with notes of his journey in the summer of 1786, and Turnor was asked to combine these details with his own knowledge of the Hayes Nelson Saskatchewan river system that he had already mapped in 1779. Hearne's advice had led to Ross avoiding the Churchill River and taking a more northerly route via the South Knife River, up to Etawney Lake, and then into Southern Indian Lake (which was a part of the lower Churchill) and from there to Cumberland House on the Saskatchewan River.[10] George Charles, Ross's assistant, had taken altitude measurements with his quadrant, but was unfamiliar with the use of the sextant, so precise observations were not available. They had not provided names, exact locations, or shapes for the seven lakes they paddled through, so when Turnor began mapping this route, he simply labelled each break in the river system as "Lake." Quite likely he was not satisfied with this part of the map, which looked unfinished, suspended above the Nelson and Hayes system.

Hearne was strongly in favour of investigating a route from Churchill to the northwest as trade at Churchill had been disrupted by the NWC, particularly by Peter Pond who had travelled to the Athabasca as early as 1779, trading with the Cree and Chipewyan in their home territories, thus making a long journey to the HBC factories at Churchill or York unnecessary.[11] In that year alone, Pond had brought out 80,000 prime beaver skins and had returned for more in 1783 and 1784. The HBC had Pond's 1785 map of this area and its waterways, and they had consulted with Hearne, who had been to the Arctic Sea on the Coppermine River in 1771. Athabasca country was an exciting new venture, not only financially, because of the vast numbers of beaver and other furs to be had, but geographically, because of the unmapped territory and river systems. Which rivers flowed north to the Arctic and which flowed west to the Pacific could finally be determined. Hearne was too ill to undertake such a journey, but the more Hearne, Wales, and Governor Wegg talked about it, the more fired up Turnor became by the prospects of a northern expedition.

While Turnor was working on his map he was introduced by Wales or Governor Wegg to Alexander Dalrymple, the hydrographer for the East India Company. Turnor would have known of Dalrymple's work for some time. Dalrymple had been elected as a member of the Royal Society in 1771, cited as "A gentleman well versed in mathematical and geographical knowledge and translator of voyages to the South Seas and other places from Spanish."[12] He had nearly commanded the *Endeavour* in 1768 on its voyage to Tahiti to observe the transit of Venus before being replaced by Captain James Cook, and he had written numerous papers on discoveries in the South Pacific and the South Atlantic. For some time Dalrymple had been interested in a union between the East India Company and the HBC in the trading of furs on the west coast. With that in mind he had been actively engaged in publishing charts of East Indies navigation and was now looking at charting areas on the west coast of North America, especially in the hope of locating a northwest passage, and, if not that, then a water route from Hudson Bay to the west coast through the inland territory. Governor Wegg had made available to Dalrymple all of the relevant maps held at the HBC offices, Turnor's maps and observations being the most recent, and Turnor and Dalrymple would have discussed the possibilities for a river route between Churchill and the west coast.

In the meantime, Philip and Elizabeth decided to marry. He was a reputable man who had good prospects, if his mapping projects continued, and he would provide social respectability for the un-married Elizabeth, if not substantial financial support. On Friday, 22 February 1788 they met in St. Mary's Church in Battersea to swear an oath of intention to marry. Turnor likely came over from Laleham, but Elizabeth, according to her oath of intention, was residing in the area, perhaps with her parents.

Philip and Elizabeth married on 13 June 1788 in St. Mary's Church, Battersea,[13] on the south side of the river Thames across from Chelsea. There had been a church there since Anglo-Saxon times, but St. Mary's had recently been re-built in the Georgian style, with modern, clean lines, a short clock tower, and conical steeple atop the tower. Its simplicity, inside and out, suited the forthright, unpretentious views of the couple.

JOURNAL TEN

Battersea

May 2006

We took the bus over Battersea Bridge, then walked along Battersea Church Road until we caught sight of St. Mary's spire, towered over, unfortunately, by concrete and glass high-rises, but right on the banks of the River Thames. I tried to erase the modern buildings and imagine the landscape of the 1780s as we walked the route that Philip and Elizabeth would have taken that day in June

Figure 24. St. Mary's Church, Battersea, Surrey (circa 1829).

1788. I imagined green pasture surrounding the church on three sides, small cottages and farms nearby. In fact, in 1788 this area was becoming well known for its market gardens, particularly excelling in asparagus and cabbage, so I read.[14] At the church I pushed open the wrought iron gate that, with its countless openings and closings, had gouged out an arc in the cobblestones.

Philip had not been a conventionally devout man; this was the conclusion I had drawn from his omission of any mention of religious observances in his journals. So, I was not surprised by this simple village church, unassuming both inside and out. The dark-stained oak pulpit towered over Quaker-like wooden pews in the nave, but the sanctuary was light and plain, with just one stained glass window, the original from the Anglo-Saxon church, and two small round windows. Philip would have seen all those features. He would not have seen the more recent stained glass windows along the sides of the church that commemorated a number of significant persons associated with St. Mary's, though he might well have seen these people in the flesh. One glass celebrated William Blake (1757–1827), the visionary poet considered mad in his own time; another memorialized J. M. W. Turner (1775–1851), the innovative pre-impressionistic painter, who, from the belfry of this church, had painted views of light falling over the city of London; and another window was dedicated to Benedict Arnold (1741–1801), the revolutionary soldier who fought in the American War of Independence and defected to the British forces in 1779, finally settling in England in 1791. He and his family were buried in the crypt. Though I'm sure St. Mary's is a church with ordinary parishioners, it seems remarkable for honouring such iconoclastic subjects.

I pictured Elizabeth and Philip at the altar with the minister, the Reverend R. Morgan. Three others are named as witnesses on the marriage license: Sarah Jennings, perhaps a friend of Elizabeth; an indecipherable name, perhaps a friend of Philip; and, finally, the clerk's name, Ezekiel Penington, who signed most of the marriages at this time. Were there any members from Elizabeth's family? I wished that Exuperious Turnor's name had been written there. Did Philip's mother attend? All in all, I suspect it was a rather plain wedding.

I wondered if Philip had told Elizabeth of his country wife or of his child. Would he have presented it as simply a business alliance, a power brokerage, like the marrying of King George III to seventeen-year-old Princess Charlotte of Mecklenburg-Strelitz, Germany?

What draws us to visit the haunts of our ancestors? What remains after 225 years? A place, solid as it is, evokes an emotional attachment, something beyond rational bare-bones fact. There was another aspect for me—an intersection of histories that seemed synchronistic. In mapping out my journey to Battersea, I discovered that William Blake was married in this same church on 18 August 1782, just six years earlier than Philip and Elizabeth. The Blakes lived for a short while in a cottage in the area. In fact, we walked to that cottage, for Blake has been the focus of my husband's academic career for forty years. How interesting it was to imagine that his subject, Blake, and mine, Turnor, might have passed one another on the lane, one who mapped the imagination, the other who mapped rivers and lakes in a world across the ocean. They would not, I think, have stopped to talk.

I can recount a number of times when, quite obliviously, I have travelled the same lanes, pathways, or streets, that my ancestor had in the 1770s, '80s and '90s. Ten years before I had even heard of Turnor's name I had visited an area very close to Laleham, wandering down the towpath by the Thames, stopping for lunch and a pint at the most ancient pub in the area. Such a route must have been taken by Turnor himself when he farmed there. Would he have sat in that very pub? Now that I knew he enjoyed a drink, it could well be. Then, in 2006 I found myself at the London Metropolitan Archives, walking the streets where Turnor spent his last days in Clerkenwell, although I did not yet know that fact.

I take all these hundreds of tiny pieces of memory, experience, and reading and try to reconstruct the picture, the map, of my ancestor. Being in the aura of the very place he was, seeing the same river flowing on, the same cobblestones, the same building, generates an electricity that stirs the imagination. I doubt, though, that he would approve of this unmathematical approach to mapping. ✳

London: Turning Point, 1788 to 1789

While in London working on his map, Turnor could not have missed the most sensational event of 1788—the impeachment trial of Warren Hastings, the former governor general of India. Hastings had worked for the East India Company since 1750, as it grew increasingly powerful and profitable. Promoted to governor general of India in 1774, he and his council disagreed about the rules of governance and about the company's involvement in local hostilities between Indian principalities. In 1787, Whig parliamentarian Edmund Burke began impeachment proceedings, citing destructively imperialistic and corrupt practices. The trial opened in Westminster Hall on 13 February 1788. From the start it was a spectacle: the robed members of the House of Commons were in attendance on one side of the hall, the House of Lords on the other, and about 200 filled the gallery, including, on this first day, Her Majesty and the princesses, the Prince of Wales, dukes, duchesses, lords and ladies, all dressed in finery, feathers, and diamonds, though, the *London Chronicle* was quick to point out, "nothing so remarkable as to attract public attention." The court was opened at noon by the lord chancellor: "Warren Hastings, you are impeached at the Bar of this House by the Commons of England, of having committed High Crimes and Misdemeanours."[15] So popular was the trial that tickets were in great demand and went for as much as fifty pounds. The Tory prime minister, William Pitt, who did not speak at the impeachment, declared beforehand that the crimes attributed to Hastings were serious and unacceptable. It was a case that would have interested Turnor, for at stake was the issue of accountability and responsibility in the governing of a colonial land and the attitude to Indigenous peoples.[16] The Hudson's Bay Company, a much smaller, considerably less wealthy enterprise than the East India Company, operating on a land less conducive to colonization, had shown more cooperation with and respect for the Indigenous population, but their moves inland and northward were creating jealousies and hostilities.

As Turnor and Dalrymple consulted over maps, they must have discussed the trial as Dalrymple, an employee of the East India Company stationed for a time in India, would have understood the complexities of the situation and expressed strong opinions about the proceedings. He had great respect for the native Indians and felt that they should govern themselves, with the powers of the company being limited.[17] Turnor likely agreed.

In November 1788, Turnor completed "A Chart of Rivers and Lakes above York Fort falling into Hudsons Bay according to an Actual Survey taken by Philip Turnor 1778 & 9 And of Rivers and Lakes above Churchill Fort Joining the Same taken from a Journal kept by Malcolm Ross and laid down by Philip Turnor" (see Plate 5). It was twenty-five by thirty-six and four-fifths inches, the largest map he had yet drafted.[18] He was paid twenty guineas by the HBC, and his map was simply referred to as a "Draught of several Inland Settlements belonging to the Company."[19] Though twenty guineas was a large sum for one map, it may be that the HBC was paying him not just for the map but for consultations from time to time. Twenty guineas, along with the sixty-odd pounds he had picked up from his HBC wage when he arrived, would not have lasted a year and a half, particularly now that he had a wife to support. Perhaps he was supplementing this with income from the farm in Laleham, where he and Elizabeth returned after their marriage.[20]

In 1788 there were alarming reports from France that the populace was critical of the king and his absolute authority, but this unrest would not fully erupt into the French Revolution until Turnor had left again for Rupert's Land. There was also a great deal of concern about England's sovereign, King George III, whose increasing illness caused great uneasiness for the government and Prime Minister Pitt. Throughout the summer King George was frequently indisposed, with reports of fever, nervous agitation, loss of memory and of speech. There were exaggerated stories as well. It was reported that he foamed at the mouth, that he ended every sentence with the word peacock, and another, that on a drive through Windsor Great Park he had stepped out of his carriage and shaken hands with an oak tree, believing it to be the king of Prussia. On 11 November 1788, the public was finally informed that the King might be unable to govern. He was ill enough that it was decided to form a regency under the profligate Prince of Wales. Fortunately, before this occurred, by February 1789 the King recovered sufficiently to resume his duties.[21]

On 29 May 1789 Dalrymple published his "Memoir of a Map of the Lands around the North Pole." His essay outlined and analyzed all the available "geographical materials" from Hudson Bay to the Pacific to the Arctic, and included a small map reduced from his larger scale map of "America." In his introduction he indicated that the resources of the Hudson's Bay Company had been freely opened to him by Governor Wegg, and he particularly praised the work done by Turnor, "being so valuable for explaining the geography of that part of the globe."[22] These "unpublished documents" he intended to "lay before the Public" at a later time, but, in the meantime, he provided thirteen astronomical observations taken by Turnor and analyzed the observations of a number of explorers, including Captain Cook, Samuel Hearne, Peter Pond, William Wales, and Captain Middleton. In comparing the observations of Hearne, Pond, and Turnor, he found Turnor's to "be unquestionably near the truth."[23] He noted that there were four degrees difference between Hearne's and Turnor's calculations of the distance between Churchill Fort and Cumberland House, which, Dalrymple felt, signified Hearne's errors in locating Lake Athabasca and Great Slave Lake.[24]

Intent on obtaining accurate observations, it is likely that Dalrymple had a hand in convincing Governor Wegg to send Turnor back to Rupert's Land to undertake the journey northwards.[25] This mission now had more significance than just the commercial interests of the HBC. Supported by these important men, Dalrymple and Maskelyne, Turnor's mapmaking and exploration took on a wider and more scientific scope—the dissemination of geographic knowledge. Turnor signed a three-year contract at eighty pounds per year on 16 May 1789.

He had been married for less than a year when he said goodbye to Elizabeth and sailed off in the *King George* on 30 May.

Stromness Harbour, *8 June to 21 June 1789*

The *King George* arrived in Stromness Harbour, Orkney Islands, on 8 June for the usual hiring and taking on of water and supplies. Also in harbour was the *John* on an expedition to the Faroe Islands and Iceland under the direction of John Stanley, a wealthy English nobleman who had a strong interest in the sciences and, at his own expense, had gathered about him a number of scientists to investigate these northern lands. Turnor met Mr. Stanley and two of his men, Mr. John Baine from Edinburgh, a teacher of mathematics, an astronomer, and a surveyor, and Mr. James Wright, a medical student in Edinburgh with an interest in botany. For two days Turnor had the pleasure of their company, and all the while, Baine and Wright kept diaries of their conversations with, and impressions of, Turnor.[26]

"So, Mr. Turnor, you are going out to Rupert's Land," began Mr. Stanley over tea the first afternoon.

"Yes, a remarkably vast land, much of it still unmapped. Thousands of miles of rivers. It is a harsh climate and there are great distances between settlements—it is not for the weak. I was there nine years, part of it as master of two houses.

"Have you been on leave in England?" inquired Stanley.

"Poor health brought me home two years ago—and I had no intention of returning to Rupert's Land."

Wright was curious. "What has drawn you back, then?"

"I was urged to return to Rupert's Land by Mr. Wales, Dr. Maskelyne, and Dalrymple—you know of them I am certain."

"Yes, indeed," Wright responded. "You come highly recommended."

Baine was less impressed. Turnor, he thought, seemed more a man of business than an astronomer, likely knowing only enough to enable him to fulfill the duty of his office in the company's service. But a few experiments together would be interesting. "We must compare notes. I am conducting experiments with the dipping needle. Come on shore with me after tea and give me your opinion."

"Gladly," Turnor responded, "and perhaps we can take some observations the next day. I have found the latitude of Stromness Harbour to be 58°59' N."

Baine concurred, having found the same on McKenzies' charts. He presented Turnor with Professor Robinson's paper on the new planet, Uranus, showed him their new sextant, which Turnor admired, and they discussed technical points of computing.

"I have cleared a lunar observation of the effects of parallax and refraction in about twenty minutes," Turnor explained. "Some of the computation I do by memory and then consult the *Nautical Almanac*."

"Interesting," murmured Baine, beginning to think Turnor more capable than he had first thought.

They compared sextants and artificial horizons. When Turnor explained that he sometimes had to use brandy in his horizon box, Baine, not understanding the ramifications of losing one's mercury in northern travel, strongly advised only mercury.

"Tell me," interrupted Wright, turning the conversation to more interesting matters, "whom do you leave back home in England?"

"I married just a year ago. It is almost my first anniversary," replied Turnor, "and I leave my dear wife behind. It was a late marriage for us both, though I knew her family and—how should I put it—she needed no courting."

"How difficult it must be for her—and for all women who are left behind when their men go off to distant lands. Indeed, how hard for you to leave her so soon," mused Wright.

"I could not refuse Wales and Maskelyne, and it is for the love of science that I go—to map the northern part of the globe, at latitude 60 degrees north and far to the west. This will be my most important expedition. As for my wife, I leave her in a fine house with £100 per annum."

"I am a bachelor," Baine replied, "and most content with that situation. But a glass of gin with a young Scottish lass is not to be turned down!"

Later that evening Turnor and Baine, the Brother Astronomers as Wright laughingly referred to them, inspected instruments and then conducted an experiment using the dipping needle, which measured the angle between the horizon and the earth's magnetic field. As it did not produce the results Baine expected, he declared the needle to be defective. On another subject regarding the computation of time, they disagreed so strenuously that Wright reported the next day that Baine and Turnor had nearly "gone together by the ears." Quite delightedly Wright noted that "our Noble Astronomer" (Baine) had proved to be in the wrong.

After taking more altitudes of the sun the following day, they all met again for midday dinner on board the *John* and after an afternoon walk and tea with Baine, wherein hogs, farming, and cornfields were the topics of conversation, Turnor took his leave and later that night the *John* weighed anchor.

JOURNAL ELEVEN

Stromness

1789

Hearing Philip's Voice

Baine's and Wright's diary entries about "Mr. Turner" were delightfully unbusinesslike, reading them was like overhearing these three men conversing over a pint, their topics jumping from lunar observations to hogs, from men of science to marriage.[27]

I could clearly hear Philip, the "blunt honest Englishman," arguing with Baine, the proud Scots surveyor, about astronomical issues, and not giving an inch to this man who fancied himself a colleague of the "celebrated Scottish engineers" of his day. Philip took on the challenge and proved he could hold his own with this man. He was indeed a Brother Astronomer.

Wright, the surgeon with a fine sense of humour, was more interested in Philip's personal life, and quite surprisingly he got Philip talking without hesitation about his marriage and his ambitions. Wright found Turnor a "communicative Gent," and in those conversations I heard a side of Philip not revealed in the HBC records. Wright prompted me to look more carefully at Philip's passionate declaration that he returned to Rupert's Land for the "love of science." I saw Philip's return, not so much as a job but as a mission to contribute geographic knowledge for the benefit of the world.

The light-hearted, even sarcastic, bantering about Philip's marriage raised questions about the nature of his relationship with Elizabeth Hallett. Was it Philip or Wright who adopted the ironic voice? Wright related that Philip left behind a "dear" wife (dear being emphasized—for sarcasm or importance?), "who, by the bye, needed no courting," and that she had been left with a fine house and in a comfortable situation, "if t'was possible in his Absence." Was Wright poking fun at the recently married man's bravado with these asides? How "dear" was she?

Philip did not leave Elizabeth with £100 per annum as he claimed; his salary was just £80 and although he could offer Elizabeth the largest part of that (as he had his mother, to a smaller degree), he did require some for his own needs (books, instruments, tea, brandy). In a letter sent to the company in the fall packet, he asked them to assist his wife if she requested it and offered up to £30, but the company chose to provide only £20 in advance from Philip's account when Elizabeth wrote in October. She was advanced £40 in May 1790 and petitioned for £30 more. She had not been left in as comfortable a position as Turnor had informed Wright. The "fine" house must have been her family's home in Uxbridge from where she wrote the company. It seems she was accustomed to a higher standard of living than was Turnor.

Nevertheless, Elizabeth, like many middle-class English women left behind by their seafaring husbands, no doubt missed him, for she returned to her spinster situation at her parents' house where she would carry on with the socially accepted activities of a woman— reading, doing needlework, looking after her parents. Elizabeth might have thought much as Anne Elliot did in Jane Austen's *Persuasion*: "We [who are left behind by seafaring men] certainly do not forget you, so soon as you forget us. It is, perhaps, our fate rather than our merit....We live at home, quiet, confined, and our feelings prey upon us. You are forced on exertion. You have always a profession, pursuits, business of some sort or other, to take you back into the world immediately."[28]

Though Turnor had "oblig[ed]" the scientists with these personal details, he did not confide to them his liaison with a Cree woman and that he had a child who was now about seven years old. But he must have thought of the parallels—that he had left his Cree wife in Moose Fort in 1787 (without any known assistance), and now his English wife a year and a half later. Like Elizabeth, Turnor's Cree wife had likely returned to her parental band, as was the practice, but her activities would have been much more of the 'world' and essential to survival than Elizabeth's. Both with Philip and without him, she, like a man, had to immerse herself in the "pursuits" and "business" of the fur trade.

These two diarists provided a rare gift—a view of Turnor's personal life, as well as a professional comment on his skills as a practical astronomer. These friendly, animated brushstrokes reveal an intimate glimpse into Turnor's character—a man who could hold his own with university-educated men; a man more social, more open, and more boastful than I had imagined from reading his journals, and a man who aspired to higher accomplishments, not for "want of money" but for "the Love of Science." This set the scene for the final chapters of his life. *

Setting Sail, 21 June 1789

The *King George*, the *Seahorse*, and the *Beaver* sloop departed for Hudson Bay; they slipped around the Old Man of Hoy, the red sandstone colossus standing guard at the entrance to the Orkney Islands, and entered the Atlantic. On 14 July they saw isles of ice and the bluffs of Resolution, and sailed into Hudson Strait. That same day the Bastille fell, and the French Revolution began, but Turnor was immune to the newest turmoil. After stopping at Churchill, the *King George* continued on to York Factory, arriving 27 August 1789.

11.

"So Much of My Life Wasted"

York Fort and Cumberland House, 1789

Turnor arrived on 27 August to a landscape much changed from what he had seen in 1778. The temporary fort, erected after York Factory had been destroyed in 1782 by the French, had been flooded a year before when the Hayes River rose over thirty feet. Although a new site had been chosen a mile upstream, only the shell of a factory had been constructed. Joseph Colen was the resident master, and Turnor, meeting him for the first time, was impressed immediately with his support for the northward expedition and his kindness. Previously in business in England, Colen had been hired in 1785 to oversee the rebuilding of the fort. William Tomison, chief of inland settlements, was first in command, however, and when at York Fort he took over from Colen. Turnor thought that, like the landscape, Tomison had changed. He was sullen and withdrawn, difficult to read. How much easier it was to read a map than read a man. Turnor could see that Tomison had set his mind against the northward journey. However, he would be returning to England for this year, and Turnor hoped Colen would be more cooperative.

The London Committee endorsed all efforts to explore and expand into Athabasca territory, but here in Rupert's Land Turnor felt the resistance. It started at Churchill where Joshua Tunstall, captain of the *King George*, let slip to someone, who passed it on to Turnor, that the committee had not trusted Turnor with the surveying watch until he had arrived in this country. Here at York Fort, Turnor and Tunstall crossed swords again:

> I was turned out of the [Council] room in the most inso-
> lent and abrupt manner by Capt Tunstall when I did not
> know that it was a Council set and [there] was talking
> upon affairs in which I was deeply concerned and Tunstall
> was talking in a ridiculous blockhead like manner and it
> has been the means of many insults since that time. Had I
> thought I had forfeited your Honors' confidence so much
> I had never come to this Country as it has made the Coun-
> try much more disagreeable than it otherwise would have
> been and may be means of the sooner sending me out of it.

Turnor harboured these ill feelings towards Tunstall for nine months before writing to London in 1790, exposing Captain Tunstall as a hypocrite who constantly declared "to all your servants that he does not care if you had not a single skin to send home in your ships."[1]

Turnor expected to set off immediately, but nothing had been prepared. George Hudson, his companion on the first trip to Cumberland House in 1778, was supposed to be his assistant on the northward expedition, but, as he had done no surveying since 1778, Colen put him in charge of managing the expedition's trading goods and supplies. In place of Hudson, Turnor chose Thomas Stayner, a young lad of nineteen, who was going to Manchester House for the winter. Turnor planned on instructing him in the taking of lunar observations. On 4 September Turnor departed with a brigade of three canoes and twelve men.

The day before departing he sat down to write letters to be sent back home with the fall packet. To the London Committee he wrote:

> I should esteem it a singular favour if your Honors would
> assist my wife in case she should apply as her happiness is
> of more consequence to my quiet of mind than any views
> of gain in this country. Your Honors former favours have
> emboldened me to make such a request, and hope to gain
> that credit with the Honourable Company and the public
> which shall secure to me their favour in England.[2]

He was buoyant and optimistic as he looked forward to earning recognition with both the company and the public on this, his most ambitious undertaking. As he anticipated, Elizabeth did require assistance and was sent twenty pounds from the company.[3] There had been no more solicitations for funds from his mother, so she may have died. Turnor was now devoted to assisting Elizabeth as much as he could. It would seem that his Cree wife was not in his thoughts.

Turnor arrived at Cumberland House on 7 October and George Hudson took charge temporarily, as he had since 1786. Thomas Stayner went on to Manchester House, supposedly to travel farther inland to the Stoney Mountains for the winter. By this time, Turnor was not sure whether Stayner was going to work out as his assistant as he had told Turnor he preferred the settled life of a trader to that of a traveller. Fortuitously, here at the house was a most promising candidate for the expedition—David Thompson. He was just nineteen, but, with his basic mathematical training from the Grey Coat Hospital and tutoring by Samuel Hearne at Churchill, he had shown skill in taking observations. He was hardy, he spoke Cree and Piikani (having spent the previous winter with the Piikani far west on the Bow River in Alberta),[4] he was young and eager—an ideal candidate for the position of assistant on the journey to Athabasca, except for one thing. He was injured.

At Manchester House, where he had been stationed the previous year, Thompson had fallen and broken his thighbone while out cutting firewood. Tomison set it as best he could, but it was too complex a break for his skills. For three months Thompson was bedridden and in pain, but in May 1789 he begged to be taken with the canoes heading to York Factory. When Thompson reached Cumberland House he could go no farther, and, once again, he was bedridden. It was August before he could walk with crutches. It looked as if it was going to be a difficult winter for the young man, who had hoped to be travelling and exploring.

Turnor's arrival was a pivotal point for Thompson. Within three days Turnor began teaching him how to use the sextant, keep a journal, and make his calculations. Thompson wrote that this set of circumstances "turned out to be the best thing that happened to me." He later wrote, "Mr. Turnor was well versed in mathematics...and a practical astronomer; under him I regained my mathematical education and during the winter became his only assistant and thus learned practical astronomy under an excellent master of the science."[5]

Thompson was quick to learn, and Turnor welcomed his enthusiasm and companionship. Using the sextant and artificial horizon to measure latitude was not difficult. It was more complicated to teach longitude. On a clear night he would show Thompson how to locate Jupiter or one of its moons with his telescope and then measure its distance to the moon. It would take hours to gather the observations, to clear or correct the data for the effects of parallax and refraction, and then to work them up using Maskelyne's *Tables Requisite* and *Nautical Almanac*. Often Thompson would sit up late, bent over his books, working only by candlelight, his eyes straining to do the work. Thompson would be a perfect assistant for the northward journey—if only his leg and ankle would heal.

When not observing and teaching Thompson, Turnor went hunting and brought in more than his share of partridges and rabbits. Whether hunting birds, sighting stars, or laying down the lines on his maps, he had the sharpest of eyes. He preferred this active life to sitting around in one of the posts dealing with correspondence and ledgers. Teaching astronomy suited him as well. He could imagine setting up a school when he retired to England. But now he was anxious to get this northward journey organized. Could he take a chance with Thompson?

Still at Cumberland House, *1790*

On 19 April 1790 George Hudson died at just twenty-nine years of age. Although he had been noticeably unfit when Turnor met him in September, he had recently taken to his bed with dropsy, a condition that left him debilitated and in pain with swollen legs and belly.[6] Some of the officers hinted that this condition had been brought on by the overconsumption of alcohol, and Malchom Ross, who took over as master, and Turnor were alarmed to discover that only one quart of brandy remained in the storehouse. There were few provisions for the men and few trading goods. Hudson had not kept the house in order, and, out of necessity, Turnor and any other men who could handle a gun went hunting daily. With no provisions laid by, it would be foolhardy to go ahead with the Athabasca expedition.

With the death of Hudson, Malchom Ross was appointed manager of the trading goods on the expedition, and, as Turnor wrote in his journal, he was "much the fitter person in every respect."[7] In fact, Turnor was delighted to have Ross with him on the expedition, as he was one of the most competent men he had met in this country.

By the middle of May it was clear that Thompson would not be able to accompany him as assistant. With all his observing and his work on the calculations by candlelight, one eye had become so inflamed he lost sight in it. Turnor had one option left. He wrote to Manchester House to request that a young man, Mr. Peter Fidler, age twenty-one, be sent up to Cumberland House to be instructed in practical astronomy. In the two years Fidler had been with the company he had proved himself a bright and hardy man. He had wintered at South Branch House, where he served as writer for Mitchell Oman, and had not hesitated to go out on a two-week venture to trade with the Plains Cree and learn their ways.[8]

Spring was backward this year, taking its time to turn warm. There was little fresh meat or pemmican, and none to be spared for the northward expedition. Delay after delay. Finally, on 3 June, Fidler arrived at Cumberland House, and the next day Turnor began an intensive training program. Fidler had some knowledge of mathematics and his mind was already "fixed on" studying practical astronomy,[9] so he was a quick and eager apprentice. As with Thompson, this was a turning point in Fidler's life, and, although there was always tension between his roles as fur trader and explorer, he would eventually become the official company surveyor in 1810.

Thompson, who was disappointed he could not proceed with Turnor, left for York Factory with the brigade on 9 June. In his annual letter to the committee, Turnor submitted a glowing recommendation of Thompson:

> In my journal which contains my observations I have inserted some observations made and worked by Your Honors' unfortunate apprentice David Thompson. I am fully convinced they are genuine and should he ever recover his strength far enough to be capable of undertaking any expedition I think your Honors may rely on his reports of the situation & of any places he may visit and should he

not be capable of travelling he may be very useful in giving instructions.[10]

Thompson made a survey on the route back to York Factory and went on in his later years, though not for the HBC, to produce a masterful map in 1814 showing more than 1.9 million square miles from Lake Superior to the Pacific coast.[11]

Though Turnor now had Ross and Fidler to accompany him on this important expedition northward, he had no other men assigned, no guides, no provisions or canoes. Even his surveying equipment was problematic, as he explained to the governors. His sextant, a standard-equipment Dollond,[12] was not accurate: "her angles vary considerably too much...so much error renders her not to be of the use of a sextant as I have not the least dependence on any angle that exceeds 110 degrees."[13] He knew how to make corrections so managed to get accurate results with the Dollond, but for future occasions he requested that the Moose Fort sextant and parallel glasses be sent to York Fort with committee orders that only men who were truly capable of taking measurements be allowed to use this equipment. His watch, as well, was unreliable, affected by extreme hot and cold temperatures. There had never been enough sextants, watches, parallel glasses, quick silver, or thermometers to deal with the rigours of the climate or the trials of travel. He was always begging. Finally, he concluded in his letter to the governors, the North was different from what it was nearly twenty years ago in Hearne's time. The NWC was now a thriving force here and, if the HBC wanted to locate a settlement in this area, more than one hundred men would be required to counter them. Perhaps the committee did not like his bluntness, but he would be straightforward and honest with them. Adding to his dismay, he had heard that the NWC master, Alexander Mackenzie, "think[s] they have discovered a river running out of the Slave Lake into Hudson Bay."[14] They were forging ahead while he sat waiting. He assured the committee he would watch for Mackenzie travelling through this summer and question him.

He had controlled his anger to some extent in the letter to the committee, but when he wrote to Joseph Colen, who had sympathy for Turnor's predicament, he was startlingly direct. So many barriers had been erected that he wondered if the company just said, rather than meant, that they had this expedition at heart. He insisted that Englishmen be assigned to this expedition, as he had discovered on his Abitibi trip that the guides did not always know the route as they claimed and could not be depended on to stay for the entire journey. Ross refused to travel with Cree guides as their only crew. Turnor demanded two well-supplied canoes, nothing less: "to be very explicit with you if two canoes cannot be procured for the purpose of executing the expedition to the northward I would be glad to return this summer to York Factory [in] time enough to return to England by the ship….My loitering my time at this place can give no satisfaction to any party and be only a disgrace to myself and so much of my life wasted."[15]

He saw his life's ambition ebbing away, his time wasted while Colen and Tomison argued about whether to mount the northward expedition or to focus on the Saskatchewan River area. This final expedition was to be his crowning achievement, and he had already spent nearly one-third of his contracted time simply waiting. He was frustrated, angry, and "unhappy." He must have alarmed Colen with his threat that "if something cannot be immediately done [I will return] and in my own vindication publish my reasons for so doing."[16] What a dramatic change this was from his letter of just nine months earlier when he hoped, with this expedition, to secure favour with the company and the public.

On 23 June, Alexander Mackenzie, Patrick Small, Angus Shaw, and William McGillivray stopped off at Cumberland House on their way to Grand Portage for the annual meeting of the NWC.[17] They were there for only two hours before pushing on, but what an interesting conversation Mackenzie and Turnor must have had—both ambitious, Mackenzie the rugged traveller, Turnor the experienced surveyor. Turnor, brief and candid as always, wrote in his journal:

> 2 pm Messrs Small, Mackenzie, Shaw and McGillivray, Masters of Canadian settlements to the northwest, arrived in their passage out. They informed me they had had a good winter both with respect to trade and provisions. Mr. Mackenzie says he has been at the sea, but thinks it is the Hyperborean Sea [Arctic] but he does not seem acquainted

with observations which makes me think he is not well convinced where he has been.[18]

Mackenzie had set out the previous year on 3 June 1789 from Fort Chipewyan, the recently established NWC settlement on Lake Athabasca (forty miles from the old Pond settlement), to find a route to the Pacific Ocean. Pond and Mackenzie had travelled together to Pond's settlement on the Athabasca River in 1787, and Pond would have told Mackenzie about his 1787 map and his belief that the river running west out of Great Slave Lake would take him to the Pacific.[19] Mackenzie followed this river (later named after him), which turned north at Camsell Bend. He did not reach his hoped-for destination, the Pacific Ocean, but arrived at Arctic tidewater on 14 July 1789, where he inscribed on a post on Garry Island (which he called Whale Island) in the Mackenzie River delta, the latitude of his location as 69°14'.[20]

Turnor would have known from their conversation that Mackenzie had never been instructed in making observations and calculating for longitude. In fact, Mackenzie did not know where he was, in terms of longitude, in relation to the Pacific Ocean, the original goal of his expedition.[21] Turnor likely suggested to him that instruction in practical astronomy would be useful before attempting his next expedition across the mountains. It would not be clear until Turnor did his own calculations that Peter Pond's map, the one used by Mackenzie, had erroneously situated Lake Athabasca closer to the Pacific Ocean by 700 miles.

Apparently there was no discussion about the river running east out of Slave Lake, perhaps because Turnor did not trust Mackenzie's observations. Nevertheless, the meeting was profitable for both men. Turnor and Ross were no doubt given information about the Methy portage and about Lake Athabasca, and Mackenzie recognized that he needed more instruction in practical astronomy. In retrospect Mackenzie would comment in his book: "In this voyage, I was not only without the necessary books and instruments, but also felt myself deficient in the sciences of astronomy and navigation; I did not hesitate, therefore, to undertake a winter's voyage to [England in 1791], in order to procure the one and acquire the other."[22] Three years later, in 1793, he was "the first person to cross the continent of North

America north of Mexico."[23] Turnor, to his credit, would become the first to accurately measure and survey Lake Athabasca.

In the meantime Colen had received Turnor's June letter and was shaken into action. He held a council and took matters into his own hands, rather than await orders from London or Tomison. When he wrote on 20 July he assured Turnor that choice goods would be sent, that Ross would look after the hiring of reliable guides, and that four HBC men had been engaged. It had been difficult to persuade the men, Colen admitted. As Turnor had told him, the company must reward men who offered to undertake these dangerous journeys. As a comparison he pointed out that Mackenzie's men received £100 over their regular wages, whereas the HBC men were paid about £25 in total. Mackenzie himself received £300 over and above his wages, five or six times Turnor's meagre £80 per year. To persuade the men, the best Colen could do was tell them he would bring their contributions to the attention of the company. Colen had nothing but praise for Turnor. Though the NWC were ahead of them in the Athabasca country, Colen wrote, "your skill, experience and perseverance will surpass them and your information of the track of country you pass [will] gain you a lasting name."[24]

Mackenzie and his men returned on 25 August and spent two days at Cumberland House. They must have talked of northward travel again, although Turnor only mentions, with some embarrassment, that Mackenzie "presented me a promissory note given him by the late Mr. George Hudson in 1787 for 150 lbs of fat which this House stands indebted for, but I could not pay it, not having 50 pounds of fat in the House."[25] Their cupboards were bare. For the past month Turnor had been sending out a young Cree hunter to bring back meat for them without much luck, except some moose flesh on two occasions. Without proper provisions Turnor could not chance heading northward. As it turned a little cooler, they began catching more fish and, finally, at the end of the month, the hunters brought in two buck and a doe moose. They began drying the flesh, and the guide for the expedition arrived with the good news that he had laid by dry provisions farther ahead on their route.

Finally, on 13 September 1790, Turnor embarked on his final and most important expedition for the HBC. Peter Fidler was his assistant and he had with him the competent and trusted Malchom Ross, accompanied by his wife and two children. They probably carried Hearne's map and Turnor would have knowledge from Dalrymple of Peter Pond's map of 1785 showing the country north of Lake Atha-basca, although it was distorted as to the area west.[26] If he did not have Cook's chart showing the west coast, he would certainly have known of the longitude of the western coast and he would have had the valuable first-hand information provided by Mackenzie. He was ready at last to prove himself.

12.

The Northward Expedition

Île-à-la-Crosse, *Fall 1790 to Spring 1791*

Turnor, whose earlier dream of voyaging to the South Seas had not been realized, hoped that this journey northward would be a chance to establish himself among the significant mapmakers of his era. At the very least he believed he could draft the most accurate map yet of the northwest which would correct Peter Pond's maps. The journey northward, although often referred to by the company as a journey of discovery, as if no one had been there before, was one of exploration, of ascertaining the correct positions of the rivers, lakes, and NWC settlements, and of assessing the viability of establishing HBC posts at Lake Athabasca. Pond, Mackenzie, and their men had been in this area before Turnor, and the Chipewyan people, or "Northern Indians" as Turnor sometimes referred to them, had inhabited this subarctic area for thousands of years.

Turnor and his men would be the first HBC men to travel the famous Methy Portage. It had been known for generations by the Indigenous peoples who guided Pond that way in 1778. Turnor was also to investigate the eastern end of Lake Athabasca, which had not been mapped, to see whether there was a route out of it to Churchill Fort. This might establish a navigable route between the Churchill River system and the fur-rich area of Lake Athabasca, and would certainly increase the HBC's competitiveness with the NWC.

Turnor, Fidler, and Ross had two canoes and a crew of four Orkneymen: Hugh Leask as steersman, Robert Garroch and Malcolm Grot as bowsmen, and Peter Brown as middleman.[1] Their Cree guide had gone ahead. On their first day, 13 September, they paddled about forty miles, travelling north through Namew Lake, then camped at the mouth of the Sturgeon-Weir River. The next day they met Patrick Small, who was accompanied by ten canoes. Turnor had met Small in June when members of the NWC, including Mackenzie, were travelling through Cumberland House to Grand Portage on Lake Superior. Small, who was stationed at Île-à-la-Crosse, was a powerful man in the NWC, holding two shares. He kindly offered to guide them if their own pilot abandoned them. Turnor and his men proceeded up the Sturgeon-Weir River, which was shoal with innocuous-looking stones spreading out like honeycombs just below the surface. It was beautiful, but a man could get his foot trapped there as he led a canoe, and they had to lead about a sixth of the total distance of the river. No wonder it was referred to by the NWC men as "the wicked river."[2]

The next day they entered rugged country, with high cliffs and rocky shores on the north side of the river. At Birch Portage, on 18 September, they met up again with Small, and this time they paddled with him and camped together. How fortuitous that was, for, at Pelican Lake on 20 September, Turnor's pilot could not be persuaded to continue, even with gifts of a coat and blanket. It is likely that his Cree guide was aware that he was entering Chipewyan territory and was reluctant to continue. Turnor gratefully accepted Small's offer to guide them. At this stop, Turnor, with Fidler's assistance, took an observation for latitude, his fourth since leaving Cumberland House, and Fidler drew his first small sketch showing Pelican Lake and an old NWC House.

On 21 September they travelled through a multitude of twists and turns to a small creek, barely navigable between granite boulders, and then carried 370 yards on the Athakiasakeapitchecon portage to the Churchill River. The Montreal traders had built an establishment here in 1774 in order to divert trade from Churchill. Waiting here to trade with Small were two Cree and three Chipewyan men. The next day was long, beginning at 5 a.m. and not putting up until 7 p.m. The Churchill River in this area, Turnor noted, was as large as a lake and had many islands in it. He added in his journal many identifying points—the indented bay, the narrow passage, the bluff of pine trees, the rapids where the carrying was best, the fresh or the slow currents, and the falls and islands—all which would help mark

Figure 25. Île-à-la-Crosse: detail from Turnor's 1794 map.

the route for future travellers. Without Mr. Small guiding, it would have been a tedious effort to find their way.

On 24 September Small left with four of his canoes, and the other five went in company with Turnor to guide him. The Churchill here was nothing like the Saskatchewan, the Nelson, or the Hayes, where a river between banks made an obvious roadway. On this part of the Churchill system it was like being in the middle of hundreds of giant amoeba with multiple arms. They would have been lost in this morass without a guide, and might well have perished, for it was now turning bitterly cold with heavy snow and winds.

They portaged on the Devil's Carrying Place, where Turnor and Fidler took another observation for latitude, and camped overnight near Trout Falls. On 28 September they paddled for fourteen hours, the route changing direction every half mile, so they made just 27 miles. Turnor was kept busy noting the mileage and the many bays and islands. With great difficulty they found the opening, covered over with grass, that would take them to Snake Lake. On 2 October, passing through grassy, swampy banks on the north and pine-covered rocks on the south, they came into Knee Lake and put up early at 11:45 a.m. so Turnor and Fidler could take observations to calculate both latitude and longitude.

Using the twelve-inch Dollond sextant, Turnor recorded three sets of observations, beginning shortly after noon and doing the third after 4:00 a.m. Turnor may have sighted while Fidler wrote down the angular distances between the moon and the sun or the moon and a star. They would take all their observations, then do the calculations when they had time.[3]

The next day they led the canoes through another strong, stony rapid; then, after travelling through Primeau Lake and Dipper Lake, they entered Île-à-la-Crosse Lake. On 7 October they arrived at Mr. Small's settlement on the west side of the lake. Over the 450 miles they paddled Turnor, with Fidler's assistance, had taken fifteen observations for latitude and one for longitude. They were the first to survey this branch of the Churchill system.[4]

Leading the canoes had been extremely hard on the men, and three were unable to carry on: "Hugh Leask not able to walk from a violent swelling in the knee which seems full of matter, Peter Brown very bad with a terrible cut in his foot and Robt Garroch with a violent bruised heel."[5] And they had no provisions. When Mr. Small offered them two houses for the winter, they decided it was best to accept.

The assistance they received from Small surprised Turnor and the tough-minded Ross, who knew the ways of the wily, competitive NWC traders. Small warned them not to trade with the Chipewyan people, and he kept the guides out of the way so Turnor and Ross could not hire them. However, without Small and his men Turnor and his crew might not have made it through the winter. On 20 October, when a hunter came in with provisions, Small gave Ross half the food for his men, "more than I expected."[6] Small also gave them four pounds of proper net thread after Ross noticed that Small's men had no trouble catching fish, whereas his men were catching nothing. In Turnor's view, the inadequate twine with which they had been supplied had been a deliberate thwarting of their expedition: "I well knew before I came from Cumberland House that the twine would not answer but if I had waited until we had been properly supplied I might have remained to the end of my contract and never have stirred this way, but I was determined to proceed this way under any inconveniences."[7] Some days they hauled up fifteen to twenty tickameg (whitefish), which were the best eating. Pike were not so good unless cooked in grease and only the carp's head was worth anything.

On 22 October they could well have suffered a tragedy when Garroch, Leask, and Brown went to check the nets and overturned their canoe. They managed to hang on to it in the icy waters and three of Small's men in one of their canoes quickly went to their rescue. When it came to survival, these men helped each other; when business was at stake, it was cutthroat.

Even with such kindness, it was not easy that winter. Turnor was good at mending nets and, as usual, made himself valuable bringing in partridges and ducks. He constructed a table to work on his mapping and observation calculations, but found it difficult to concentrate. Soon, there was nothing but fish to eat, and not even enough of that for all the men. "We can hardly live as is; if some supply does not come in the winter I do not know the consequence of it," wrote Ross in his journal on 14 November. Finally, after a month of nothing but fish, Turnor brought home five partridges and a rabbit, and eight partridges the next day. Mr. Ross was thankful for "that industrious gentleman Mr. Turnor."[8] The partridges and rabbits might have been dull eating if they had no fat to lard them up while cooking, but there were no complaints. It was not until 20 December that they traded a few articles with a Chipewyan hunter who came in with moose flesh, fat, and "beat meat."[9]

New Year's Day, 1791 This was an opportunity to celebrate better things to come and to look forward to the goals of the new year: reaching Lake Athabasca and Slave Lake. As many of the NWC were Scots whose custom it was to celebrate Hogmanay with visiting and drinking, they came over to the HBC house. Ross wryly commented that it cost him a "gallon of Brandy and 3 lbs of Brazil Tobacco." However, Turnor and Ross, aware of their good fortune in being guided by one of Small's men, presented the guide with some cloth, tobacco, knives, and brandy. Pointedly Ross wrote, for "His Honors" to read, that this guide had shown "great attention and kindness…which is more than an Indian pilot would have done…and I believe more

than one of your Honor's servants would have done for one another."[10]
Although the code of assisting and sharing in dire conditions was
honoured by both sides, Small and his men had gone beyond the call
of duty. Perhaps Small detected Turnor's and Ross's frustration with
the HBC and was subtly luring them away to the NWC. Perhaps over
their New Year's glasses of brandy Small made an offer.[11]

On 19 January, five Chipewyan hunters came in and pleaded for
one or two HBC men to accompany them to their wintering location
north of Primeau Lake. When inland, the company often encouraged
their men to winter with an Indigenous band if provisions were running low. Turnor and Ross hoped that sending out two men would
reduce the burden at Île-à-la-Crosse. Fidler and Leask volunteered,
and it was hoped that not only would they find better provisions, but
they would learn the language and ways of the Chipewyan people.
They took with them small presents of brandy, tobacco, ammunition,
and knives and went off with the band until April.

February, March, and April were three of the hardest months
Turnor had yet faced in Rupert's Land. Only a few Chipewyan hunters arrived with just enough fresh meat to keep the men alive. On one
occasion Turnor, with more colourful language than usual, remarked
that the provisions brought in were so "poor" and "dirty" that they
"would rather have disgraced one of Your Honors' carrion trees."[12] The
carrion tree had been recently introduced to England from China.
It grew quickly, sending its foliage so high that it was also called the
tree of heaven. The HBC must have planted some of these trees near
the company buildings in Fenchurch and Turnor must have caught
a whiff of them in the spring when the male blossoms gave off an
utterly repugnant odour. But Turnor and his men were so starved for
food that they were glad to hold their noses and eat the provisions
brought in.

On 22 March, with a hungry stomach fuelling his bad temper, he
wrote a lengthy complaint to Joseph Colen at York Factory. Without
the help of Mr. Small they would have starved, he told Colen. They
were heartily laughed at by the NWC, who thought them badly provisioned by the company. He, Ross, and Fidler had been eating hand
to mouth, and "for the sake of a small supper at night" he had been
out all day long, every day, hunting rabbits. There had been not one
ounce of oatmeal or barley for him, or Ross, or Fidler, yet the other

four men, who had been separately provisioned at the beginning of the journey, had four times the quantity of meal. Did the company think that he, Fidler, and Ross could "live upon air?" The other four men also had more liquor, sugar, and chocolate. Even the tea, he complained, was so bad he would not even have brought it had he seen it beforehand. He was at his lowest point:

> I have many a time last winter prayed you might know the want of a little oatmeal. But I suppose you think, "let them come to the Factory & I will fill their bellies and they will forget it all." Some times I can hardly believe myself that you should be so unkind. We are now too far out of your reach for you to send us any thing. I am very glad you have reason to believe what I informed you concerning this expedition was true, but I cannot help thinking that you ought to have been fully informed by the Honorable Hudson's Bay Company at the time I came out and not to have been left so much in the dark. I wish to put the best construction on what has passed, but yet a hungry, hard worked man will be out of temper.[13]

Though terribly "displeased," he was glad that Colen would now realize how much this expedition had been jeopardized. He mentioned no one but Tunstall by name, but he must have been thinking about Tomison and his role in this. He had a long and dangerous venture ahead of him, and he must make it work. However, he wanted it known that all the covert manoeuvrings going on among the leadership the committee, Tomison, Colen, Tunstall, and whoever else—were dangerous. Men's lives were at stake.

Fidler and Leask arrived back on 13 April, and Turnor was thankful that "they had lived in plenty."[14] As a bonus to their wintering with the Chipewyan people, they had found a man to serve as pilot for their journey north and to build canoes for them. During this time a number of the NWC traders came in with their furs, and Turnor was astonished to see so many taken and of such good quality. It was all the more evident that the HBC needed to establish a route to the Athabasca.

Northward to Athabasca Lake, *30 May to 28 June 1791*

Île-à-la-Crosse Lake was clear of ice and, after repairing all the canoes and packing up their nine-day's worth of provisions, Turnor and his men departed for Lake Athabasca on 30 May. There was a good breeze, but it was rainy, and they put up sails on their canoes and moved quickly through Clearwater Lake to where they expected to meet their Chipewyan guide. They found him the next day and carried on into Peter Pond Lake, where they met with six canoes of Chipewyan people who wished to travel with them.

On 1 June, after stopping to take an observation for latitude, they came to the mouth of the Methy River (La Loche River) running out of Peter Pond Lake. Incredibly, in this vast northern region, once again they met up with Alexander Mackenzie. He was on his way to the Grand Portage *rendezvous* on Lake Superior, then to Montreal to sail for England, where he intended to learn more about astronomy and practical observations. Turnor's urgings had taken root.

Mackenzie noticed, as he remarked in a note that day to his cousin Roderick Mackenzie, that Turnor and his party were "ill prepared for the undertaking," but apparently he made no comment to Turnor.[15] The next day, 2 June, Mackenzie set off early to gather together his canoes, men, and hunters for the journey south. Turnor was held up by his guides, and when they finally got underway on the Methy River, they travelled only about 8 miles before the guides wanted to hunt. How lucky that stop was for Turnor. At 5 p.m., Mackenzie, his French clerk, Mr. Leroux,[16] and a group of Cree hunters[17] pulled up beside them.

Looking out to the burnt woods surrounding them, Mackenzie offered his advice.

"It is not wise to take the Methy Portage. Aye, it is the route we have come from and the shorter road, but there are no provisions to be had that way. I am telling you straight. You can see for yourselves. Above the portage, it is like this—the woods are burnt all round. There is no game, no birds, no moose, nothing to be had. You would require a month's provisions to travel that way."

"I have barely seven days' provisions," replied Turnor. "We intended to trade for provisions with the Indians above."

Mr. Leroux interjected, "The Southern Indians [Cree] tell me the Chipewyan band have left that ground for the Athabasca. There will be no trading for provisions there. But the Indians tell me there is another route. It is round-about, to the west by way of Swan Lake, but they say there is buffalo and moose meat, plenty in that track."

"Is this true?" asked Turnor, looking to his own Chipewyan guides for advice.

"Yes," the Chipewyan man replied, "but we have not been on the whole river. We know only the ends. No white man has ever gone this way."

"What is your opinion, Ross?" asked Turnor. "If we go before the current we cannot miss the way. Though, if it should prove full of falls and no person knows them, it may prove tedious as well as dangerous."

The Chipewyan and Cree men consulted amongst themselves which route would be the best route to follow. After some time, Turnor's Chipewyan guide came to inform them that they must take the south route through Swan Lake.

Turnor looked at Ross and Fidler, "It is the only thing we can do. Want of provisions obliges us to try it."[18]

In the note to his cousin, Mackenzie also wrote that Turnor's expedition was one of "discoveries only,"[19] so there was no need to worry about the HBC trading with the local bands. However, Turnor was carefully recording any evidence of the NWC business that he could. He noted fifteen canoes filled with bundles, and Mackenzie himself had to put twenty packs in his own canoe, even though, as master, he would not commonly have done so. Another settlement up the Peace River sent sixty packs of furs. Turnor was gratified to see such wealth in the area, for it would make his explorations all the more valuable. On the other hand, it was distressing to see how far ahead of them the NWC was.

On 3 June 1791, Turnor and his men set out on their unmapped southwestern track. Garson River was, at first, as wide as the other branch, but it soon narrowed and twisted and turned so drastically that they went around the compass, from north to south and back again. Their eighteen and a half miles of paddling amounted to only five and a half miles of westerly distance. The next day was the same. The country was pleasant enough, willows crowding close to the river, but, still, they paddled double the progress they made. On 5 June, after fourteen hours of paddling, they made just twenty-three miles. They put up and the guides killed four swans, two geese, a beaver, and

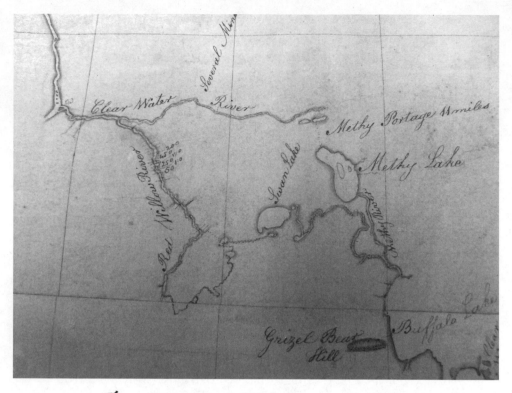

Figure 26. Detour around Methy Portage via Red Willow
River (Christina River): detail from Turnor's 1794 map.

a few ducks. They had tired muscles, but full bellies. The following
day, after Turnor and Fidler had taken their observations, they arrived at Swan Lake (now Garson Lake, on the border of Alberta and
Saskatchewan). A gun accident the next day nearly lost them their
guide. A moose had been killed, but the new four-foot gun Ross had
given their pilot had burst about eighteen inches from the breech.
The poor man was so downhearted he refused to carry on, and it was
with difficulty they persuaded him to proceed. It could have been
much worse. Reporting to the governors, Turnor described the break
as the worst he had ever seen, the metal being as thin as a counterfeit
halfpenny. He hoped his words would result in better guns for trade.

For the next few days they worked long hours for little gain. The
land was swampy, the streams so narrow they had to cut away the
banks in order to make a turn. But it was green, silent, and serene;
the land seemed to float, thought Turnor. Only one of their guides

had ever been this way, so each carrying place had to be searched out. Turnor took observations for latitude almost every day and described in detail the location of each portage in case this route should be chosen for travel again.

They passed through Watchusk Lake and found the Newby River. Provisions were plentiful: moose, buffalo, swans, geese, ducks, and beaver. Two days later, on 12 June, they put up for the night at Red Willow River (Christina River), which would take them north to the Athabasca River.

On 16 June, while the hunters were at work drying meat, Turnor sent Fidler off to examine the carrying place. Turnor could not go himself as he did not have English shoes with him, which were needed for such a long tramp through the woods. On his first trek in 1778, it had been the reverse—his English shoes had been useless in the shoal water and on the clay banks. It was a long trudge for Fidler, five and a half hours, through swamp, mossy woods, thick pines and junipers. An area of wind-fallen trees would have to be cleared before the canoes could be carried through. But it could be done. The route was just as difficult the next day—high banks, a serpentine course with strong rapids. "It is too dangerous," wrote Turnor, "to turn a point in a rapid without knowing what is below."[20] What took them seven hours should have taken five, had any one of them known the river.

The worst was still to come. On the 18th they came to the head of a falls that looked very bad. Ross and Leask walked down about a mile on the east and then two miles on the west side, but found they would not be able to shoot it. Garroch and Grot walked down farther and still could not find the end of the falls. Hearing all this, the Chipewyan people refused to proceed. Turnor knew that they did not trust canoes, particularly in bad water, but he scoffed at their suggestion to return to the Methy Portage or to leave their canoes and walk all the way to the Pillicon River (Clearwater River)— forty kilometers or more. "The fall must have an end and we must see it," he told them.[21]

The next day they were still undecided. Ross was not satisfied, and he was the most experienced of them. The two Chipewyan guides were sent out to find the end of the rapids so they could be reassured, and Fidler and Leask went to investigate how to manage the passage down. After nearly twelve hours of walking, the guides reported, they had still not seen the end and again pleaded with Turnor to return. Leask and Fidler walked two hours past where the guides had been. They could see it was dangerous, twelve miles of continuous rapid, but they felt it could be done with a few carrying places. On his walk back along the north shore, Fidler was fascinated to discover great quantities of bitumen, "a kind of liquid tar oozing out of the banks on both sides of the river in many places, which has a sulphurous smell & quite black like real tar."[22] He was also amazed to find salt springs right next to fresh springs and, in a dry riverbed, he discovered a curious assortment of fossilized shells. Millions of years ago this had been an inland sea full of marine life.

It had been an exhausting trek for Fidler. His shoes had been quite worn out, his feet bruised and so sore he had difficulty getting back. For nine days he was unable to walk at all, with his feet "opened and…running much matter." Nevertheless, they brought back the "joyful tidings" that, though they would have to make a few carrying places, it was manageable. This "crisis," wrote Ross in his journal with some anger, was the result of not having established a trading settlement in the area first so that they could procure provisions and local guides who knew this route.[23]

They got underway the next day with short mileage on the water and a number of carries. They made only five and three-quarter miles; it was tense, but they managed well enough. A glass of brandy was a happy reward at the end of the stretch. The Chipewyan people were two reaches behind. After one of their canoes overturned and they lost that cargo, they chose to lead the canoes from the bank with the women and children carrying their goods through the woods.

The course continued with its twists and turns, Turnor noting every quarter mile a new direction. In spite of their initial fear, they had dealt well with these rapids and Turnor had time to look around him. Nine years ago on the Abitibi he had been overwhelmed by that river, which stole his sextant and left him awestruck by the formidable height of the granite banks. Now, as he looked out, he reported "banks which are 100 yards high or upwards and as steep as earth can well hang together,"[24] double what he had seen on the Abitibi, and yet he was taking all this in his stride. Finally, on 21 June they came to the Clearwater, the river they would have taken after the Methy Portage, had they gone that route. Glad they were safe and well fed,

Turnor felt that, given their circumstances, they had made the only logical decision—to take the new and longer route.

They continued on another seventeen miles, stopping at the NWC house (now Fort McMurray) that Mackenzie had told him had been abandoned, but they could see very well that there was birch rind and pemmican locked up in the warehouse and potatoes thriving in the garden. Another half mile and they came to the Athabasca River, the land on the east still exceptionally high—so high it would be impossible to climb it—the land on the west side low and covered with aspen. The river was wide here, the breeze light, so they put up their sails.

The next day Turnor took more observations, and in the afternoon the Chipewyan people caught up to them. The days were longer now and they could paddle from 3:00 a.m. to 8:00 p.m. in daylight. All was going well, except for poor Fidler whose feet had been so badly bruised while checking for the end to the falls that he was unable to walk and had to be carried in and out of the canoe.

This was good country, Turnor thought. There was poplar, willow, and birch in abundance, fit for building large canoes. With hills, tree cover, and grasslands, it was ideal for moose and buffalo. Saskatoon bushes lined the banks. The Chipewyan people, comfortable at last, were now ahead of them. They told Turnor to keep to the eastern branch to get into Lake Athabasca. However, in the thick, foggy weather, confronted by numerous small river branches, Turnor and his men took a couple of wrong channels and found themselves twice in a small lake called Jack Lake. Unconcerned about not being on the proper track, Turnor watched in amazement as thousands of geese and ducks rose like dark clouds out of the lake. Finally, in the late afternoon, they made their way back to the main river.

A fresh wind was blowing and there were flying clouds on 28 June when they set off at 3:00 a.m. They came into Athabasca Lake at 7:00 a.m., the land around was low-lying and covered with willows. They crossed the bay, about six miles, and came to Fort Chipewyan, the NWC settlement, that sat high on a sandy point (Old Fort Point). Alexander Mackenzie's cousin, Roderick, the head clerk of this area, greeted them. Turnor had nothing but compliments for Fort Chipewyan: "I think this the completest inland house I have seen in the country. This is the Grand Magazine of the Athapiscow Country

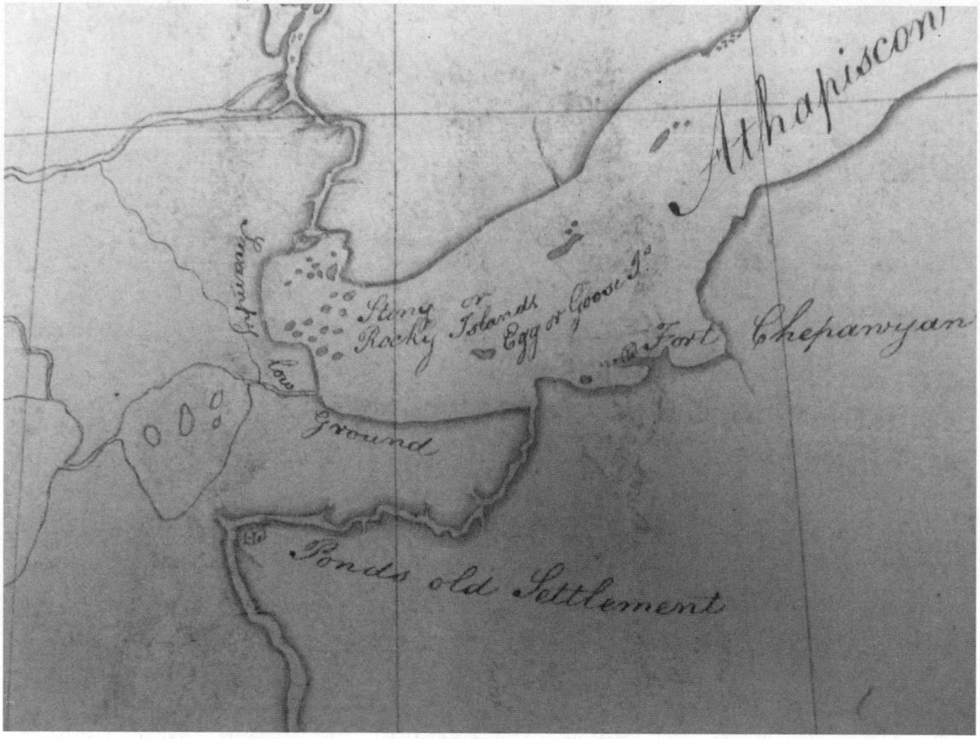

Figure 27. Fort Chipewyan on Lake Athabasca:
detail from Turnor's 1794 map.

and I am informed they have sufficient quantity of trading goods in this country for at least two years to come."[25] Ross pointed out that the NWC had a well-organized system established here. The fort was on a high hill with bays around it and, though the land around did not have game, the men took care to set up a network for bringing in provisions. There were three Indigenous peoples who came regularly to trade: the Cree, the Beaver River people, and the Chipewyan. It was the best house Ross had seen in the interior, and how he envied it.

Fidler sketched the location and Turnor took two observations for latitude on 29 and 30 June. Both days were windy with flying clouds, not the best conditions for taking observations. He recorded 58°37'34" N on 29 June and 58°37'30" N on 30 June.[26] Though Turnor did not record in his journal the date on which he took observations for longitude, his mean longitude measurement for Fort Chipewyan, noted in 1794 in his *Result of Astronomical Observations,* was 110°25'13" W.[27]

On four different occasions between this time and his winter stay at Fort Chipewyan he observed nearly four hundred lunar distances with his sextant.[28] The computations to find longitude would have taken hours, so he probably worked on them at his leisure during the winter months. Turnor was the first to correctly fix the longitudinal position of Fort Chipewyan.

Great Slave Lake, 2 July to 26 July 1791

Turnor wanted to push on to Slave Lake, but Ross fumed that there were no guides ready to take them. Their northward expedition had been hindered not only by Tomison, who had done little to support their efforts, but also by the NWC, who were doing all they could to keep guides away from them. "In my humble opinion," Ross wrote in his journal for the eyes of the London Committee, "nothing will be made of this expedition, so much at your Honor's heart, until a trading party takes place, and that at 2 different settlements."[29] A trading party would establish a base with provisions, canoes, and home guard guides and hunters from which to mount these explorations. The NWC was successful because they already had five settlements established in the area.

However, Ross found a Chipewyan guide, and on 2 July at 8:30 p.m. they were underway for Great Slave Lake. On the second day out, travelling northwest, they came to a portion of Athabasca Lake called Lake of the Paps (or rocky islands) and Turnor, who lately had provided location names in both the Cree and the Chipewyan language, offered a small lesson regarding the Chipewyan name for Lake of the Paps, which was Thew Tooah. "Thew is pronounced," he wrote, "by pressing the tongue very hard against the upper teeth." He continued "Athapescow [Lake Athabasca] in the Southern Indian tongue [Cree] signifies open country such as lakes with willows and grass growing about them or swampy land without wood [and] Kytehelleca in the Chipewyan tongue implies the same meaning but that name does not properly belong or is applied to any part but the South end."[30] During his first nine years in Rupert's Land, with the assistance of his guides and his country wife, Turnor had learned some Cree, and now was keen to understand Chipewyan. Fidler, who had spent a winter with the Chipewyan band, could help him. They entered the

Slave River, for which he again gave the Cree name, Archathinnu Seepe or Waucon Seepe or Slave Indian River, and the Chipewyan name, Besschow Dezza or Great Knife River.[31]

Full of islands and with numerous branches joining in from both sides, the Slave River hardly looked like a river. Turnor diligently documented all the details of this landscape every quarter or half mile. At 7:30 p.m. on their second day out, after thirteen hours of travel, he discovered that the sextant had been left at the NWC House. "I had particularly enquired and was assured it was in the Canoe," he added to his day's entry. Nevertheless, he could not work without it, so he set off at four in the morning in his own canoe with his paddler to retrieve the sextant. Thirteen hours and forty-five miles later he found it where it had been stored at the house. He rested there for only two hours before setting off on the return trip. As he paddled he had plenty of time to think of the value of this expedition, of the numerous frustrations and hindrances he had experienced, and of his future in this country. When he passed the small river running to the Peace River, he thought of the advantage the NWC had in this country, for up the Peace River they had two settlements that provided them with all the provisions they needed for their expeditions and for their journeys back to the Grand Portage to carry out their furs. If only the Hudson's Bay Company could see that this was the best strategy to build up their enterprise in the North. Would they make use of his surveys? Perhaps he wondered if he might return to explore the Peace River another year.[32]

Ross, Fidler, and the guides had gone on ahead, so he followed in their path, making notes all along the route. He finally stopped for food and a good rest after nearly 120 miles of travel in two days and a night. Early the next morning, 6 July, he reconnected with the other canoe, and they immediately got underway. Thirty-five miles down river they pulled up at the mouth of the Dog River (Fort Fitzgerald).

A summer storm hit the next day with an easterly gale, thunder, and rain, so they lay by, knowing that they had dangerous waters ahead of them. At 2:00 p.m. they started off and "shot three strong shoots,"[33] followed by four carries. The last carry of the day was at the head of a large falls, twenty feet perpendicular. Turnor was told that a NWC man and a Chipewyan man had drowned there a few years ago.

The next day they had more difficult falls to navigate, and Hugh Leask, Turnor's steersman, nearly lost the canoe and its cargo. Unable to get his canoe up on the bank without assistance, he had tied it carefully, he thought, to a willow tree while he carried a bundle over the trail. When he returned, she was adrift. How Grot managed to catch it at the head of a falls, one yard from going over, was a miracle. On their next carry at Grand Rapids (Fort Smith), Turnor again heard of this river taking its toll: two canoes and five men drowned a few years earlier trying to shoot the falls. It now bears the name Rapids of the Drowned.

Turnor took his observations at the foot of the falls on 9 July. They were now above latitude 60° north. Below the falls they could make time and easily paddled twenty-five miles until they put up for the evening.

It was good hunting ground: low-lying land covered with willows and pines. The Chipewyan hunters went off for a few days and came back with geese and swans, and a Cree hunter killed a moose, which Turnor and his men helped cart back. Then the meat had to be dried and beaten for travel. The Chipewyan men went out to hunt again, and this time killed a buffalo, which had to be prepared. Ross was impatient to be underway:

We are waiting for our pilot such is the slow process of business when rested involuntarily upon the Chipewyan, which is always very dilatory and slow. I am obliged to break upon my instructions received from the chief at York Factory which would have been good instructions if upon a trading party, but not when joining along with those insolent careless race of Chipewyan solely depending upon them for provisions & pilotages. If I should lavish in the expending of your property [be more generous with the trading goods], I hope your Honours will pardon ignorance as I am not better acquainted with your wishes having no knowledge of it but what I hear from Mr. Turnor who urges that your Honours have the expedition much at heart, which makes me give more than I would willingly do. The Canadians was by some means acquainted with your intended expedition to the Northward which they have taken care to have every Indian out of our way that could have been of any use in giving intelligence or promising provisions so that we labour under various disadvantages.[34]

Eager to get going, Ross started off the following morning. Turnor, more patient, waited until the following evening for the Chipewyan pilot and his men to return from hunting.

On 19 July they arrived at the mouth of the Slave River and entered Great Slave Lake.[35] The current was strong and the water high. Turnor was struck by the "great flush of water" coming down from the Rocky Mountains, "as if a head had been penned and opened all at once." He noted with great interest how the river banks with their trees were broken away with the flood, carried out into the river, making it appear that the trees were growing from the bottom of the river. It astonished him that sixty-foot-high pines had only ten feet of their tops showing above water. There were good woods around, plenty of provisions, and he and Fidler marvelled at the flocks of geese and cranes, Fidler reporting that at one point the entire width of the river was covered with young geese: "we had nothing else to do but paddle the canoe into the middle of them, and kill as many as we pleased with a stick." From starvation a month ago to such plenty here on Great Slave Lake. However, they might have to do the hunting themselves, for, as Turnor noted: "This would be a fine country for provision was the Chipewyan who inhabit this part willing to part with it [the provision] but it is not easy to get it from them."[36] They were not like the Cree, who were more willing to trade and guide.

In the early morning of 22 July they came to a point of woods where the NWC were building a new house, just west of the eastern branch of the Slave River. The master, Péché, one of Peter Pond's men, had been up here for three years, winters and summers, living with a Chipewyan band, unable to go south for fear of the gallows. Turnor and his men had heard by word of mouth about the incident at Peter Pond's House on the Athabasca River in 1787 between Pond's men and the rival NWC trader, John Ross, a partner of Pangman and Alexander Mackenzie. When John Ross discovered that Pond and his men were forcibly dragging the Chipewyan men into their house to trade, he confronted them and was shot dead by Péché. In order to avoid inquiry into this incident, Pond's company joined John Ross's party and they began trading together with no opposition.

Putting aside any distrust he had of Péché, Turnor took the opportunity to question him about his travels on Great Slave Lake. When he was travelling with the Chipewyan people, Péché told him, they saw a great lake, which they called Dock-an, so named because they kill deer there by pushing them into the water; but Turnor was told that name was given to many lakes in those parts. Because the Chipewyan people only crossed the rivers and lakes, not following them to their rise, it was difficult to determine which rivers they were describing. Péché himself saw one very large river running eastward, which Turnor thought must be a branch of the Wager, which runs to Wager Bay and into Hudson Bay. It was one of the rivers mentioned to him in England by Dalrymple, who was bent on finding a route between Hudson Bay and Great Slave or Athabasca Lake that would ultimately join the Atlantic and the Pacific oceans.

Three days later, after the arrival of eleven canoes of Chipewyan people who provisioned and traded with them, Turnor received more information. He met a Chipewyan man, Shewditheda, who knew the water routes flowing east from Great Slave Lake. How frustrating it was, Turnor thought, that he had not yet learned enough Chipewyan language to understand him. He found a Cree guide to interpret, but Turnor could not be certain, after the conversation had been filtered through two levels of translation, that he had comprehended all that Shewditheda had to tell him.

"At the far end of this lake [Great Slave Lake]," Shewditheda gestured, "a fall falls out of another large lake we call Dinnanethatooah." He reached down and drew in the earth two lakes, a large one and a smaller one, joined by a narrow band.

Turnor knew the second lake as Northern Indian Great Lake, and he would later label the narrow band drawn by Shewditheda as a carrying place.

Shewditheda continued, "There is a carrying place to another lake out of which a river, a large river, runs to the sea." He drew that in the earth and the interpreter said that he had understood all this.

"The end of this lake, where we are, is very far, and is full of islands. Dinnanethatooah is long but not wide and full of islands also. These islands have trees but the land all around is barren. The river bold deep ~~river~~ River without any falls in it but rather strong current and no woods growing about it the under is his discription of it

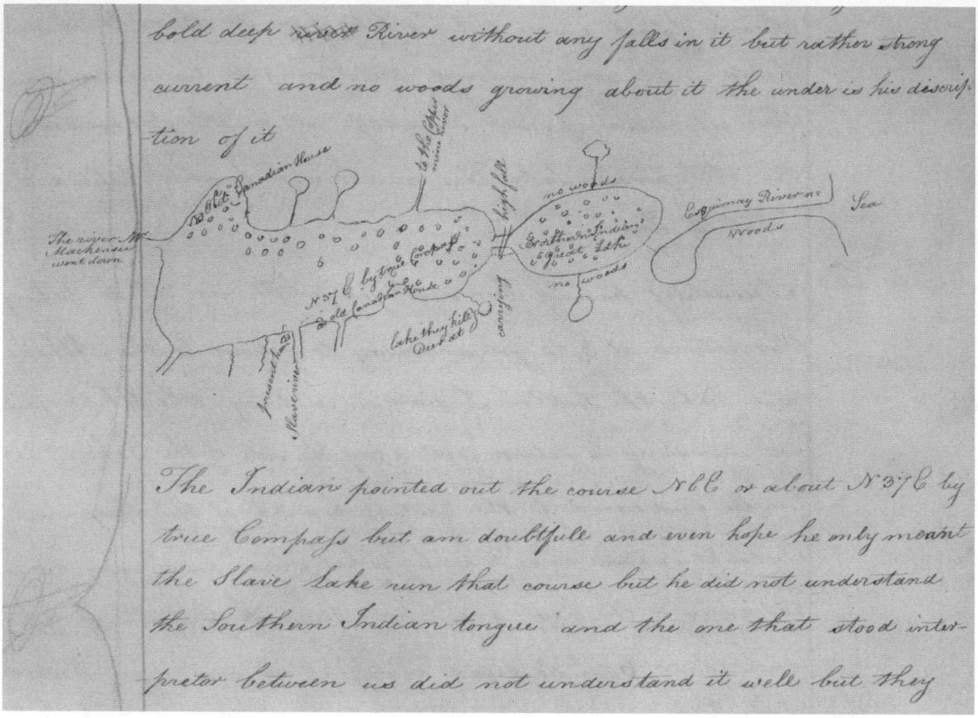

[handwritten map with labels: "The river Mackenzie went down", "old Canadian House", "N 37 E by true Compass", "old Canadian House", "to the Oppis... no woods", "high fall", "no woods", "Southern Indian's Great Lake", "no woods", "Esquimay River or", "Woods", "Sea", "Lake they killd Deer at", "carrying"]

The Indian pointed out the course N b E or about N 37 E by true Compass but am doubtfull and even hope he only meant the Slave Lake run that course but he did not understand the Southern Indian tongue and the one that stood interpreter between us did not understand it well but they

Figure 28. "Shewditheda's map of Great Slave Lake, Northern Indian Lake and Esquimay River to the sea." Sketched by Turnor in his journal, 25 July 1791.

which runs to the sea is called Esquimay." He talked as he drew: "It is a bold deep river without falls and no woods growing about it."[37]

"Will you take us there?" asked Turnor.

"It is too late to go and return. There are no provisions ready for such a journey."

Turnor sketched out in his journal the map he had seen and as he had understood it from Shewditheda, or at least what he understood twice translated. The Cree interpreter said he understood, "but they always say they understand what is said to them," wrote Turnor in his notes.[38]

Though Shewditheda had described the Northern Indian Great Lake as "very long but not very wide" (which would describe in some degree Artillery Lake), he did not draw the lake as such but rather as an oval. Perhaps, thought Turnor, Shewditheda was only interested in the relationships of waterways and not their exact proportions or directions. Or had it been the translation?

Could the Esquimay River be part of the Wager River? Shewditheda had pointed out the course at about N37E by compass. Did he mean that only Slave Lake ran that course? Or did he mean the entire course to Hudson Bay, which would take them farther north to Wager Bay? But Shewditheda's insistence that the river was short, coupled with what Turnor had heard at Île-à-la-Crosse of such a river, made him believe that the route described would run to Chesterfield's Inlet.[39]

Finding a river route to Churchill where the HBC had a factory would be much more beneficial, and since Turnor had determined that Lake Athabasca and Churchill lay at the same latitude, he felt it wiser to return to Athabasca and survey that lake than to spend time at Slave Lake. He pointed out in his journal that the London Committee had mistakenly thought "that the Athapiscow [Athabasca] Lake laid in a much higher latitude than what it does,"[40] and Dalrymple would have thought the same, but now that Turnor had corrected that misconception with his observations, it would be more likely a viable route could be found from Lake Athabasca.

At 3:00 a.m. on 26 July, Turnor and Fidler began taking their observations for the latitude and longitude of the NWC settlement. He also estimated the size of Great Slave Lake at 175 miles eastward and 110 miles westward from the NWC house, which was quite accurate.[41] They concluded their work at 3:00 p.m., at which time they got underway to return to Lake Athabasca. For the next ten days progress was slow but without incident, except for Malchom Ross's canoe being damaged by a deadhead on 28 July. They needed to hunt, then dry the meat before a fire or in the sun, and beat some into pemmican. All this could not be hurried, and by 5 August Turnor was concerned that they might not get to Athabasca by 14 August, the date on which he had arranged for Fidler to go with Roderick Mackenzie's men up the Peace River in order to survey that portion. Leaving Malchom Ross to deal with the meat-drying and the pilots, Turnor took Fidler in his canoe, along with Garroch and his steersman, Leask. They arrived at the NWC settlement on 12 August, only to discover that Mackenzie had sent his canoe several days ago, apparently a clerical error not a deliberate act.

Surveying Lake Athabasca, *15 August to 30 August 1791*

As Fidler had missed going to the Peace River country, Turnor took him along with Leask and Garroch on his survey of Lake Athabasca. Ross would decide on the location of their winter house when he arrived back at Fort Chipewyan.

On the first day out, Turnor and his men sailed across the bay and then along the southern shore. He and Fidler took two observations for latitude. On the second day they travelled close to the shore, which was sandy and stony, covered with small scrub aspens and purple-tinged willows.[42] They ventured up the banks where they "could then see about 3 miles east and round to SSW all a rising sandy desert of a yellowish white colour with a chance scrub pine standing singly." Near William River, as far as they could see, it was sand with just the tips of pine trees peeping over the tops of the dunes.[43] It was an amazing sight to behold so far north.

Uncharacteristically, Turnor launched into descriptions of the landscape. On 18 August they sailed six miles across a bay where the "sandy hills drifted like snow drifts in ridges 20 feet in the face." After making their way along the point, they came to the mouth of a river. He and Fidler had been told that, using small canoes, the local people could take this river to Île-à-la-Crosse. The mouth of the river opened "from SE through high sandy hills which when seen off the mouth of this river look like fields of ripe corn between ledges of woods such as are seen in the hill countries of England." Fascinated with this view, Turnor was not only pulled back emotionally to his home country, but he was equally captivated by the story given him by a Chipewyan man. Intertwined in his journal with his factual account of directions and distances, he provided the Chipewyan explanation for this unexpected phenomenon of the sand dunes: "the Chipewyan who are not without their fables call this river the Great Beaver or Giant Beaver River. A species of beaver formerly was at this part and turned up all this sand but there was a species of giant Indians who killed all those beaver and whose race is likewise extinct."[44] According to the legend, the giant hunter thought he had speared the giant beaver and killed it, but he had not, and it thrashed around and kicked up all the sand that created the dunes. Giant Beaver River (now McFarlane River) connects through Mudjatick River to Île-à-la-Crosse and to the Churchill River, which flows east to Hudson Bay.

Another narrative closely related to the giant beaver creation tale centres on two battling giant hunters. This story about naming describes the territory of the people called Thilanottinè ("Those who dwell at the Head"). Two giants, "He Whose Head Sweeps the Sky" and "Bettsinuli," engage in battle. Bettsinuli, the stronger one, would have killed the good giant had it not been for a Dene man who cut Bettsinuli's ankle with an axe made from a giant beaver's tooth, causing him to fall backwards with his feet in the west and his head in the area of Île-à-la-Crosse. Thus, these Chipewyan people described their home territory as the place where the head fell, north of Île-à-la-Crosse near the headwaters of the Churchill River.[15]

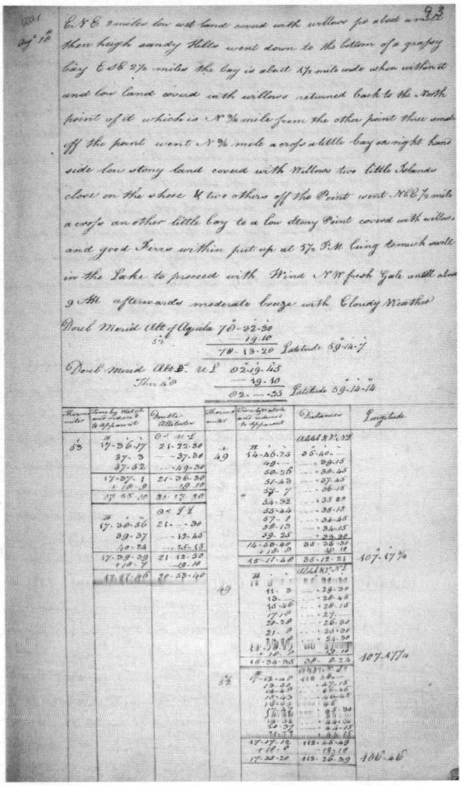
1791 Augt 18th
E N E 2 miles low wet land covered with willows for about a mile then heigh sandy Hills went down to the bottom of a grassy bay E S E 2½ miles the bay is about 1½ mile wide when within it and low land covered with willows returned back to the North point of it which is N ¾ mile from the other point three small off the point went N ¾ mile a cross a little bay on right hand side low stony land covered with Willows two little Islands close on the shore & two others off the Point went N E E ½ mile a cross an other little bay to a low stony Point covered with willows and good Firrs within put up at 5½ P.M being too much swell in the Lake to proceed with Wind N W fresh Gale untill about 9 AM afterwards moderate breeze with Cloudy Weather
Doub Merid Alt of Aquila 78°-32-30 / 19-10 / 78-13-20 Latitude 59°-14-7
Doub Merid Alt ... 82°-19-45 / 19-10 / 82-...-35 Latitude 59-14-14

Figure 29. Turnor's astronomical observations, 18 August 1791, taken near mouth of McFarlane River on Lake Athabasca.

Six miles on, they put up for the night. After a few hours' rest Turnor and Fidler were up taking observations for latitude and conducting sets of observations for longitude. As recorded, from 2:46 a.m. until nearly 5:57 a.m. they observed three sets of lunar distances.

On 20 August they came to the end of Athabasca Lake at longitude 105° 29′, about 180 miles from Fort Chipewyan. They entered the Stone River, which Turnor was told could lead to Churchill water. How advantageous that route might be he could not personally judge, as they only went up it about three and a half miles. However, his guides told him that when they "get into the Churchill water at Athakiasakeapitchecon they proceed down the river to the mouth of a river called the Deer River which runs out of the Deer Lake

[Reindeer Lake]," and that "the navigation of that river is not bad."[46] At Stone River Turnor left a "Lopt pine" as a marker,[47] which David Thompson noted four years later in 1796 when he reached the Stone River via the Churchill route. In 1807, Fidler arrived at the same spot where he and Turnor had left their mark, but it was gone. Fidler concluded, as had Thompson, that this Churchill route, though shorter, was not practical.

On 21 August, after a breakfast of jackfish, they started back down the lake on the north side to Fort Chipewyan. Though it was a cloudy, thundery day, they sailed for three and a half hours. The next day they sailed again until a heavy gale drove them to find protection on a small island in the lee of two large ones. The only place to pitch their tent on the rocky island was over an old swan's nest that, Turnor noted, made them a comfortable bed for the night.[48] The north side was more rugged, with low, rocky islands, some with small firs, pines, and birch. In his fifteen-day journey, he and Fidler had taken the observations needed to calculate eleven latitude and eight longitude positions. He had seen desert on one side, boreal woods and granite on the other. The last leg of the journey was to cross from the north to the south shore. The winds were still heavy, so they took on stones for ballast, and, after some difficulty, arrived at 10 a.m. on 30 August. He had circled the shores of Lake Athabasca, located by observation the mouth of the Stone River, a potential route to the Churchill system, and had also fixed accurately the latitude and longitude of Fort Chipewyan on Lake Athabasca.[49] He now had enough information to map a route from York Factory to Great Slave Lake. On their return journey he would take measurements over the Methy Portage.

Winter at Lake Athabasca, *September 1791 to May 1792*

While Turnor was making his way around Lake Athabasca, Ross and his men arrived at Lake Athabasca on 18 August, selected a location for the house, only six hundred yards from the NWC settlement (as they could find no better location), and began laying the foundation. It was the first Hudson's Bay Company house in the Lake Athabasca area. Ross had been tempted to make their winter quarters south of Île-à-la-Crosse on the Beaver River, closer to the

HBC settlements on the Saskatchewan. Even now, with Turnor's return, they contemplated going, as they wanted information from Tomison at Hudson House about plans for further expeditions in the North. However, Turnor quickly reasoned that he could feed his men better here and, furthermore, they could gain intelligence of the NWC trading practices.[50]

Their house, twenty-four feet long, had a partitioned-off area of ten feet by fifteen feet for Turnor's quarters where he could more quietly work on his calculations. Ross built for himself and his family a separate place, eighteen feet by fifteen feet. Watching Ross's family on the journey and here at the House, Turnor must have wondered how his Cree wife and son were faring. Joseph, now seven or eight years old, would be learning the routes to and from Moose Fort, travelling with his mother and her people. Knowing the hardships he had dealt with on this northward trip, Turnor may have been thankful his family was near Moose Fort.

Four canoes of Chipewyan people came in on 2 September, and Fidler was asked to winter with them. He readily agreed as he wanted to learn their language and customs. This also served Ross well, for not only did he have one less person to feed, but Fidler could keep an eye on the Chipewyan people, who owed him debt for some traded goods

At the end of September two NWC men arrived and, as always, news was exchanged. Turnor heard from them that at Grand Rapids, on Lake Winnipeg, they had met Tomison, who reported that he had lost a man, cargo, and a canoe on the rapids. But they had no letters for Turnor—not a single line from Tomison. Turnor had proposed to Tomison that he and Ross would return to Athabasca next summer if they could be supplied. Was there not to be another northern expedition or a permanent trading house established in this area? He would have been more disheartened if he had been aware that, at this very time, Joseph Colen at York Factory was writing his annual letter to the London Committee, informing them that Tomison was dead set against the northward expedition and had done what he could in a subversive manner to withhold men and canoes.[51] Tomison had deliberately avoided writing Turnor.

In early October many canoes of NWC men came in to the Athabasca settlement, twelve canoes on one day alone, before all departed to their various wintering places. It rankled Ross and Turnor to see the number of men working for the NWC and the great stock of trading goods and European provisions they were bringing in. Ross was embarrassed, but accepted the kind offer from Roderick Mackenzie of eighteen pounds of pork, twenty-eight pounds of flour, and nine pounds of white sugar. He wrote in his journal: "I am very sorry that any of your Honours servants should be at the necessity of receiving such things."[52]

The winter was long and Turnor grew sick of fish, mostly tickameg, which turned soft after December, although they could keep frozen stores. If they had had more nets they would have been able to catch more fresh trout, sturgeon, and pike, but, as Turnor wrote, he had discovered that "Mr. William Walker ordered two of them [nets] to be secreted from us at Cumberland House when he knew they was the only two nets we had to take with us into the North."[53] The six nets they had were of short length and poor twine. Each day one had to be taken up, washed in scalding water, dried, and mended (which Turnor did himself), and then reset the next morning.

Finally there were signs of spring: a gentle thaw, light rain, even some mosquitoes flying around above the snow, geese flying, and, in the evening, the mating calls of the moose. Fidler returned on 10 April in good health from his winter with the Chipewyan band. Although Fidler told him it had been an agreeable winter, his tales told another story. Turnor, nearly forty years old to Fidler's twenty-two years, did not think he could have taken the hunger and cold in the Chipewyan camp. Fidler was incredibly resilient, managing with few outer clothes, just a leather coat and shoes, no toggy (blanket coat) or socks, and no tent, just a bed under a pine tree, until he and the Chipewyan people arrived at Slave Lake. Halfway through the winter he had to rip off the sleeves of his leather coat to make shoes for himself, and he had to beg for a blanket to wear like a petticoat when they stopped walking and his body heat dissipated. He survived on the same fare as the band. Some days, Fidler told Turnor, they shared a beaver's tail or a partridge among ten of them. A few days there was nothing but berry hips. Once they shot a wolverine and greedily ate it before it was even cooked through. "A delicious morsel," he said. "What cannot hunger do?" He had heard that some years ago at a NWC house on Slave Lake, the men were so starved that "one man was eaten by two others through necessity." So neutrally did Fidler mention this that it carried no judgement other than a comment on the utter harshness of the North. Other times, Fidler said, they were "wallowing up to the eyes in good meat," with moose, bear, and geese. He learned the customs and the language, and once, because he spoke both Cree and Chipewyan, he persuaded the Chipewyan people he was with to abandon their plan to kill the Cree people over an old grudge. He kept his own journal, made sketches of the areas he visited, and took observations for latitude. He had the smaller five-inch brass sextant, but no watch, so he was unable to observe for longitude.[54] Once or twice he froze his fingertips while holding the brass instrument in freezing temperatures. All in all, as Turnor wrote in his journal, Fidler was "a very fit hand for the country."[55]

The Chipewyan people with whom Fidler returned had left their women behind for fear the NWC men would take them. Fidler, Turnor, and Ross were distressed to see this common NWC practice of taking the women by force, not just for themselves but for trade among their men:

> The method by which they get most of the Chipewyan women is by the [NWC] Masters seizing them for their husbands' or fathers' debts and then selling them to their men from five hundred to two thousand Livres and if the father or husband or any of them resist the only satisfaction they get is a beating and they are frequently not satisfied with taking the woman but their husbands' or fathers' gun and tent likewise.[56]

These masters were nothing better than pimps, wrote Ross. He had seen an aged father, walking with the help of a cane, knocked down and beaten by them for protecting his daughter, and he noted that a master sometimes took three women for himself.[57]

This practice could only lead to violence, and in fact an incident took place at the NWC settlement just as Turnor was packing up to leave. Mistapoose, a respected chief who had accompanied Mackenzie to the Arctic, passed by the HBC house with eighteen men carrying guns and a woman with a hatchet, all vowing vengeance against the NWC men for taking their women. However, the Chipewyan people were afraid to confront the NWC men, so they dropped off their weapons in the woods before proceeding to Fort Chipewyan, where they argued and disputed, but finally had to leave without their women.[58] Turnor was told by the NWC men that the Chipewyan people "had never behaved so insolent to them as they have done this year," which they blamed on Turnor and his men for raising the band's expectations of trade with the HBC. Turnor and Ross were concerned about the trading of women and felt that the presence of the HBC in this area might moderate that situation as the Chipewyan people would trade with them. In the past some Chipewyan people had traded at Churchill, where they were "well used" and received "plenty" for their furs, but the journey fatigued them as, being fearful of the water routes, they had to go overland.[59] Turnor's urging of the company to build a settlement here and his assessment that this would be lucrative territory for the HBC, with about three hundred hunters bringing in furs, ended with an explanation. He hoped he had not been "unnecessarily partial" in believing the assurances of the three Chipewyan men who had been their pilots and who had taken in Fidler for the winter.

On 30 April, when the river was mostly clear of ice, Turnor and his men began hauling by hand the furs and cargo to the mouth of the Athabasca River to be ready to leave for Cumberland House as soon as possible. By now Turnor was suspicious that Tomison and also William Walker, master at South Branch House, had no intention of supplying him and Ross for a return trip this summer to the Athabasca area. Walker, who had originally been distrusted by Tomison, was now being recommended by Tomison as his successor in 1793, so the two were working together. They had never wanted a trade to be started in the North. Turnor disputed their claim that it was impossible to provide men, canoes, and supplies for a northward expedition, and he reported to the London Committee, "I made some inquiry and I shall communicate my information in its due place."[60]

Turnor was convinced that there was great opportunity in the Athabasca area. The Peace River and the Slave River people could provide ample provisions; the fishery was plentiful in the late fall and they could freeze the fish for winter use; there was birch rind for canoes, plenty of geese, and natural salt in the area to cure them. The NWC were reaping great profits, twenty thousand Made Beaver from the Athabasca area and even more from the Churchill country north of Cumberland House. Their only opposition from the Hudson's Bay Company was Chatham House on Wintering Lake. Turnor had heard the NWC traders admit that keeping the HBC focussed on competing with them on the Saskatchewan River was to the NWC's advantage; "that while they can draw the attention of the Honourable Company's servants [to the trade] up the Saskatchewan or to southern parts they can afford to oppose them at a trifling loss, so long as they can keep the North to themselves."[61] This was an ideal time for the HBC to move up north, for the Chipewyan people were not happy with the NWC. They received few goods for their furs, and felt the goods were inferior. A gun cost five times as much in a trade with the NWC as it did with the HBC, and the Chipewyan people wanted the cloth that they could only get from Churchill. For Turnor, however, it was not simply a business matter, but a question of the company's integrity—and his own. "In my opinion," he wrote, "neglecting to send to the Northern parts after such repeated promises must lessen the Honourable Company in the eyes of the Indians and greatly discredit their Servants to the no small satisfaction of the Canadians and greatly injure those poor Indians that dared show themselves as our friends."[62] It was a breach of trust, he felt, to make promises to the Chipewyan or the Cree people that were not kept.

Though he and Fidler had done their work well, clearing up the confusion between the two large lakes and fixing their positions, it was with a sense of futility about the company's future plans that he left for Cumberland House on 9 May 1792.

13.

"No Small Breach of Trust"

The Methy Portage, 1792

Still, Turnor harboured some hope that, in person, he might be able to persuade Tomison at York Fort to agree to supply another expedition north. Right now though, he needed a guide for the trip to Cumberland House, particularly over the Methy Portage, which he had heard was difficult to locate. They stopped at the NWC Settlement farther up river, but, as usual, any available guides had been sent away so that the HBC men could not induce them to their trade. There was little they could do but carry on.

The route to the junction of the Clearwater and Christina Rivers was easy enough. A year ago, on their detour of the Methy Portage, they had come down the Christina to this point. This time they would travel east on the Clearwater River to the famous Portage that joined the river systems of the Arctic watershed and the Hudson Bay. Because the Athabasca River and all waters north of the Methy Portage drained into the Arctic basin, this territory was not protected by the HBC charter, and the NWC, as Turnor had seen, had comfortably gained a foothold there. Mackenzie had taken this route north from Île-à-la-Crosse to Lake Athabasca in 1787, from where he set out on the journey that took him to the Arctic. Now, five years on, it was Turnor mapping the portage route for the HBC. He could only hope that the company would make use of his surveys and begin to challenge the NWC in this northern area.

Every switch in compass direction, every distance, every change in terrain, all were meticulously jotted down in his journal. They passed Pine Portage with its ragged rock banks, and on 20 May began looking for the Methy Portage. Without a guide, they spent the better part of a day locating the entrance to the portage. Banks of small willows, grass, and swampy land camouflaged any opening. Garroch was put on land to try to find it. They took a few wrong tracks, but eventually put up on a "piece of fine meadow"[1] at the left-hand side of the carrying place.

Starting at 4 a.m. the next day, they began their carrying along the portage, sometimes on a level trail, other times over steep hills that were a hundred yards or more to the bottom. "If a person was to make a slip to either side he would be sure of being at the bottom before he stopped,"[2] wrote Turnor in his journal. The men walked and hauled in four or five stages for nine and a half hours, advancing just over two miles a day. Ross, carrying with the men, wrote, "I am not able to give your honours any remarks worth your notice as hard labour & hunger are my constant companions & employs all my attention how to overcome them."[3] Turnor had taken time at the beginning of the portage to take an observation for latitude, and throughout he recorded all his distances and descriptions of the terrain. Towards the end of the day, when the men were hauling up to the final stage, he went searching for much needed fresh water, which luckily he found at a nearby lake, probably Rendezvous Lake, so named because the traders from the North with their furs met there with the Montreal voyageurs coming up with goods. Exhausted and preoccupied with their work, Turnor, Fidler, and Ross all failed to comment on the spectacular Clearwater Valley panorama that Mackenzie later described as "a most extensive, ravishing and romantic prospect."[4]

The portage was twelve and a half miles: five long days of hauling their heavy bundles and canoes, the days warm, the mosquitoes and black flies tormenting them. It left them totally spent. But Turnor felt a sense of completion. The effort was worth it, for he understood the value of this passage—it was the gateway to the Athabasca area and to both the Arctic and the Pacific oceans. They celebrated with a feast of the five ducks that Ross had shot.

The following day they pitched and repaired the canoes, which had been dried out by the sun and loosened by the jarring as they were carried on the men's shoulders. Then they set off for Methy Lake (Lac La Loche), where Fidler drew a small sketch of the lake and two NWC trading houses.[5] With ice on the lake and cold, rainy weather, they were stalled there for two days. Though they put their nets out, all they had to eat was "a piece of poor jack fish roasted."[6] They went down the Methy River and arrived at the south branch (Garson River) where they had begun their detour route on the trip out. The detour had cost them almost double the mileage, but it had been the right thing to do, for game and fish were definitely scarce on the Methy Portage, just as Mackenzie had warned. They continued on to Buffalo Lake (now Peter Pond Lake), and finally, after a delay of five days due to ice and then two days of burning woods, they arrived at Île-à-la-Crosse on 8 June, where the NWC summer master, Mr. Graham, greeted them with as much kindness as Patrick Small had in October 1790. He offered them anything they needed. Ross, always wary, wrote Graham a receipt for some provisions, but this was declined, and he was told that Mr. William McGillivray, in charge of the Athabasca territory for the NWC, had left orders to treat them well, as he had been kindly looked after by the HBC at Cumberland House.

Two days later they set off through Île-à-la-Crosse Lake, carried on through Primeau Lake, Knee Lake, Snake Lake, and Black Bear Island Lake. Though there was no need to take constant measurements, having paddled this course in the fall of 1790, Fidler sketched some of the lakes and Turnor took an observation for latitude at the east end of Black Bear Island Lake. On 17 June, at Trout Lake, they met up with six canoes of Chipewyan families. Turnor could only get a few dried trout from them. "They never give you anything like the Southern Indians [Cree] who never let an Englishman pass them without giving some provision…but a Chipewyan loves first to make a bargain,"[7] he wrote in his journal. Earlier, back at their Lake Athabasca location, Turnor had noted that the Chipewyan people were the most "politic Indians" he had yet met.[8] They never traded all their furs, hoping to make better deals with the competition.

Here at Trout Lake they had an interesting tale to tell Turnor and his men. William McGillivray had told them that the NWC master, Mr. Small, had gone to England to obtain medicine that would kill all the English and any Chipewyan who went to the English to trade. Not so, retorted Turnor and his men, spinning their own tale of deception. Our company has better medicine. We are not afraid of the NWC, he told them, as they get all their trading goods from our country, and it is plain to see that they do not get the best blankets, guns, or cloth. While that seemed to convince them, Turnor, with no apparent irony, said that the Chipewyan people "are such liars themselves that they readily believe other people to be so."[9] Such trading games made *all* the players "politic."

They went over the height of land between the Churchill River and the Saskatchewan system, and into Pelican and then Merion Lake, where they had the sails up and went too far south, causing a three hour return against a heavy gale. Other than fish and gull eggs, they had eaten only a small beaver from a Cree man and his wife, and a little moose meat from the Chipewyan hunters. Turnor's shooting of a young black bear the next day "was very acceptable"[10] to the men and made up for the extra hours of travel.

They arrived at Cumberland House on 27 June. This track, between Île-à-la-Crosse and Cumberland Lake, had not been as bad as he remembered it from 1790, when his mind had been taut with anxiety. Second time round, it was always easier—though never uncomplicated. Magnus Twatt was in charge at Cumberland. The house was almost as poorly supplied as it had been in 1790—no brandy and no trading goods. It was clear that Tomison was not preparing for another expedition north.

Mr. Ross's canoe was not fit for travel up to York Factory and he would have to make do with an old one from here. It was interesting, thought Turnor, that Tomison had left three new canoes at Manchester House. This was "no great proof of the impossibility of getting canoes,"[11] as Tomison claimed, just the impossibility of anyone other than Tomison using them.

They set off for York Factory on 30 June, taking the southern track into Lake Winnipeg. This route was familiar to Turnor, and the journey relatively easy. They came through the Echimamish River, the route he had mapped in 1779, and into the Hayes River with no difficulty. He had the route in his head so well that he could relax, and for the first time in his journals he had time to complain about the insects. They came off the land in clouds that nearly blinded them. The bull dogs (similar to a horse fly) were terrible, "their bite is as sudden as the sting of a bee."[12] The mosquitoes, though, were the worst and on a portage they entirely covered a body so that no inch of skin could be seen. So bad were they that the men preferred to stay on the water paddling, rather than put up on shore for rest or food.

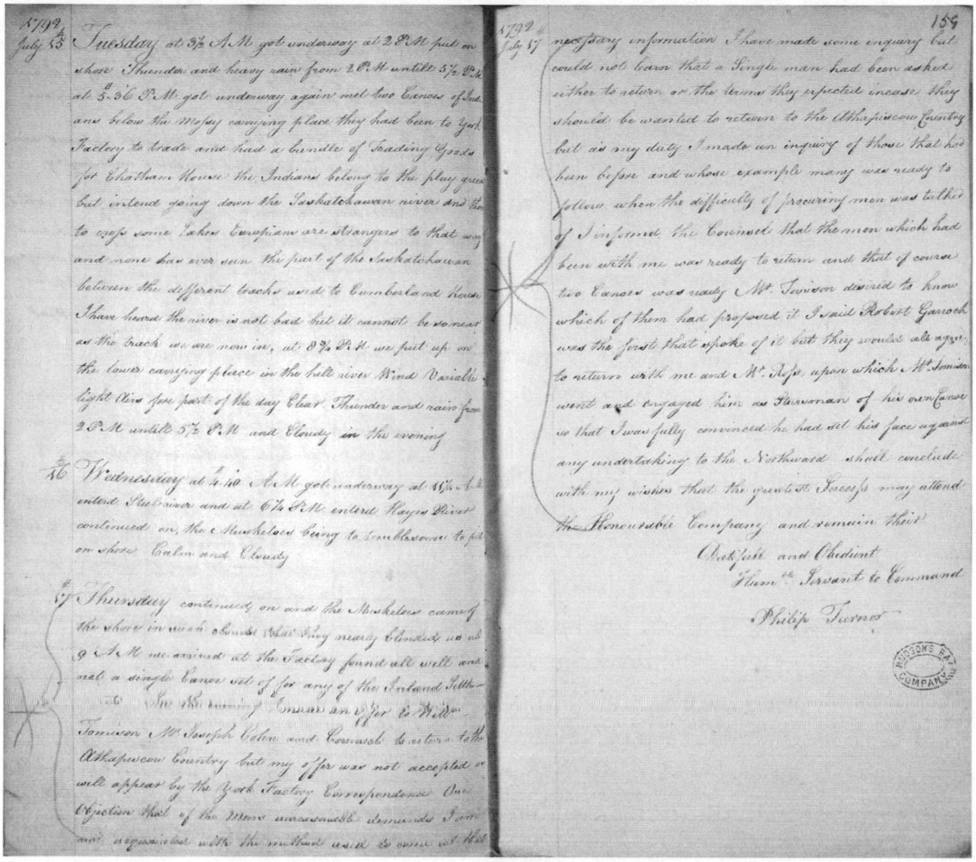
1792 July 15 Tuesday at 3½ A.M got underway at 2 P.M put on shore Thunder and heavy rain from 2 P.M untill 5½ P.M at 5.36 P.M got underway again met two Canoes of Indians below the Mossy carrying place they had been to York Factory to trade and had a bundle of Trading Goods for Chatham House the Indians belong to the play green but intend going down the Saskatchawan river and then to cross some Lakes Europians are strangers to that way and none has ever seen the part of the Saskatchawan between the different tracks used to Cumberland House I have heard the river is not bad but it cannot be so near as the track we are now in, at 8¾ P.M we put up on the lower carrying place in the hill river Wind Variable light Airs fore part of the day Clear Thunder and rain from 2 P.M untill 5½ P.M and Cloudy in the evening

16 Wednesday at 4.40 A.M got underway at 11½ A.M entered Steel river and at 6¼ P.M entered Hayes River continued on, the Muskettoes being so troublesome to pitch on shore Calm and Cloudy

17 Thursday continued on and the Muskettoes came off the shore in such clouds that they nearly blinded us at 9 A.M we arrived at the Factory found all well and not a single Canoe set off for any of the Inland Settlements. In the evening I made an offer to Willm Tomison Mr Joseph Colen and Council to return to the Athapescow Country but my offer was not accepted as will appear by the York Factory Correspondence One objection that of the Mens unreasonable demands I am not acquainted with the method used to come at that

159

1792 July 17 necessary information I have made some enquiry but could not learn that a single man had been asked either to return or the terms they expected incase they should be wanted to return to the Athapiscow Country but as my duty I made an inquiry of those that had been before and whose example many was ready to follow when the difficulty of procuring men was talked of I informed the Council that the men which had been with me was ready to return and that of course two Canoes was ready Mr Tomison desired to know which of them had proposed it I said Robert Garrock was the first that spoke of it but they would all agree to return with me and Mr Ross, upon which Mr Tomison went and engaged him as Steersman of his own Canoe so that I was fully convinced he had set his face against any undertaking to the Northward shall conclude with my wishes that the greatest Success may attend the Honourable Company and remain their

Dutifull and Obedient
Humble Servant to Command
Philip Turnor

HUDSON'S BAY COMPANY

Figure 30. Final journal pages of Turnor's journey northward, 1790–1792.

"Truth is the child of time," *1792*

They arrived at York Factory on 17 July 1792 in the morning. After unpacking and settling in his quarters, Turnor opened a letter from Joseph Colen, the resident master at York, dated 12 July. It was a response to the letter Turnor had written, in great mental and physical distress, from Île-à-la-Crosse sixteen months before in which he had accused Colen of unkindness in not properly supplying the northern expedition. Colen, who had just received the letter, was shocked by Turnor's accusations and immediately wrote to vindicate himself:

Dear Sir [Mr. Turnor]

Some time has elapsed since I heard several flying reports said to have come from you that greatly hurt my feelings. It was said that both yourself and Peter Fidler were sent away from Cumberland House on your journey of discovery without any supplies or provisions, and that I had not sent any for that purpose. I assure you every article in my power was sent you, though I will acknowledge that no supplies I could send you from hence were equal to the undertaking in which you were engaged. As many underhand attempts were made to frustrate your first efforts, I concluded the reports I heard were the invention of prejudiced minds and I made myself easy. But when your letter dated [22 March 1791] from Île à la Crosse was delivered me by Mr. Tomison yesterday [11 July, 1792], I was astonished. It roused every passion in my breast and I found those reports too well founded. I find myself deceived and you most grossly injured. The supplies I intended for your outfit at Cumberland House were never delivered you. From the neglect with which you have been treated I conclude the Honourable Committee have been acquainted, and for my own vindication I trouble you with this letter that you may make proper enquiries....I wish you to examine Mr. Malchom Ross to whom I gave the liberty to take of any articles, provisions, stores in the warehouse, and in order to prevent the men that accompanied you from being encumbered in their canoes to Cumberland, natives had in charge many articles for you which Mr. Walker promised to see delivered on their arrival there....I wish you had made the necessary enquiries before you passed so harsh judgement on my conduct and if you had found any the least backwardness in me in affording you proper necessaries I should think myself undeserving protection or support—I wish no favour—Truth is the child of time and will discover the party who has acted with such duplicity towards you.[13]

With his heartfelt and direct comments, Colen restored his position in Turnor's trust and narrowed down the guilty parties to Tomison, Walker, and Ross.

That evening Turnor attended the council meeting with the other officers, Chief William Tomison, Joseph Colen, and Thomas Thomas, the surgeon. He asked permission to address them.

"Sirs, I have had a good passage, every circumstance considered, and would very much like to return to the Athabasca country. Provide me with six canoes, and I will conduct a party there next spring, after which I will employ my utmost endeavours to discover a shorter route by way of the Nelson or Churchill Rivers. By all the information and intelligence I have gained from the Indian people and from the Canadians, along with my own experience of the country, I am fully of the opinion that it is necessary in the company's interest to immediately erect a settlement on Athabasca Lake and another one on the Peace River. The furs are of the finest quality, prime winter beaver and some marten. The Canadians have made this the bulwark of their enterprise and are drawing upwards of twenty thousand Made Beaver. I've made calculations. If you consider that their total expense to the Port of London does not exceed £3,000, including wages, trading goods, and provisions, you can readily see there is a great profit to be made. Athabasca has abundance, but the Churchill area is even wealthier in furs. I know that the Canadians have carried away from that country north of Cumberland House between forty and fifty thousand Made Beaver every year. I have heard …."

"Mr. Turnor, sir," interrupted Tomison, "we have established ourselves along the Saskatchewan, which is also lucrative, and we have no means of supplying both areas. We cannot provision a northern expedition."

"You would not need to provision it. If you would establish a house up the Peace River, there are grasslands with plenty of buffalo and moose, and those men could bring provisions to Lake Athabasca. And there is a fine fishery. In fact, there is nothing wanting there except cedar for canoes, but pine has been used successfully."

"There are no men available. It is impossible."

"Men may as well be sent out there as loiter their time at York Factory," retorted Turnor.

"Mr. Turnor, do not forget your position."

"Sir, I must speak about what I have seen. Neglecting to send men and goods to the northern parts after repeated promises to the Indians is lessening the reputation of the Honourable Company in their eyes and greatly discrediting the servants with them. It also injures those poor Indians who dared show themselves as our friends."

"It is a long, difficult route and the men consider it an unreasonable demand upon them."

"I have made a point of inquiring about this from the men. I could not learn of a single man who has been asked and who refused. The men who travelled with me are willing to return and two canoes are ready now."

"Who," asked Tomison, "proposed such a thing?"

"Robert Garroch has agreed, as have all the men, including Mr. Ross."

"No," replied Tomison angrily, "this will not happen. As chief of inland operations I have determined that the Saskatchewan area is to be developed before we consider the North. Your work is done here."

"I can tell you, sir, that the Canadians are laughing. They draw you to the Saskatchewan territory, so they can keep the North to themselves."[14]

Tomison was adamant. He dismissed the council, and in apparent retaliation he spoke immediately to Robert Garroch, engaging him as his own steersman. Tomison had set himself against any undertaking northward in spite of encouragement from the London Committee that further forays into the North should be made. It would not be until 1802, ten years later, that a settlement would be established on Lake Athabasca by Peter Fidler. By then it was too late, for in the ten years both the NWC and its offshoot, the New NWC or XY Company, had grown too strong for the HBC, and Fidler was literally forced to leave in 1806.

The war of words continued. Writing to Tomison, Colen, and the council on 19 July, Turnor formally reported on his journey of discovery. He outlined the specifics of the journey, the latitude and longitude of Athabasca Lake, the "information and intelligence gained both from the Natives and the Canadians joined with [his] own experience," and concluded with his recommendations to the company to move into the Athabasca area.[15]

The council, instructed by Tomison, replied, repeating the same arguments as before: there would be no expedition northward until the summer of 1794; they would require twenty-four men for such an undertaking, who could not be spared from other settlements; and the men would expect more pay. They concluded with the wish that Turnor explore the Nelson River towards Chatham House until ship time. Turnor countered all their points regarding the expedition northward except one: "The only argument that bears weight with me are the demands of the men which you do not think yourselves sufficiently empowered [by the London Committee] to comply with. Undoubtedly men will expect more for residing in those parts, than in a country where their provisions drop into their mouths without any trouble." He could not resist this final stab of irony at the man he suspected of failing to provision his northward journey. With that he capitulated: "As you are in full possession of my opinion from our conversation I do not think there is an occasion to burthen the subject."[16]

On 24 July Turnor answered Colen's personal letter, explaining carefully that, when he discovered how he and Fidler were badly supplied, he thought that Colen, like others in command (clearly he meant Tomison and Walker), had adopted a duplicitous attitude towards him and the northward expedition, deliberately placing obstacles in his path. Though his men, Garroch, Leask, Grot, and Brown, had been supplied with oatmeal, barley, and tea, he, Ross, and Fidler, who were to receive provisions separately sent from Colen to Walker, had received nothing. "In my constitution I greatly suffered and under the Canadian noses [at Île-à-la-Crosse] I, Mr. Malchom Ross and Peter Fidler was glad to take stale Jack fish heads out of the dust to afford some relief to the cravings of nature while the others could afford a little oatmeal in their fish liquor." Along the journey to Lake Athabasca, the men would give him and Ross a bit of their oatmeal and barley, but there was not enough to share, and at Lake Athabasca over the winter, though they had some fish, the steady diet of it, along with the very cold weather, proved a great hardship for Turnor:

> I was several times reduced to the necessity of supporting myself with a stick, and once for the continuance of a month I was in so bad a state that I was bordering upon

a dysentery and upon every call of nature the quantity of blood that came from me surprised all our people, but I never could be brought to own that I thought the provision was the cause of it. I did not go to state the difficulties to the men who are fond enough of catching at such things, but on the contrary I offered immediately I arrived at York Factory to return to the northern parts and run all risks though I am not able to bear the hardships many can.

Turnor exonerated Malchom Ross, whom "I ever shall respect," and he apologized to Colen: "instead of censure you deserve my warmest and sincerest thanks which I now give you as flowing from my heart." He told Colen that it was William Walker (master of South Branch House) who "abused us both" by not turning over the supplies he was ordered to.

Turnor next addressed the rumours that had been so injurious to him and to Ross over this period. They had been accused of drinking rum at Cumberland House that had been supplied for the northward expedition, and Ross had been accused of being so intoxicated for four days that he was incapable of doing his duty. All this was false: "This Rum was never tasted until the 31ˢᵗ of October [when they were wintering at Île-à-la-Crosse]," and as for Mr. Ross, Turnor stated, he is "remarkable for sobriety and good conduct." Furthermore, Turnor wrote, "a greater injury was offered us both by a gentleman, high in station in this country, a charge of the highest nature, that of neglect of duty." To clear himself of this slander Turnor "took the liberty of mentioning it before [Colen], Messrs Tomison, Thomas Thomas senior, Thomas junior, William Cook, Charles Isham, George Sutherland and David Thompson." They all stated openly that they did not know who had laid this accusation, but all believed the rumours to have no foundation of truth. Believing the "gentleman" who levelled the accusation to be Tomison, Turnor specifically addressed him, and Tomison "declared before the whole [group] that he thought we [Ross and Turnor] could not have done more than we did." When he said these words in front of the men, it was as if he "condescended to eat his words" about any neglect of duty. Turnor believed he had been cleared in the eyes of his fellow officers and went no further: "I did not choose to involve the Factory in broils to the injury of business but treated him in such a pointed manner as to convince him that I knew him to be the person." Generously Turnor added, "he [Tomison] has merits but he should not sport with people's characters as that is deceiving those by whom he is employed and highly entrusted. Such conduct strikes me as no small breach of trust."[17]

Turnor was bitterly disappointed not to be re-assigned to explore routes to the Athabasca country. He had spent his best years in this country and wanted to contribute more. He would lay all these matters before the company when he arrived home. He could do no more here, but in England he would draft the largest and most accurate map of this northern territory to date.

Journey to Chatham House, *July to August 1792*

It was painful for Turnor to sit about at York Factory watching the men prepare for their inland journeys, carrying on without him. Fidler, Ross, and Isham were all being sent out. Tomison kept to himself, although his officious presence was felt. Turnor had agreed to go up the Nelson River to Chatham House, a recently established HBC house on Wintering Lake, and he wanted to get underway. He opened a new marble-covered journal and began his last record for the Hudson's Bay Company:

> 1792
> Mr. Colen having expressed a desire of sending up to Chatham House a canoe with some brandy…and as I had a desire of seeing the lower part of the river again I immediately promised him to man a canoe the next day out of the men who had just come from the northward with me and accordingly instantly engaged Hugh Leask my former steersman, Malcom Grot who had been head or bowsman to Mr. Malchom Ross and Peter Brown who had been a middle man in my canoe.[18]

Colen advised him that they should wait for Tomison to leave before making any further arrangements. With all the contracted men busy, Turnor could only employ those who were waiting for the ship. Arch Linklighter was one of them, but he refused to go unless paid forty shillings.[19] He stirred up the other men, persuading them that it was both too dangerous and too late. They might miss the ship. A council was held. Linklighter was reprimanded, put on half-food allowance, and grounded. That settled down the men, but Turnor could see that they were demanding more than they had in the past. Though Turnor had been a proponent of the men receiving proper payment for dangerous trips and explorations, and had always believed that officers needed to "share some difficulties with the men,"[20] he had no patience for their "intermedling" in general affairs. They were always holding a "council" to discuss the master's conduct and always played it to their own advantage.[21] Turnor intended to look into this matter. Perhaps he was becoming cranky.

Finally, on 31 July, not soon enough for Turnor who felt they were deliberately held up, he and his canoes left York Factory. Hugh Leask was his steersman. Grot was not available, but Peter Brown was his middleman and James Johnson, "an invalid," was bowsman. The other canoe had three men: Edward Wishart, William Flett Senior, both "capital hands," and Andrew Codagill.[22] Two Cree lads, inexperienced in these larger canoes, were hired to help. Turnor grumbled that his canoe was "weakly manned"[23] compared to the other canoe, and yet he took on four hundredweight more. It was not a good start.

They went around Marsh Point and into the Nelson River. This was the same track Turnor had taken in 1778, just off the ship from England. He had to smile as he recalled his first time tracking and how he wore out his two pairs of English shoes. He had been green for sure. It was not an easy river, but now he knew what was around the corner.

Tracking in the face of the high, stony banks demanded constant attention. At times the river narrowed to the width of a canoe, and with ragged rocks and heavy current they had to be careful. He was testing the river this time, to see if it was a feasible transportation route for flat-bottomed boats. At Gull Falls, ten days in, they were handing a line around a rocky point when the heavy current knocked him and William Flett right off their legs, but the line brought them safely to shore. Gull Falls, as he recorded, "is all one continued exceeding heavy rapid in a constant raging foam."[24] They had four carries to make, but the next day they were in Gull Lake, which was easy going.

After another difficult day of handing and carrying they were in Tasquiau Lake (Split Lake), where they were able to sail at four miles an hour. They entered Grass River, a part of the Saskatchewan River, on their thirteenth day out, and on 15 August they were about fifty miles from Chatham House. They had just paddled to Picacasinne Powestick, meaning one stone fall (Standing Stone Rapids), where a single obelisk-shaped rock stands alone, eroded from the rest of the cliff. It reminded Turnor of the Old Man of Hoy in the Orkneys.

Here matters took a turn when Turnor learned to his surprise that three NWC men were currently at McKay's House,[25] nine miles from the HBC Chatham House. He had understood that no NWC men stayed there during the summer months, perhaps hearing this from Mr. Mckay himself, whom Turnor had met near Pelican Lake about two months earlier. Knowing that there was only one man at Chatham House, that he did not understand Cree, and that the Cree in this area were traders with the NWC, Turnor was concerned. He recalled his own fears in 1778, three weeks into his first trip to Cumberland House, when brandy caused the Cree guides to shoot into his tent and to tear it down. The Eagle Hills attack might have been in his mind as well.[26] He explained in his journal that the NWC men "would wish no better sport than by giving the Indians a little liquor setting them upon the single man [at Chatham House]."[27] Turnor decided that they could not leave the supplies of brandy and trading goods with just one man. He tried to persuade one or two of his travelling companions to stay at Chatham House until the wintering servants arrived, but they were concerned that they might miss the ship and wanted to start back immediately.

Perhaps he was losing his nerve after the difficulties of his northward journey, but once again the lack of foresight and planning angered him:

> If I had known of this before I left York Factory I would not have proceeded without one or two of the men which are to winter at the place; it's surprising to me that all the men knew it and that I never heard of it.[28]

They had gone 275 miles on a difficult river and now must return without delivering their goods. He made the best of a bad situation and cached the cargo here so the men coming up for the winter could carry it on to Chatham House. There was some satisfaction, once again and for the last time, in having seen this river that had educated him fourteen years ago. And it was better than waiting around York Factory.

He took an observation for latitude, and they started back. Running a rapid the next day, his bowsman turned the head of the canoe into an eddy. At the same time a squall of wind caught them, water filled the canoe, and they overturned. They lost the sextant, compass, a small glass, and a few other articles. Fourteen years ago, on his first trip out and not far from this spot, he had lost his bottle of quicksilver. He had not been so unflustered then.

At Split Lake they met up with James Spence, one of the York Factory men en route to Chatham House, laid up at this place because of the rain. As always, Turnor spoke about the waterways to the Cree guides accompanying Spence. They described a small river (Assean) leading into the Little Churchill River and then on to the Churchill River that might be a faster route to Île-à-la-Crosse. Or there might be a route from the Churchill River through Reindeer Lake and Wollaston Lake into the east end of Lake Athabasca. If only he could have made another journey northwards to explore these possibilities.

On 20 August they came into a part of the Nelson River that was full of islands and rapids. They passed Gull Falls, Kettle Falls, and finally Hell Gate Falls. Turnor made notes that he would flesh out in his journal about the possibility of bringing boats from York Fort as far as Hell Gate Falls. Canoes from inland could meet them there and transfer the furs to the boats. The canoes would be saved from travelling farther down through the gravelly shoals that stripped the birch rind from their bottoms and made them almost impossible to mend.

On 24 August they turned the point of Marsh and saw the *Seahorse* already there.

JOURNAL TWELVE

A Map in the Mind

I did not inherit any propensity for geography or cartography from my four-times-great-grandfather. At Moose Fort I had to ask whether I was looking towards James Bay or towards the Moose River going up to the Abitibi. The clearest and most thrilling overview I had of the territory that Turnor mapped was on my flight in the small plane following the Nelson and the Hayes to York Factory. From that bird's eye view I could see, laid out like a gargantuan map, the details and connections that Turnor stored in his mind.

On the floor of my study, I have laid, side by side, the maps of Quebec, Ontario, Manitoba, Saskatchewan, and Alberta and outlined in red his many thousand miles of travel—nearly fifteen thousand by my count. The online topographical close-up maps allowed me to see tree cover, rapids, rock, and shore, but not connections of one river to another. I could zoom in on places like Standing Rock Rapids, but nothing helped me visualize the entire network of rivers in this north country. Where did the Churchill and the Nelson or the Saskatchewan meet? The Cree at Split Lake told Turnor about a small river, the Assean, navigable up to a carrying place that led to the Churchill River. He could immediately see the possibilities—such a route would avoid the worst part of the Churchill and it would be a shorter track to Île-à-la-Crosse. He could see a passage from the Churchill to Lake Athabasca via Reindeer and Wollaston Lakes. Whether it was viable was a different matter. His mind worked in 3D mode. He could travel over these splotches of lakes and tendrils of rivers as if he had Google Earth in his head. ✳

York Factory, 24 August to 17 September 1792

The men were not sitting around now. When the ship was in, there was plenty of work, unloading the trading goods, English provisions, building materials, packets with orders and correspondence, and then loading the furs and the packets with journals, maps, and correspondence. The shallop, the long boat, and the sloop worked all day, back and forth to the *Seahorse*. Turnor used this time to write out a copy of the journal of his last trip, and for the last time he signed off:

> went up to the Factory at which place I had the happiness
> to hear everything was well and am with the greatest respect
> *The Honourable Company's Obedient Servant*
> *Philip Turnor*[29]

He had no time to make a chart of his last journey, but started collecting all his information about the trip to Athabasca and packing up Fidler's maps and his own notes.

He said his good byes to David Thompson, who set off on 5 September, proceeding to Sipiwesk Lake, south of where Turnor had just been. Fidler had already been re-assigned to the Saskatchewan River settlements and had left in late July. Thompson was instructed to continue Turnor's investigation of a route to the Athabasca, and the two men would have looked over maps and thoroughly discussed possible routes. No doubt they talked of Tomison. Thompson had witnessed Turnor's confrontation with Tomison at the council meeting over the deliberate stalling and dangerous compromising of the Athabasca expedition and the accusation of neglect of duty. In fact, this might have been in the back of Thompson's mind five years later when he fell prey to the same treatment and defected to the NWC.

Turnor recommended both Thompson and Fidler to the London Committee, but probably thought that Thompson would be his replacement. At this time Thompson was a favourite with Tomison, and Tomison was still the most powerful man in Rupert's Land. Thompson was treated generously, not only given a raise in salary but, at no cost to himself, he had been given a sextant and other materials for his surveying, unlike Turnor who had to return his equipment and had bought a watch from his own salary. But there was nothing to indicate resentment on Turnor's part, and both men always spoke highly of each other.

Turnor sailed for England on the *Seahorse* on 27 September. As he watched York Factory recede, the red of the HBC ensign a small dot of colour on the horizon, he must have been filled with ambivalent emotion. His Cree wife and son were of his past now, but he must have thought of his son, now ten years old and the only progeny he was to have. He was parting from colleagues, some of them dear friends, a few antagonists. He would never again hear Cree or Chipewyan spoken, he would never see the scrub pines or black spruce, hear the rapids that tensed his muscles and quickened his heartbeat, never curse the marl banks, or marvel at the granite canyon walls higher than a ship's mast.

Would he, too, disappear like that small dot of colour? Success—a "lasting name," as Joseph Colen had phrased it—how could that be measured? Would he be remembered for his northward expedition and his observations of Lake Athabasca? Would he be remembered for his service to the company and his reputation as a surveyor? Tomison had tried to disgrace him, but he had not buckled:

> When I look back I tremble to think upon what ground
> I have stood; when such an assertion as fell from so great
> a height, it must rebound so often, that by some means
> it must come to the ears of the Honourable Committee
> to cultivate whose good opinion has and shall ever be my
> study; it is a duty I owe to myself.[30]

He had been true to himself. He still had maps to make, and they would show that he expanded the company's knowledge of Rupert's Land and the world's knowledge of North America.

14.

"A Permanent Foundation"

London, *1792 to 1795*

As Turnor sailed east to England, his former apprentices, David Thompson and Peter Fidler, journeyed west to survey unmapped territory. Thompson, in an attempt to discover a route from the Churchill River to Lake Athabasca, paddled into Sipiwesk Lake. Fidler, travelling with the Piikani people,[1] rode horseback west and south from Buckingham House on the North Saskatchewan where, in a few weeks, he would see the Rocky Mountains for the first time. On 14 December Fidler was camped at "Spitcheyee River."[2]

JOURNAL THIRTEEN

Connections and the Aura of Place

Spitzee — I knew that name from my youth, though we had anglicized it from Spitcheyee (Piikani) and Ispitsi (Siksika). Now I realize I had looked out to the Rockies from that same river, the Highwood, at which Fidler had stopped.

I grew up in High River, a small town on the banks of the High-wood River nestled between the Rocky Mountains and the prairies. I had not heard of Fidler in my school days; there was not then, or now, to my knowledge, a plaque commemorating his visit here. But I did know that Ispitsi, meaning high, referred to the river (which disastrously floods on occasion) and to the high cottonwood trees along the banks of the river. At Spitzee Crossing or Fort Spitzee,[3] about five miles west of town where the river was low enough to ford, the Siksika came regularly to camp. Nearby was a unique tree formation—two large cottonwood trees side by side, with the limb of one grown into the trunk of the other. Known as the Medicine Tree, it was a spiritual and healing place for the Siksika.

Fidler was six weeks in this area. He wrote about "Old Woman's Buffalo Jump," south of High River, where he had been mystified when he saw a herd of buffalo thundering along the prairie suddenly disappear. He travelled along Pekisko Creek through the tall prairie grass with the mountains sharp and white on the horizon, and past where the famous Bar U Ranch was established in the 1880s—places where I had picnicked as a girl. Farther southwest he saw King or Chief Mountain still sixty odd miles away (across what is now the Canadian–United States border). A towering promontory, it was a powerful spiritual place for the Indigenous peoples. Fidler was the first European to travel this far southwest, and the Piikani were delighted to show off their specimen white man to the Snakes, who had never before seen such a being. Fidler further astonished them by lighting his pipe by means of his burning glass (convex lens), which was fixed in the lid of his tobacco box.[4]

Fidler sent Turnor sketches and observations, and on first looking closely at this section of Turnor's 1794 map I saw the dotted lines he used to show Fidler's track to and from the mountains. And there, with some excitement, I saw that Turnor had drawn in Spitcheyee River, running into the Bow, then into the South Saskatchewan, and, though Turnor's map did not show this, into Lake Winnipeg and, finally, Hudson Bay. Here was another instance where my research became much more than an amassing and ordering of historical detail. Through this shared place, Spitcheyee/Spitzee River, I caught a glimpse of 'my' own landscape as it had been over 200 years ago when the Piikani people brought Fidler here. ✳

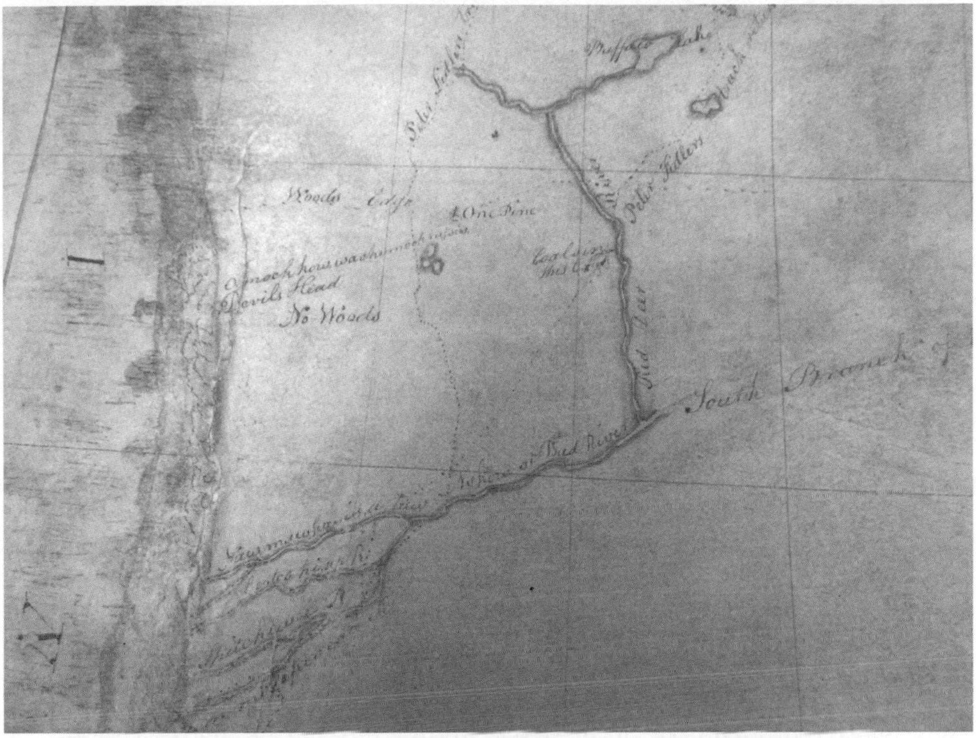

Figure 31. Spitcheyee (Highwood) River running into
the Bow River: detail from Turnor's 1794 map.

Mapping the Northward Journey, *1792*

On 17 October Turnor arrived off the Isle of Wight and was taken ashore by the pilot boat. He took a coach home to Elizabeth, but it is unknown whether she was residing in Battersea where they were married, in Laleham where Turnor had returned in 1787, or in Uxbridge from where Elizabeth wrote when Turnor was in Rupert's Land. They had been apart for nearly three and a half years. It would be an adjustment to resume domestic life after his rugged travels. Where would they live? He hardly knew how to tend to an English wife. For her sake he tried to quickly adapt to the activity and noise that unsettled him.

A week after he arrived he went to the Hudson's Bay Company offices at Fenchurch. His task now was to draft a map of his route to the Athabasca country. He may have worked at the company offices where he had access to all the current maps, his own from past years and others that were available at that time. He began, as usual, with a sheet of blank rag paper, carefully inking in a graticule of degrees and minutes and then pinpointing his locations on the map. The first map he drafted was in fourteen sheets: "the Track from Cumberland House to Isle la Crosse with the Magnetic Bearings."[5] It formed the basis for the second map, "A Chart of Lakes and Rivers in North America by Philip Turnor those Shaded are from Actual Survey's [sic] the others from Canadian and Indian information"[6] (see Plate 6). On this map, twenty-six and a half by thirty-nine and a half inches, he set down his recent journey from York Factory to Great Slave Lake.

As he drafted this map he could feel himself on the rivers once again. In his mind's eye he saw the granite walls or the clay banks, the pines and the willows, rapids and portages; he could hear the steady, rhythmic dip of the paddles, the thunder of falls ahead, the lull of lakes and marshes. The map of this country would forever be in his memory. He charted the main arteries from York Factory and Albany Fort, which he had shown on his previous maps. Above and below the Nelson and the Hayes he left blank space. The Indigenous people knew these lakes and rivers, but he did not. He had wanted to explore more thoroughly the Stone River running into Lake Athabasca and a possible route between Reindeer Lake and the Churchill River, but that would be up to someone else now. Referring to his notes, he wrote descriptive comments in fine, unembellished strokes. On the Saskatchewan River he noted its "sandy clay banks," a portion of "bad river," and where it became "Meadow Country full of Buffalo and Wolves" as it made its way towards the Stony Mountains which were its source. Over the Athabasca and Peace River country he profusely entered his comments. Beyond Île-à-la-Crosse he mapped both his initial route on the Christina River and his return track on the Methy Portage. All along these rivers he noted the good and poor fisheries and hunting grounds. Beside the Athabasca River he wrote "upon this part plenty of good birch rind." Fort Chipewyan was "a good place for fish." He noted the NWC house on Great Slave Lake, and that Slave River had "bad water." The eastward waters out of Slave Lake that he had spoken about with Shewditheda are indicated in five faint dots. On the Peace River, for which he only had information from the NWC men and the Indigenous people, he wrote, "About this river Beaver and Buffalo are very plenty and furs and provision is procured at a very easy rate." At the eastern end of Lake Athabasca he noted, "The fishing at this end of the Lake is not well known but it lays well for trade."[7] This map was a basis for his final map of 1794, and it was his argument for establishing trade in Athabasca country.

Accuracy was always his chief concern. At the same time that he was drafting in the Athabasca and Peace Rivers in October 1792, Alexander Mackenzie was on the Peace River, ascending it towards his wintering place at the junction of the Peace and Smoky Rivers (Peace River town) before beginning his famous trek to the Pacific, the first man to make that journey. It was likely that Mackenzie had been given Turnor's calculation for Fort Chipewyan before setting out, which would give him the distance to the Pacific. He would arrive at Dean Channel, one of the longest inlets into the Pacific Ocean, on 22 July 1793.[8]

For the next two months Turnor worked steadily on his maps and was paid, retroactively in December, one guinea per week until "further orders."[9] This amount, if paid for a year, would be about the wage he initially earned in Rupert's Land, and would be an adequate lower middle-class wage.[10] Likely he was already looking into establishing a navigation school.

He met with the HBC committee and reported on the state of affairs in the various settlements in Rupert's Land. He stressed, as he had done in his journals, that the company must find a way to compete with the NWC in the North, where the furs were plentiful and of superior quality. Tomison had been a good man, but was now so fixed on expanding the Saskatchewan River trade that he could not see clearly the vision for the North. Though Colen, chief factor at York, was keen for the discovery of a new route to the North, he was weak against Tomison and his only strategy was to subvert Tomison's orders when Tomison was away from the fort. Just this fall, Colen had sent Thompson out in September, although he had been poorly supplied. There was also troubling news that Churchill and York Factories were competing with each other, an unprofitable development.

It was not just the trade itself that was evolving, but the men had changed. In Turnor's early years in Rupert's Land they had worked hard. Now they complained openly. There was a lack of cooperation among the leaders as well as among the men.[11] Company direction itself was partly responsible. More men needed to be hired and they needed to be better paid and better supplied for the long, difficult journeys. Turnor would no doubt have told the London Committee how the NWC treated their men and warned them that if they did not reward their own men they would lose them.

The committee, however, was ambivalent about his advocacy of a change in policy and leadership for Rupert's Land. Though they agreed that the Athabasca country was promising, they did nothing to permanently replace Tomison. In fact, Tomison would be censured, retired, and then hired again on four different occasions.[12] It was true that, with the French Revolution erupting and a possible war with France, there were fewer men for hire from the Orkneys, but Turnor felt strongly that Tomison was the obstacle to realigning the company's direction.

There was an air of fear about rebellion and change in general. The Bastille in Paris, the symbol of the aristocracy and the old regime, had fallen to the revolutionaries in 1789. At first this was greeted with approval by England. However, when the revolutionaries ruthlessly abused their power, William Pitt, the Tory prime minister, backed away from supporting them. Stability returned to England, although there were several factions of discontent: the middle class, who wanted better working conditions and took hope from the overthrow of the French regime; and the upper-class Whigs, who saw an opportunity for parliamentary reform. In France during the September Massacres of 1792, the revolutionaries killed hundreds of imprisoned nobility, and the First French Republic was declared on 22 September. With this shocking turn of events, order, stability, and a return to conservatism were called for in England, and this mood may well have permeated the offices of the Hudson's Bay Company. The HBC governor, Samuel Wegg, and the deputy governor, Sir James Winter Lake, preferred the status quo. They would stick with the old master they knew—William Tomison.

Turnor would have heard all this news at the Hudson's Bay Company offices, or the coffee houses, or from the newspapers, which were full of the debates taking place in France over the fate of King Louis XVI, who had been imprisoned since August of last year. Finally a decision was made. *The Evening Mail* declared: "The Convention of

France has found Louis XVI Guilty—DEATH!!!"[13] On 21 January 1793 he was executed by guillotine. Nine months later France's Queen Marie Antoinette was executed. Maximilien Robespierre commenced the Reign of Terror, which resulted in the killing of tens of thousands of those loyal to the King. France marched into the Rhineland and the Netherlands, taunting England to come to the support of her allies. Pitt was reluctant to declare war, and finally, on 1 February, France declared war on Great Britain and on Holland. With fleets being sent to the Mediterranean and to the West Indies, with men being pressed into service, it was a tense, unsettling atmosphere in London.

Turnor's "Chart of Lakes and Rivers" was finished by the end of 1792, and he began planning his final map for the company which was to be a composite of all he had surveyed as well as any new information available. He also worked on a pamphlet that would provide the latitude and longitude observations of the significant places he had surveyed throughout his travels in Rupert's Land and northward. The company still depended on his experience and knowledge of Rupert's Land, and he was regularly called to the HBC offices for consultations on various matters: the building of boats for York Factory, the choice of astronomical instruments for Ross and Fidler, or the will of a former colleague, Germain Maugenest, who died in November. Turnor continued to mentor Fidler and communicated directly with him. He chose a package of instruments to be sent out in May 1793, a Ramsden sextant, a watch made by Jolly, a Dollond thermometer, and other necessary equipment, and Fidler sent at least some of his surveying information directly to Turnor rather than to the company. Of course this information was useful for Turnor's maps, and perhaps he checked Fidler's calculations before passing everything on to the committee. Turnor also advised about employees and his recommendations were taken seriously. He was partly responsible for Ross being named Master to the Northward, and he recommended his wife's nephew, Henry Hallett, for service in the company, although Hallett had a troublesome career.[14]

Rotherhithe, *1793*

By 1793 Turnor had taken a place at Prospect Row, Dock Head, Rotherhithe, where he taught navigation and lunar observations.

This may have been solely a business location, although, as he was not financially well off, he and Elizabeth may have taken up residence there as well.[15]

Rotherhithe was well situated for teaching navigation, for it was on the south side of the Thames, five miles from the Royal Observatory at Greenwich, and at the centre of London's shipping business. The Pool of London, upstream from Rotherhithe to London Bridge, was teeming with vessels, over three thousand coming and going every year. Docks and wharves outlined the snout-like peninsula of land to the east, an area rich with the history and stories of sea travel and seamen. The *Mayflower* had sailed from here to America in 1620, and more recently Rotherhithe had been home to Prince Lee Boo, a Palau Islands aboriginal man, brought here in 1784 by the East India Company.[16] At the numerous wharves, Savory Mill Stairs, Cherry Garden Pier, King & Queen Stairs, Cuckold's Point, Dock and Duck Stairs, pilots plied their trade, guiding ships, loading and unloading cargo—and transporting people, as there were only three bridges across the Thames. Timber ponds (where lumber was stored and/or seasoned) and granaries of corn, flax, and hemp were located at East Country Docks. Howland or Greenland Dock, around the peninsula to the east, was the largest commercial dock and could handle 120 merchant ships. It was also the base for processing whales. Whale meat, cut in strips onboard the ships, was brought back to be boiled down to oil for lamps and lubrication for machines. The smell of the rotting flesh aboard the whalers as they came in and the stink and steam from the blubber boilers on the dock often made this area an unsavoury place.[17]

However, Dock Head, where Turnor settled, at the top end of St. Saviour's Dock, was near Bermondsey and it was more residential. Close by was Cherry Garden Pier which led to a Commons where Londoners came to buy cherries, play games and relax, and nearby was a market garden, later known as Southwark Park. Farther south there were spas with chalybeate springs that were advertised as curing anything from melancholy to indigestion, anemia and gout. Turnor may have been suffering from the rheumatic attacks he had in Rupert's Land, and the closeness to a spa might have been useful.

The sea air at Rotherhithe, however, was not always salutary, for the area down by St. Saviour's Dock, known as Jacob's Island, was evolving into a slum area, not yet at its worst although it had a dark history. The river Neckinger entered the Thames at this point, so named because, a century earlier, pirates who ransacked the moored ships were hanged by the neck for their misdeeds. Farther east dank, stagnant air hung over marshy fields and tidal ditches. In the fall and winter months Turnor must have pined for the bright skies, the clean, crisp scent of spruce, and the unsullied snow of Rupert's Land.

With a population of about ten thousand in Rotherhithe, there was a great need for schools. A free school for the sons of seamen had been established, and there was a schoolhouse near St. Mary's Church, but there was an opportunity for many more schools. If Turnor took on six to eight boys, he could probably earn about four to five pounds per year.[18] This small salary would supplement his guinea per week from the HBC, but was hardly adequate compared to his salary of eighty pounds per annum for the last six years of service in Rupert's Land.

In 1794 Aaron Arrowsmith printed *Result of Astronomical Observations made in the Interior Parts of North America*, Turnor's collection of his observations of key locations in Rupert's Land. Arrowsmith's world map, printed in 1790, had brought him to the attention of the Hudson's Bay Company. They abandoned their policy of secrecy, allowed him access to their map collection, and granted Turnor permission to publish his work with Arrowsmith. Turnor's sixteen-page pamphlet contained the latitude and longitude of places from York Fort on Hudson Bay and Cumberland House on the Saskatchewan River to Athabasca and Great Slave Lakes in the north, Frederick House and Lake Timiskaming in the south. He also included the observations of other accurate surveys: Fidler's results in 1792 and 1793 as far west as the Rocky Mountains; David Thompson's results from Chatham House in 1792 and 1793; Mr. Vandriel's[19] of Michipicoten and Lake Winnipeg in 1791; and Captain Cook's of Nootka Sound in 1778. The "Advertisement" inside the pamphlet announced the particulars of this publication:

> THE RESULT OF ASTRONOMICAL OBSERVATIONS in the Interior Parts of North America, have chiefly been made at the Expense of The Honorable GOVERNOR and COMPANY OF ADVENTURERS OF ENGLAND, Trading into HUDSON'S BAY; and printed by Permission of the COMPANY; to which

the Public stands indebted for the many Positions so accu-
rately settled by MR. PHILIP TURNOR and Others in their
Service; which has laid a permanent Foundation for the
GEOGRAPHY in that Part of the Globe.[20]

To see his name brought to the public's attention and to see praise
for his endeavours was no small measure of satisfaction for Turnor.
This pamphlet and his upcoming map would be a fitting culmination
to his career: twelve years and nearly 15,000 miles of travel, hundreds
of hours of observations and calculations, ten maps drafted, and five
years as master of two different posts.

By the autumn of 1794 Turnor had nearly completed work on
his final, composite map (the complete map is reproduced in colour
on this book's endsheets). He had worked on it in nine sheets, each
sheet slightly different in size.[21] First, he had established his graticule,
laying down his lines of latitude and longitude in black ink, precise
as usual.[22] He used the Mercator projection with parallel lines, his
longitude interval being one and a half inches. In graphite he plotted
all the locations he had personally surveyed from Hudson Bay to
Great Slave Lake and south to Lake Superior and Lake Timiskaming.
On all the routes he had travelled he drew with a firm hand, showing
islands by small dots, settlements with a house, and portages with
a line across the river and a distance noted. He glued together with
a flour paste the nine pieces before inking over the graphite and
applying colour, his river lines flowing across the joins.[23]

The lakes and Hudson Bay were coloured with a blue wash. He
used different ink colours to mark areas that had been surveyed by
others and noted their names in his "References" list: Mackenzie,
Vandriel, and "others."[24] The map showed Mackenzie's route to the
Arctic, and one of the salient features on the map was the notation in
the upper left called "The Sea," where Turnor provided information
about the post Mackenzie erected in 1789 on which he wrote his
name and the latitude of Whale (Garry) Island. The area was washed
originally in pale red and strikingly scripted in India ink.

Turnor noted unreliable information in pale grey ink. He could
not show Mackenzie's 1793 journey to the Pacific Ocean as he had not
yet seen the details. The Peace River, which Mackenzie would take,

trails off, but the outline of the Pacific coast, known from Captain James Cook's voyage, was drawn in.

The "others" included work by Donald McKay, Edward Jarvis, and Fidler. At the HBC offices Turnor had pulled out the 1791 "Genl: Map" (General Map) drafted by Jarvis, showing territory explored by Donald McKay, who until 1790 had been in the employ of the NWC. McKay knew the territory west of the Albany and Moose River areas from Lake Nipigon to Lake of the Woods and into the Assiniboine country. Marking the territory south of the Assiniboine, Turnor wrote on his map, "Mr. Donald Mackay track with 4 Canadians in Feby 1780...after 12 hours on horse back he discovered the Great Missouri." This material filled a significant gap on Turnor's map.[25]

In 1792 and 1793 Fidler had travelled with the Piikani people from Buckingham House on the North Saskatchewan into the foothills. As he had continued to communicate directly with Turnor rather than the London Committee, his journal or correspondence or both were sent to Turnor on either the 1793 or 1794 company ship. Turnor was provided with enough details to locate Buckingham House, the farthest west location at that time of a HBC house,[26] and to draft in the Stone (Rocky) Mountains south to the bottom of his map at the forty-sixth parallel. He drew the Bad (Bow) River and its tributaries,[27] and the Red Deer River, though he apparently did not have enough information to know where the Red Deer River joined the South Saskatchewan.[28] Turnor drew Fidler's journeys on his map with dots to indicate tentativeness. Fidler's description of his first sight of the Stone (Rocky) Mountains, which he saw from the Red Deer area ("awfully grand stretching from SSW to WbS by compass, very much similar to dark rain like clouds rising up above the horizon on a fine summers evening")[29] may have inspired Turnor's thick, cloudy dark line representing the mountain ranges on his map. In his pamphlet, underneath the latitude and longitude for a location near Stom-mixepisconneeheattatti (Buffalo Pond River), Turnor added what appear to be details from Fidler's journal: "Mr. Fidler went from this place E.S.E. 4 ½ miles, then S. by W. 12 miles, and then arrived at the Tents of the *Cattanahowes* [Kootenai], three miles within the Stony Mountain on December 31, 1792."[30] At latitude 49°52'03" North and longitude 114°47'19" West, this was the farthest south and west point reached by Fidler within sight of King or Chief Mountain, which lies just south in what is now the United States.

When mounted on canvas, Turnor's map was over six by eight feet, and it covered 46° to 70° North and 72° to 138° West—exceptionally large.[31] Positioned in the centre-top piece of the nine pieces, and overlapping on the top left and right, was an impressive cartouche, designed by Edward Dayes, draughtsman to the Duke of York[32] (see Plate 7). Well known at this time, Dayes frequently produced designs for important publishers, so his was a significant embellishment for Turnor's map. Dayes produced a nicely balanced scene in subtle greens and browns, with pine trees leaning outwards on either side to suggest expansiveness, blue mountains rising on the left, a body of water in front of the mountains, two elk on the right, a buffalo on the left, and three beaver in the centre foreground. It was dramatic, it was emblematic of Rupert's Land and the company, but Turnor might well have smiled at the cow faces of the elk and the hunched haunches of the beaver, the placid water of the lake, and the buffalo perched on a boulder—not exactly what he had witnessed. In between the trees the elegant script declared:

To the
Honourable the Governor, Deputy Governor
And COMMITTEE of the
Hudson's Bay Company
THIS MAP
of Hudson's Bay and the Rivers and Lakes
BETWEEN the Atlantick and Pacifick OCEANS
Is most humbly Inscribed
By their most obedient & dutiful Servant
Philip Turnor

Tomkins of Foster Lane signed his name on the face of a boulder as the "scripsit" who had rendered the flourishes of variegated script.[33]

With his large map nearing completion, his remuneration from the HBC coming to an end, and, perhaps, his school not bringing in what he had hoped, Turnor decided to seek additional employment. On 18 August 1794 he met with Nevil Maskelyne, the Astronomer Royal, who lived at the Greenwich Observatory, not far from Rotherhithe. If they had not met in person before, they were certainly familiar with each other's work through their mutual friend, William Wales. Maskelyne was the pre-eminent astronomer in England and admired throughout Europe. In 1767 he had initiated the publication of *The Nautical Almanac*, the valuable resource that saved surveyors and navigators hours of time in calculations of latitude and longitude. By publishing (for up to five years in advance) the predicted lunar distances from the sun and certain stars at different Greenwich time intervals during the day, the *Almanac* permitted a surveyor or navigator anywhere in the world to determine his longitude. The surveyor would compare his lunar distance with that in the almanac and the difference between local and Greenwich time would provide his longitude.[34]

Tabulating this data for *The Nautical Almanac* was the job of Maskelyne's computers. Between four and nine computers would perform the calculations for each lunar distance that appeared in his annual publication. It was time-consuming and repetitive work requiring accuracy and knowledge of the use of mathematical and astronomical tables. A computer would be required to perform a dozen or more calculations for each observation, knowing that an error might result in a navigational disaster.[35]

At their August meeting Turnor was hired as one of the team of computers. Maskelyne, in his usual meticulous notation, recorded that he loaned Turnor twenty texts of astronomical tables and materials, ranging from "Mayer's Tables" and "Lalande's Ephemeris" to "Charles Mason's Lunar Tables of 1780" and *The Nautical Almanac* from 1795 to 1800—all required to conduct the calculations for each observation.[36] He also loaned Turnor his own "manuscript book of calculations," for Maskelyne was particular about the way in which calculations were performed. Turnor's first assignment was "for examining, correcting & recomputing various calculations of the moon's place made formerly at the Royal Observatory," and for "reducing and comparing with the nautical almanac several observations within the same period which had not been calculated before."[37] Turnor left that day with a huge bundle of books but with a lighter step, knowing he had work after his map was completed.

Just as Turnor was completing his map, the ship from Hudson Bay arrived with David Thompson's newest map showing the Burnt-

wood River area between the Nelson and Churchill Rivers and into
Reindeer Lake that he had surveyed in 1793. Turnor himself had
not travelled this area, but it was precisely the connection between
Reindeer Lake and Lake Athabasca that he had hoped to pursue. He
erased his own markings and drafted in Thompson's latest results,
leaving the light green wash on his map looking smudged.

It was finished—and he was satisfied that his map exhibited the
most complete information of northern North America that had
been seen to date.

Turnor presented his map to the company some time before 14 January 1795, because on that date the secretary was "ordered...to pay Mr.
Philip Turnor £100 in consideration of his services in having surveyed
the company's several settlements and explored several New Straits,
laid down the same in a large and accurate map. And also that the
secretary do procur the Company's arms to be engraved on the outer
case of the watch which Mr. Turnor used in his surveys and that the
same be given to him as a mark of the Committee's regard for him."[38]

But Turnor's map in this state was not published. Rather,
Arrowsmith's map dated 1 January 1795 used Turnor's map as its
foundation, but he did not show the Burntwood area surveyed by
Thompson, nor did he include the Bow River, although he drew in
one of its tributaries (Bull Buffalo Pond River), which had been documented in Turnor's pamphlet. Arrowsmith incorrectly presented
the Red Deer River running into the North Saskatchewan River and,
although Turnor himself did not accurately portray the relationship
between the Red Deer, Bow, and South Saskatchewan Rivers, he
understood it better than Arrowsmith. However, Arrowsmith was
able to add more information along the western coast and south of
the forty-ninth parallel than Turnor could.

Arrowsmith may not have added the Thompson and Fidler material because these areas appeared rough and tentative on Turnor's
map, and Arrowsmith was always reluctant to include unconfirmed
information on his maps.[39] Or, perhaps, Arrowsmith's map had already been engraved by October or November 1794, too late to make
any alterations.

Arrowsmith's map was decorated with a handsomely lettered
cartouche acknowledging the HBC:

A Map / Exhibiting all the New Discoveries / in the Interior Parts of / NORTH AMERICA / Inscribed by Permission / To the Honourable Governor and Company of Adventurers of England / Trading into Hudsons Bay / In Testimony of their liberal Communications / To their most Obedient / and very Humble Servant / A. Arrowsmith.[40]

Turnor was not personally acknowledged on the cartouche, but Arrowsmith was indebted to him for the accurate mapping of the "interior parts," the routes from York Fort, the regions along the Saskatchewan River, the country north to Great Slave Lake, west to the Rocky Mountains, and south to within sight of Chief Mountain, this latter information supplied by Peter Fidler.[41]

Arrowsmith's map and a "Pamphlet" were advertised together in *The Morning Chronicle* and several other newspapers on 13 and 14 March 1795:

NEW DISCOVERIES
This Day is Published,

A MAP, exhibiting all the New Discoveries made in the Interior Parts of NORTH AMERICA between the latitudes of 40 and 70 North to Longitude 45 and 180 West, from Greenwich, accompanied with a Pamphlet containing a Catalogue of the results, Astronomical Observations, how determined, with Observers' Names, Date, etc. The size of the map is 5 ½ feet by 3 feet. Price in sheets £1 1s

By A ARROWSMITH, Charles Street, Soho Square[42]

The pamphlet referred to must be Turnor's *Result of Astronomical Observations*, which notes on the cover that it was "printed for A. Arrowsmith." Thus, Turnor, named in the pamphlet and praised for laying "a foundation for the Geography in that Part of the Globe" was explicitly connected to the production of Arrowsmith's map.

On First Seeing Turnor's Great Map

2008

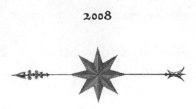

I recall the unveiling, when I first saw Turnor's magnum opus. Two archivists carried in the rolled-up scroll. They put it down at the bottom of a large table and slowly unrolled it, revealing bit by bit the inked routes in red, green, blue, and brown. Eight and a half feet wide by nearly six and a half feet high, it overlapped the edges of the table. The bottom was discoloured and torn. That would have been the part most touched as many fingers traced the trade routes over its 223-year life. For a time it must have hung in the Hudson's Bay Company offices, displaying the expanse of their enterprise, but for the next 200 years it had been rolled up and forgotten.

It was impossible not to be drawn to the cartouche dominating the map. On this first viewing, and before I had read much of Turnor's life, I mistakenly thought Turnor had drawn the cartouche as well as the map. Nevertheless, such an extravagant adornment denoted a work of significance. His name, inscribed with elegant flourishes, bestowed on him an importance and dignity I had not expected.

Photographs, I discovered, were unequal to the task of representing it whole and coherent. I tried, by standing on a chair, to get the entire map, but that distance made it unreadable. Its magnitude cannot be contained in a single photographic image, but must be seen by the eye.

The map itself seemed like a stunning achievement. I did not yet understand or appreciate his perseverance, the hardships, and skills that went into the making of this map. I did not know about the cooperation of so many people: his fellow canoeists, his Cree guides and paddlers, his Cree wife. He may have simply wanted adventure

Figure 32. Author viewing Turnor's 1794 map for the first time.

when he arrived in 1778, but when he left in 1792 he hoped to have contributed to public knowledge. Was it enough that he had mapped his life's work here on this map, knowing that, as the foundation for Arrowsmith's map, it would go out further into the world? Or did he feel unfulfilled and disappointed that it had not been published? Perhaps he would be astonished, but certainly gratified, to hear that over 200 years later his map has been described by today's geographers as a "masterpiece,"[43] and "one of Canada's greatest cartographic treasures,"[44] and that this period of mapping for the Hudson's Bay Company, 1778 to 1794, "may fairly be designated the Turnor period."[45] ✳

Turnor, the computer, *1795*

Turnor turned to the job he had talked about with Maskelyne well over a year before. He received his first payment on 18 January

1796 in the amount of fifty-six pounds and 4 pence.[46] The time taken and the amount paid suggest that these were involved calculations, although it is difficult to know just when in 1795 he began the work.

His second assignment was "for calculating the moon's longitude from observations and comparing them with the Tables for 28 observations,…for correcting some original computations of the right ascensions of the moon and planets,…and to reduce them to the standard of Dr. Maskelyne's two catalogues of stars of the years 1766 & 1784." Eleven months later, on 28 December 1796,[47] he was paid twenty-two pounds, 16 shillings, and 9 pence. For this year, 1796, he managed well financially: he had earned nearly eighty pounds from Maskelyne alone and perhaps more from his school. Also in that year he received nearly twenty-five pounds from the HBC for consulting work.[48] Of course, it was more expensive living in England than in Rupert's Land, where he had room and board supplied. His rent was fourteen pounds, but food and clothing were becoming increasingly expensive.

The headquarters for the HBC had been moved late in 1794 to larger quarters at 3 & 4 Fenchurch Street, not far from the former building.[49] The company was doing well although they dropped the dividend from 8 per cent to 6 per cent in 1795, where it stayed for the next six years. It was hard times in England, which was still at war with France and suffering huge losses in both the Mediterranean and the West Indies. The harvest had been poor and working people were starving. There had been local bread riots in 1792 and 1793, but in September 1795 they were widespread. As the King drove to Parliament House on 29 October, the streets were "choked" with people, two hundred thousand in number, and the King was "violently hissed, and hooted, and groaned at, with incessant vociferations of 'No Pitt, No War, Peace, Bread.'"[50] Prime Minister Pitt and the French War were blamed for causing severe starvation among the poor. While the large farmers and the grain merchants were making money, the poor were suffering. One news story told of a single mother whose children died with pieces of straw in their mouths—all they could find to eat. Turnor and his wife were fortunately solvent enough in 1795 and 1796, though with food shortages and the war continuing, they too would come into hard times.

Clerkenwell, *1797 to 1799*

Turnor continued computing for Maskelyne. 1797 was a lean year with just ten pounds received from Maskelyne on 9 December. In 1798 he made a liveable salary of about fifty pounds, but he was not well. Conditions were still wretched in England, although, fortunately, the tide had turned in the war with France. In February 1797 Horatio Nelson, fearless and arrogant, broke orders, sailed from the rear to the front line, challenged three Spanish warships, and led Britain to victory over the Spanish in the Mediterranean. In August 1798 he defeated the French in Aboukir Bay, and the Mediterranean was firmly in the hands of the British.

In 1798 Turnor and Elizabeth moved to No. 9 Chappel Row, Spa Fields, Clerkenwell.[51] Turnor may have become afflicted once again with the dreadful bouts of rheumatism he had suffered in Rupert's Land, or he may never have fully recovered from the toll his travels and poor diet had taken on him. By the end of his time in Rupert's Land, he had admitted to Joseph Colen that he was no longer able to "bear the hardships many can."[52] Aside from the usual debilitating swelling of his joints, he may more recently have been experiencing heart palpitations.[53] Perhaps he and Elizabeth purposely chose Spa Fields, which was well known for its mineral waters, reputed to cure many complaints from heart and rheumatic conditions to skin diseases and nervous disorders. There were cold baths at Coldbath Square and mineral waters at Spa Fields that were considered as curative as those at Tunbridge Wells.

He may have been drawn to Spa Fields for its association with dissension and radicalism. Here the Countess of Huntingdon, a dissenter and a charity worker, oversaw the Spa Fields Charity School and headed the chapel, which welcomed Methodists, Presbyterians, Quakers, and non-believers who had left the official church. Although Turnor was married and buried by the Church of England, he appeared not to practice the faith of the traditional Church of England.

At the end of his first year in Clerkenwell, his mentor, William Wales, died at age sixty-four, which must have saddened Turnor. Not well himself, struggling to make a decent living, he pushed on, and in May 1799 he began correcting proofs for the *Nautical Almanac* of 1800, and then for 1805. In June he requested from Maskelyne, as he had not done before, cash advances of nearly four pounds. Either he was not well enough to do more work, or he was not supplied with it. He made just over twenty pounds in 1799, hardly enough to live on. His situation had become desperate.

If the news reached him in the fall that his son, Joseph, now fifteen or sixteen, had been hired on as a labourer at Moose Fort, that would have stirred many memories. Joseph was his only (known) progeny. This news would carry with it bittersweet thoughts of his own achievements. He thought of the years he had spent as an officer in the HBC in charge of surveying journeys when he was full of ambition and pride for the challenging work he was doing. Now it was simply survival.

Correspondence from Peter Fidler had reminded him of Rupert's Land over the past seven years since his departure. They had continued their strong relationship developed on the Athabasca journey in 1792. Fidler would send his latest surveys and observations directly to Turnor, who would pass them on to the committee. Perhaps Fidler did this out of loyalty to and respect for his teacher, or perhaps he did it to reassure himself that his calculations were accurate. This practice, however, did not please the governor and committee, and Turnor received a letter in October 1799 to that effect: "They thank you for the communication of Mr. Fidler's location. They however think he should have likewise wrote himself to the Board."[54] They perhaps sensed that Fidler, in spite of his hardiness, dedication, and voluminous sketches, did not have the confidence and independent spirit they wanted, for he was not appointed to succeed Turnor as official surveyor until 1810.

The same letter from the governor and committee, the last communication Turnor would receive from them, began on a contentious note: "The Governor & Committee of the Hudson's Bay Company are much surprised at your thinking they have shown to you any marks of neglect much less of contempt."[55] Whatever the particulars of this disagreement were, Turnor felt dismissed, receiving neither the attention nor, perhaps, the payment he felt he deserved. It resurrected in his mind the old battles and his feelings of a breach of trust.

Near the end of 1799, on 21 December, Turnor received two pounds from Maskelyne for his computations. On 27 December Turnor gave him corrections for page two of the 1805 *Nautical Almanac,* and this was the last time Maskelyne saw him.

JOURNAL FIFTEEN

Imagining Turnor's Last Days

February 1800

He was not well. He tried again to work on the astronomical calculations for Maskelyne, but his mind was as thick as the fog outdoors. He shook with fever and chills. He could not bear to even move a limb, so swollen were his ankles and knees. His wrists were too inflamed to hold his pen steady. This was worse than the violent affliction he suffered in Rupert's Land at Brunswick House. Seventeen eighty-three it was, on the Missinaibi River. It took him three months to recover. He thought of the willow bark tea she had made him.

But it was different now—such an oppression in his chest.

The spas had been no help.

My poor Elizabeth, he thought. What will become of her?

He looked at the books on his table. *The Nautical Almanac*, Lalande's *Ephemeris*, Mayer's tables, Gardner's *Logarithms*. He called Elizabeth and reached for Taylor's *Logarithms*.

"Take this to the pawnshop. Get the most you can. Ten shillings, if you can bargain well. Settle for seven if necessary. Tell Mr. Ward that I will pay the rent as soon as I get on my feet again."

He wondered—could he appeal to the company for money? The company—God knows he had done good service for them. ✳

"Mr. Turnor Died," 1800

In his diary Maskelyne simply wrote, "1800 March 1 Mr. Turnor died."[56] Turnor had been struggling to make ends meet and dealing with a weakened constitution, perhaps a heart condition, but as he was still working on assignments for Maskelyne, it would seem that his death had not been imminent. His widow, Elizabeth, must have been in shock at the loss of her husband at just forty-eight and at being left in such an impoverished state. On 6 March Turnor was buried at St. Marylebone.[57]

Maskelyne went to Turnor's lodgings on 7 March and methodically wrote in his notes that he "received of Mr. Ward, [Turnor's] landlord, the following books" which he then listed. Taylor's *Logarithms*, however, "was never returned; it had doubtless been pawned, or disposed of."[58] The landlord was holding the books as rent payment and, to retrieve them, Maskelyne paid Turnor's rent of ten pounds ten shillings. Turnor had left some completed calculations, and, meticulously as always, Maskelyne calculated the amount due for the work. The final notation on Turnor's account was Maskelyne's note that the payments he owed Turnor "may be considered as equivalent to the value" of the rent that Maskelyne had paid the landlord.[59] Though poverty stricken, having had to pawn one of Maskelyne's books, Turnor, in the end, balanced his account.

Turnor's death was not remarked on by the HBC. However, on 26 March the secretary noted in the minute book a plea from Turnor's widow: "Read a petition from Elizabeth Turner [sic] wife of Philip Turnor geographer to this Company lately deceased, praying for some pecuniary assistance. Ordered that the Secretary do give the said Mrs. Turnor twenty guineas.[60] There is no further mention of her. She may have returned to Uxbridge or to Battersea to live out her days on the family farm. Elizabeth Turnor disappeared from history, almost as anonymously as did Turnor's Cree wife.

The "lasting name" that Joseph Colen predicted for Turnor and the credit with the "Public" for which Turnor himself wished shone briefly in 1795 when Arrowsmith acknowledged his use of Turnor's map for the foundation of his important 1795 map. In its fifth state, this map was studied by President Jefferson and was of utmost value to Lewis and Clark on their 1805 expedition to the Pacific,[61] though Turnor's name might have been forgotten by then. Fidler and Thompson carried his name further, remembering him as a valued teacher and continuing to survey and make maps to his high standard of accuracy, indeed surpassing him in scope. Just as Turnor marked his name on the rock at Marten Falls, he has marked his name on the history and geography of Canada, and with the current restoration of his major map, his reputation is re-emerging.[62]

Epilogue

I would not creep along the coast but
steer out in mid-sea, by guidance of the stars.[1]

Turnor, literally and figuratively, ventured afar "by guidance of the stars." He was not satisfied with farming in Laleham, but sought adventure beyond England. He grew out of the Age of Enlightenment, marked by a philosophy of empiricism and knowledge based on human observation, which led into the scientific excitement of the late eighteenth century in England. Samuel Coleridge was to call this period the "second scientific revolution," dated approximately from Captain James Cook's first voyage to the South Seas in 1768 to Charles Darwin's to the Galapagos in 1831.[2] Though Turnor was a man of lesser rank and wealth than many of the famous astronomers, navigators, and scientists of this era (James Cook, captain and navigator of three world voyages; Nevil Maskelyne, Astronomer Royal; Charles Green, astronomer on Cook's first voyage; Joseph Banks, botanist on Cook's second voyage; William Herschel, astronomer; and William Wales, mathematician and astronomer), he had a similar ambition to steer into unmapped territory.

Turnor, in fact, had dreamed of travelling to the South Seas, but, as he put it, was "disappointed."[3] Perhaps he had applied for a position on the first or second of Captain Cook's three round-the-world voyages, but his destiny proved to be in Rupert's Land where he aspired to know and map with exactitude as much of this territory as he could.

In 1781, while Turnor was trudging through snow to East Main using the stars to find his latitudes and longitudes, on the other side of the Atlantic another astronomer, William Herschel, was standing sure-footed in Bath, gazing heavenward through his seven-foot reflector telescope, mapping the glittering solar system. On 13 March 1781 Herschel discovered a new planet, Uranus, the seventh in the solar system. He was honoured at the Royal Society with the Gold Medal for best work in a scientific field, although he remained nonchalant about his achievements. It was left to the poets to celebrate the wonder and excitement of Herschel's discovery, who, with another world explorer, Cortez, was mythologized in John Keats' sonnet "On first looking into Chapman's Homer:"

> Then felt I like some watcher of the skies
> When a new planet swims into his ken;
> Or like stout Cortez when with eagle eyes
> He star'd at the Pacific—and all his men
> Look'd at each other with a wild surmise—
> Silent, upon a peak in Darien.[4]

Turnor's 'Uranus' was his pinpointing of Lake Athabasca and Great Slave Lake and the composition of his 1794 map of northern North America. Knowing the latitudes and longitudes of these lakes, he could fix their relationship with both the Pacific Ocean to the west and Hudson Bay to the east. Though not as brilliant a discovery as Uranus or the Pacific itself, and though he was not immortalized in poetry, he was publicly acknowledged by the renowned mapmaker Arrowsmith, for "[laying] a permanent foundation for the geography in that part of the globe."[5] Nothing remarkable was heard of Turnor until 140 years later, when J. B. Tyrrell published *The Journals of Hearne and Turnor* in which he wrote, "[Turnor] had blazed the way into the interior of Canada, and his pupils, Thompson and Fidler, were to take up the work where he left it, and carry it onward gloriously."[6] Since then Turnor has been respectfully, though not prominently, mentioned by scholars, and in 1991 Richard I. Ruggles did much to bring him out of the shadows.

Turnor felt his work in Rupert's Land unfinished, but his accomplishments are many. He was a mapmaker, a surveyor, an analyst, a trader, and a teacher, and, in England on his return, a teacher and a computer. As one of only two official and trained surveyors hired by the HBC,[7] he was at the forefront of map production in the latter years of the eighteenth century, producing ten maps. He largely travelled places known already to Europeans (with the exception of the survey of Lake Athabasca and his detour around the Methy Portage), unlike the next generation of explorers and mapmakers, Thompson and Fidler (his students) and Mackenzie, who travelled unmapped areas. But Turnor was a model to them in terms of standards of accuracy and practices of mapmaking. Recognizing the collective enterprise of surveying and mapping, the building on previous work, he credited those who provided him with information: Fidler, Malchom Ross, the NWC, the Cree and Chipewyan guides.

Turnor was in Rupert's Land before an official policy of Christianizing and civilizing had been established and before the beginning of Indigenous reserves in the 1830s.[8] His era was largely one of cooperation with and dependence upon the Indigenous people. However, his mapmaking was part of the British imperial plan to explore and claim territory. Turnor thought of his maps as official documents of geographical knowledge, which they were, but they were also maps asserting control by the HBC of Indigenous territory. Naming was also a stamp of ownership, although once Turnor was inland and once he knew the Cree language he used Cree place names for rivers and lakes when he could. Trading posts were named by the company. On his large map, Turnor designated the Indigenous territories of the Snake, Blackfoot, Shoshone, Creek, Big Belly, Stone, and Chipewyan peoples.

Turnor's surveying and mapmaking have been my primary focus, but his legacy also lies in his progeny. His descendants must number in the thousands, for his son and his wife had thirteen children. At least twenty newfound fourth cousins have contacted me, wanting to learn more about this man and his family. For someone who has always regarded herself as a British-Canadian, I was awakened to my Cree roots through Turnor.

His story and his achievements owe much to his Cree wife and to the Indigenous people with whom he worked. I now have a clearer understanding of the role of women in the fur trade, though I was disappointed not to locate any specific references to my four-times-great-grandmother. She is not mentioned in Turnor's journals or correspondence. In fact, women in general are seldom mentioned in the documents of this period.[9] I wished for more from Turnor—some note in the company's account books allotting funds for his child and Cree wife. I am left to imagine her life, and can only judge by her son's stature in the HBC that both she and his father deeply influenced his life.

My four-times-great-grandmother was Cree, and my three-times-great-grandmother was identified by her daughter Charlotte as "Emma Turner Half Breed."[10] They lived in the camps around Moose Fort, probably as members of the Home Guard. My great-great-grandmother, Charlotte, was British-Cree. Charlotte and James Harper (Orkney-Cree) came in 1844 to St. Andrew's Parish with their firstborn child, Philip, and took up farming. Their second-born, Nancy Ann, "the gutsy one" who did not go to school but desperately wanted to read, married John Low Loutit (Orkney-Cree) in 1867 in St. Andrew's Parish, and they became farmers. Their eighth child, my grandmother Mary, married an Englishman from Norfolk who, after serving in India, came to Canada to start a new life. They lived in St. Andrew's Parish as well, on land inherited from Mary's father through his service to the Hudson's Bay Company.

Though Mary did not talk about her mixed heritage, other Turnor descendants did. Dorothy Turner, a fourth cousin who traces her lineage through the male line to Philip Jr., grandson of Philip Turnor, was raised in Moose Factory along with her eight siblings. Pearl Weston, the author of *Across the River*, indicated that her family knew the stories of Turnor and his country wife. Another cousin, ninety-nine when I interviewed her in 2007, was matter-of-fact about her heritage: "My father [Peter Loutit] said that eighty per cent of the people in this area [along the Red River] have some Indian blood." She recalled that people of mixed ancestry in the 1930s were referred to as "halfers." Her grandmother, Nancy Ann, "would have thought you designated a person as native or not by the culture they adopted....If you lived along the Red River, you were of the white culture; if you lived up north in Indian communities, you were Indian."[11]

Turnor introduced me to Canada's northern geography and early history, to the men who mapped this land, and to the Cree and Chipewyan men and women who showed him the routes. On my own voyage of discovery I travelled to some of these northern settlements—Moose Fort, Norway House, York Factory, Churchill. Other places I travelled mentally with Turnor as he paddled the northern rivers, and I now am alert to the names and locations of First Nations communities like Kashechewan, Cross Lake, or Attawapisak. Though distant, my connection through Turnor to Indigenous people has helped me see with a more personal lens. More strongly than ever I am dismayed by the great needs Indigenous communities have for the fundamental necessities of life (schooling, medical care, housing, clean water), about which little is done by Canadians and our governments. But I am also more aware of Indigenous people's achievements in politics, the professions, and the arts.

A few years ago, when I was attending a Red River Reunion held at Lower Fort Garry, I was told by a participant that my great-grandparents, John Low Loutit and Nancy Ann Harper, had been married at St. Peter's on the east side of the Red River near Selkirk, and that their wedding registration was displayed in a glass showcase in the church.

St. Peter's is a small church, the second-oldest stone church in western Canada. It was constructed in 1853 under the supervision of Archdeacon William Cochran. Stone was quarried from the banks of the Red River to build its foundation and walls, and from that solid rectangle was raised a simple roof and belfry tower. This was the church that served Chief Peguis, a Saulteaux-Ojibwa who had moved to this area in the 1790s with his people. Because most of the people who came were of Saulteaux, Ojibwa, or Cree heritage, it was called the "Indian Settlement." The way to the church now is from Stone Church Road, but in its early days it would have been up the long stone walkway from the river as most of the traffic came from the river, much as it did with the Hudson Bay forts. The inside of the church is plain. A small stained-glass window with a delicate blue and yellow quatrefoil design is all that decorates the front. Above the altar the word *Kanatiseyun* is written, a combination of Saulteaux and Cree that translates as holy or clean. The pews are hand-hewn, each one unique. The glass showcase at the entrance was opened at a page in the marriage registry.

I wandered around the graveyard, reading the plaque in honour of Chief Peguis and noting two Harper graves that might belong to my ancestors. As I walked down to the river's edge, I imagined Nancy

Figure 33. St. Peter's Church, Selkirk.

Ann in a simple dress, her red hair flowing over her shoulders, and John Low Loutit in his best shirt and jacket arriving by boat with a wedding party, walking up the path arm-in-arm to be married. They were only three generations away from me, and, because I had seen a black and white photograph of each of them, I could visualize them when they were just twenty-five and twenty-one.

In the green silence of the churchyard, I sat on the bench contemplating my ancestors and the river when quite suddenly I was awakened from my reverie. A woman stood before me and asked, "So you are a squaw too?" Or was it a statement? The harshness of the word startled me. My romantic thoughts about Nancy Ann and John's wedding vanished, and I spluttered that I was here doing family genealogical work, looking for Loutit and Harper gravestones. Nothing more was said.

I have thought many times since about this encounter—why she approached me and why I was hesitant. In fact, I learned soon after that my great-grandparents, Nancy Ann and John Low, were married

Figure 34. (Left) Nancy Ann Harper: great-granddaughter
of Philip Turnor. This is the oldest photo in the author's
possession of one of Philip's descendants.

Figure 35. (Right) John Low Loutit:
husband of Nancy Ann Harper.

in 1867 at St. Andrew's Church. The visit to St. Peter's had been a
false lead—yet it led to a moment of enlightenment.

Nancy Ann might have been called a squaw. Her mother, Charlotte, likely was. I thought of the decades of discrimination, of era-
sure, of exploitation perpetrated against Indigenous people. And
I thought of the terrible injustices recently exposed by the Truth
and Reconciliation Commission, and the racism and violence that
continue against Indigenous women. I now believe that this stranger,
this woman who spoke to me, was offering an invitation—to 'hear'
the injustices, to connect, and to recognize that we are all involved
in travelling the road to reconciliation and change.

Chronology

Note: the beginnings and ends of these periods are not definitive

1752

26 NOV.....................................Philip Turnor baptized at St. Mary's, Battersea.

1754

1754–1763...................................Seven Years' War between France and Britain and their allies.

1768

1768–1771...................................James Cook's first voyage to the South Pacific. Joseph Banks, naturalist, accompanies Cook.

1769

...................................William Wales at Churchill observes transit of Venus.

1771

17 JULY....................................Samuel Hearne reaches Arctic Ocean overland.

1772

1772–1775...................................James Cook circumnavigates the world. William Wales accompanies him as astronomer.

1774

SUMMER....................................Samuel Hearne establishes Cumberland House.

1775

APR. 1775–SEPT. 1783 .... American War of Independence: France and Thirteen Colonies at war with Britain.

1776

1776 –1779 .... On James Cook's third voyage to discover a Northwest Passage, he enters Nootka Sound on Vancouver Island.

1778

APR. .... Turnor hired as surveyor by HBC for three years at £50 per year.

29 MAY–11 OCT. .... Turnor sails to York Factory, Rupert's Land, then canoes to Cumberland House by Upper Track.

1779

.... Alexander Dalrymple appointed hydrographer for the East India Company.

MAR.–JUNE .... Turnor surveys to Hudson House and returns to Cumberland House.

22 APR. .... Eagle Hills incident (North Saskatchewan River).

24 APR. .... Sixteen-share partnership of Montreal traders.

JUNE–SEPT. .... Turnor surveys to York Factory by Lower Track and works on first map.

SEPT.–OCT. .... Turnor takes sloop to Severn and Moose Forts.

DEC. .... Turnor snowshoes to Albany Fort.

1780

FEB.–AUG. .... Turnor surveys Albany River to Henley House and, after recovering from bad health, surveys to Gloucester House.

SEPT. .... Turnor at Moose Fort. Works on second map.

DEC. .... Turnor snowshoes to Albany Fort charting coastal headlands and returns to Moose Fort.

1781

JAN.–MAR.	From Moose Fort, Turnor snowshoes and surveys to East Main House.
13 MAR.	William Herschel discovers Uranus.
APR.–JULY	Turnor unable to reach Mesakamy Lake. Surveys to Michipicoten on Lake Superior.
JULY–AUG.	Turnor unable to reach Lake Abitibi via French River.
7 AUG. 1781–OCT. 1782	Turnor's journal is missing.
AUG. 1781–MAR. 1782	Turnor at Moose Fort. Signs contract for three years at £60 per year.
SEPT.	Turnor marries a Cree woman (à la façon du pays).
FALL 1780–1782	Smallpox epidemic hits inland posts.

1782

25 MAR.–13 APR.	Turnor goes to Albany Fort with plans for Henley House.
13 APR.–23 MAY	Turnor back at Moose Fort.
23 MAY–2 AUG.	Turnor surveys up Abitibi River, loses sextant. Returns via Mesakamy Lake.
JUNE	Son, Joseph, born to Turnor and his Cree wife at Moose Fort.
2 AUG.–30 SEPT.	Turnor works on third map.
9 AUG.	Prince of Wales Fort attacked by French.
24 AUG.	York Factory surrenders to La Pérouse.
30 SEPT.–14 OCT.	Turnor canoes to Brunswick House. Becomes master.

1783

1783–1801	William Pitt the Younger, Prime Minister of England.
FEB.–APR.	Turnor is too ill to attend council at Moose Fort.
JUNE–SEPT.	Turnor travels to Moose Fort. Works on third map and fourth map (a copy). Men prepare defences against possible French attack.
3 SEPT.	American War of Independence ends.
9–22 OCT.	Canoes to Brunswick House. Second term as master.
WINTER 1783–1784	Formation of North West Company (NWC).

1784

24 MAR. 1784–19 OCT. 1785	Turnor's journal is missing.
24 MAR.–3 APR.	Turnor canoes to Moose Fort.
19 MAY	Turnor signs contract for £80 per year for 3 years.
14 JUNE–8 AUG.	Turnor winters at confluence of Frederick House River and Abitibi River.

1785

16 JUNE	Turnor establishes Frederick House 52 miles farther south.
19–25 JULY	Turnor canoes to Moose Fort.
26 SEPT.–18 OCT.	Turnor returns to Frederick House.
19 OCT. 1785–27 JULY 1786	Turnor is master of Frederick House.

1786

27 JULY–2 AUG.	Turnor canoes to Moose Fort. In bad health.
18 SEPT.–18 OCT.	Turnor canoes to Frederick House. Second term as master.

1787

1787	NWC merged with McLeod and Co, including Alexander Mackenzie and cousin, Roderick Mackenzie.
7 JULY–10 AUG.	Turnor begins survey of Montreal traders' settlements (no notes extant).
14–20 AUG.	Turnor canoes to Moose Fort. In bad health.
9 SEPT.–15 OCT.	Turnor sails for England.
OCT. 1787–NOV. 1788	Turnor begins drafting fifth and sixth maps (latter not located). Meets with Wales, Maskelyne, Dalrymple.

1788

13 FEB. 1788–1795	Impeachment trials of Warren Hastings, first governor general of India.
22 FEB.	Marriage banns between Turnor and Elizabeth Hallett.
13 JUNE	Turnor marries Elizabeth Hallett at St. Mary's Church, Battersea.

NOV. 1788–FEB. 1789	King George suffering fits of madness (porphyria).
26 NOV.	Turnor paid 20 guineas by HBC for two maps.

1789

1789	Dalrymple publishes "Memoir of a Map of the Lands around the North Pole."
16 MAY	Turnor renews contract with HBC for three years at £80 per year.
30 MAY–8 JUNE	Turnor stops at Stromness. Meets Stanley Expedition.
21 JUNE –27 AUG.	Turnor sails to York Factory.
14 JULY	Alexander Mackenzie reaches Garry Island (Arctic Ocean).
14 JULY 1789–1799	Fall of Bastille and beginning of French Revolution (overthrow of the monarch and establishment of Enlightenment ideals).
2 SEPT.–7 OCT.	Turnor canoes to Cumberland House.
10 OCT.	Turnor begins training David Thompson for northward expedition.

1790

4 JUNE	To replace injured Thompson, Peter Fidler arrives at Cumberland House to be trained as assistant on northward expedition.
10 JUNE	Turnor complains in letter about stalling of expedition.
23 JUNE	Mackenzie and 3 NWC traders arrive.
13 SEPT.	Turnor leaves for North with Malchom Ross & Fidler.
6 OCT.	Winters at Île-à-la-Crosse Lake.

1791

WINTER	Few provisions for Turnor, Fidler, and Ross.
30 MAY–28 JUNE	Turnor resumes trip to Lake Athabasca. At mouth of Methy River meets Mackenzie, who advises the Swan Lake detour.

2–22 JULY .... Turnor continues on to NWC
house on Great Slave Lake.

25 JULY.. Turnor reproduces Shewditheda's
map showing route to Hudson
Bay (seventh map).

26 JULY–30 AUG. .... Turnor arrives back at Lake Athabasca
and conducts survey of the lake.

30 AUG. 1791–9 MAY 1792............. Turnor winters at Fort Chipewyan.

1792

1792–1802... French Revolutionary Wars
arising from French Revolution:
France and Britain at war.

APR.–OCT. .... Captain George Vancouver surveys
west coast of North America from
Straight of Juan de Fuca to Alaska.

9 MAY–17 JULY .... Turnor heads back to Cumberland
House and onward to York Factory.

17–25 JULY .... In a series of letters and meetings
Turnor discloses Walker's and Tomison's
efforts to thwart the expedition
and clears his own reputation.

25 JULY.. Fidler sets off to winter with the Piikani.

31 JULY–24 AUG.............................. Turnor's last assignment: Chatham House.

5 SEPT. .... Thompson leaves for Sipiwesk
Lake en route to exploring eastern
end of Lake Athabasca.

17 SEPT.–17 OCT.............................. Turnor sails for England.

24 OCT. .... Turnor engaged by HBC in
drawing maps and compiling his
observations at 1 guinea per week.

12 DEC. .... Turnor is paid for eighth map
(not extant) and ninth map.

14 DEC. .... Fidler reaches the Spitcheyee River.

1793

JAN.–DEC. .... Turnor establishes navigation school at
Rotherhithe. Works on his observations
pamphlet and on his tenth map.

22 JULY.. Alexander Mackenzie
reaches Pacific Ocean.

1794

18 AUG.	Maskelyne hires Turnor to do computing.
FALL	Turnor publishes his pamphlet of observations. Turnor completes large, final map.

1795

1 JAN.	Arrowsmith publishes his first map of North America.
14 JAN.	HBC pays Turnor £100 for his map and presents him with an engraved watch.

1796

18 JAN.	Maskelyne pays Turnor for computing work.
5 FEB.–16 NOV.	HBC makes four payments to Turnor for consulting work.
28 DEC.	Maskelyne pays Turnor for computing work.

1797

9 DEC.	Maskelyne pays Turnor for his work.

1798

23 APR.	Turnor is living in Clerkenwell. Receives payment from Maskelyne.
8 OCT.–19 NOV.	Maskelyne makes two payments to Turnor.

1799

9 JAN.	Turnor given work by Maskelyne.
8–17 JUNE	Maskelyne gives Turnor two advances.
8 JULY	Maskelyne pays Turnor.
4 OCT.	London Committee's final note to Turnor.
7 OCT.–21 DEC.	Maskelyne makes two payments to Turnor.

1800

1 MAR.	"Mr. Turnor died."
7 MAR.	Maskelyne pays off Turnor's debt to landlord.

26 MAR. .... HBC reads a petition for money
from Elizabeth Turnor.

1803

1803–1815 .... Napoleonic Wars (France
against Britain and Europe).

1804

1804–1806 .... Lewis and Clark Expedition: first
American expedition to cross western
United States. They carry Arrowsmith's
1795 map, additions to 1802, based on
Turnor's 1794 map.

Acknowledgements

The Hudson's Bay Company Archives are the foundation of this book, and I am greatly indebted to the patient, knowledgeable staff who helped me explore Turnor's story through a maze of journals, correspondence, maps, minutes, and agenda books. My sincere thanks go to Sjoeke Hunter (microfilm archivist and micrographics coordinator) and to the HBCA archivists James Gorton, Ian Keenan, Leah Sander, Mandy Malazdrewich, Anna Shumilak, and Bronwen Quarry for guiding me through the database and for answering my numerous questions. Ala Rekrut (Manager, Preservation Services) has undertaken the restoration of the 1794 Turnor map, and she and Lisa Friesen have helped me understand the construction of Turnor's maps. I am grateful to Maureen Dolyniuk, the Keeper of the Archives, who initiated and moderated the 2016 Rupert's Land Colloquium session on Philip Turnor.

My gratitude goes to staff at the following libraries and archives for their professional assistance: the Staffordshire Record Office, England (for research regarding Turnor's parentage); London Metropolitan Archives (for genealogical work); Cambridge University Department of Manuscripts (for the Royal Greenwich Observatory papers); Harvard University Collection of Historical Scientific Instruments (Sara Schechner, curator, for information on surveying instruments and her help in choosing images); Special Collections at the Toronto Reference Library (for assistance with images); and Trent University (for secondary materials and for use of the microfilm facilities).

I am indebted to three readers of my early manuscript: Trent Professor Emeritus and author John Milloy, aboriginal issues consultant

Harve McCue (Waubageshig), and novelist Frances Itani, who all kindly agreed to comment on my manuscript prior to its submission, and who continued to offer suggestions and encouragement.

I am grateful to scholars and researchers who helped me at various stages of my writing: especially to Dr. Jennifer Brown for her interest in my project, her many constructive editorial suggestions, and her continued support; to Mary Croarken (Warwick Honorary Research Fellow) for pointing out Turnor's work as a computer; to Dr. Jennine Hurl-Eamon for her interest and for locating a research assistant at Cambridge; to Adrian Leonard (Cambridge) who sent me Maskelyne's files on Turnor; to David Malahar for his valuable suggestions regarding Turnor's 1794 map and his interest in the restoration of the Turnor map; to Andy Korsos for answering my map questions; to Peter Broughton, who patiently attempted to teach me how to use a sextant and who answered technical questions about Turnor's astronomical observations; and to Dr. Barbara Belyea for her sharing of information and encouragement as I was completing my book.

I gratefully acknowledge the Symons Trust Fund for Canadian Studies for financial support and for their confidence in my project.

A special thanks to Rick Isaacson who incredibly ran Sextant Rapids (a Category 4 rapids) and took photos for me.

And to a stranger in a churchyard who asked me a blunt question, I say, 'I am listening.'

The impetus for this project came from my uncle-by-marriage, Bob Campbell (deceased), a family genealogist who traced our beginnings in this country to Philip Turnor and his Cree wife. My Aunt Vivian (Campbell) and Aunt Anna (Warrington, deceased) were the tellers of family stories. Thank you also to my first cousins for their interest, especially to Karen, Louise, and Ken for their stories.

One of my first routes to discovering Turnor was Pearl Weston's family history, *Across the River, A History of the Turner, Thompson, Campbell Families*. As a four-times-great-granddaughter (Joseph Turner Jr. line), Weston wrote in a personal, engaging manner which immediately drew me to Turnor's story.

Through this project I discovered many new relations, and I would like to acknowledge their enthusiasm, support, information, and interviews: Anne, Isobel, Ruth, and Marvel Loutit (from Nancy

Ann Harper line); Arthur Poirier (Joseph Turner Jr. line); Wesley Turner (Joseph Turner Jr. line); Pam Jarrett (Joseph Turner Jr. line); Dorothy, Mrytle, Trudy, Sue (Philip Turner line); Valerie Walker (Jane Turner line); Karel Horsley and Jenn Ambrose (Jane Turner line); Frank Godfrey (Jane Turner line); Marianne Hall (Richard Turner line). I am most grateful to Dorothy Turner, and her siblings and mother, Daisy, for their time and kindness during my visit to Moose Factory.

A small group of non-fiction writers—Mary Breen, Molly Cartmell, Erica Cherney and Isabel Henniger—gave me the opportunity to read aloud a few chapters, and I greatly appreciate their support.

I am fortunate to have a group of friends who were always ready to listen and to offer encouragement: Michelle Berry, Susan Calder, Laura Dunbar, Joanne Findon, Julie Gagne, Janet Greene, Troon Harrison, Sharon McCue, Craig Paterson, Betsy Struthers, Katie Syrett, Florence Treadwell, and Fred and Annette Tromly. Many thanks to Dave and Kay Carver who ferried me around Staffordshire—to churches, cemeteries, numerous villages, and pubs—seeking Turnor connections.

To my editor, Karen Clark, who through this long process towards publication encouraged me and offered wise advice—thank you. I am indebted to my publisher, Bruce Walsh, for his enthusiasm for the book, to Duncan Campbell for the beautiful cover and book design, and to Donna Grant, managing editor, and Marionne Cronin, copy editor, for their diligent work. Many thanks to Morgan Tunzelmann and Melissa Shirley for getting my book out to the public.

My family have been my mainstay. They surely heard more than they cared to hear over many years, but they never failed to spur me on. Thanks to my sister Linda Robbins and niece Elizabeth for their interest and for keeping me well stocked with HBC blankets and mugs. To Geoff (who travelled with me to York Factory) and to Bernadette and to Sara a huge thank you for your steady, loving support. To Orm, my first reader and editor, who had more faith in me than I did in myself, I cannot say enough thanks.

Notes

All sources in the "Notes" are abbreviated. The full form will be found in the "Bibliography."

The initials HBCA refer to the Hudson's Bay Company Archives.

The initials SRO refer to the Staffordshire Record Office. *Journals of Hearne and Turnor* published by J. B. Tyrrell will be sectioned as follows to indicate the author of the quoted text:

> Turnor refers to Philip Turnor's journals (III–VII & IX)
> Hearne refers to Samuel Hearne's journals (I–II)
> Fidler refers to Peter Fidler's journal (VIII)
> Tyrrell refers to Tyrrell's "Introduction," notes, appendices and maps.

When quoting from manuscript sources I have amended the punctuation, spelling, and capitalization used in quotations in order to facilitate comprehension. I have not changed, omitted, or added any words.

Prologue

1   Bob Campbell, Family Tree, 24 October 1992. No birth date has been located for Philip Turnor; however, his christening date is recorded as 26 November 1752, St. Mary's Battersea. As I found out through my research, Turnor did not take his Cree wife back to England.

2   In this period of fur trade history an Indigenous woman who had a relationship with a fur trader was often referred to as a "country wife" and their union was sanctioned, not by clergy, but by the custom of the country or *à la façon du pays.*

3   Children born to Mary (Loutit) and William V. B. Goff. Dorothy (1906–1968); Edith (1910–2005); Barney (1912–2006); Anna (1915–2009); Haig (1919–2006); Vivian (1923–).

4   Author's interview with Vivian Campbell and Anna Warrington, June 2002. My mother, the eldest in the family, died in 1968. She never talked to me about family history, although on many occasions we visited her mother, sister (Edith), and brother (Haig) living in Lockport, Manitoba (St. Andrew's Parish), the settlement that had been established for retired HBC servants in the 1800s. My aunts, Vivian and Anna, provided most of the personal history of the immediate family.

5   See Figure 1. John Low Loutit was born in 1841 at Rocky Mountain
     House to Low Loutit (Orkney) and Jane McDougall (Cree-Scots).
     James Harper was born in 1813 at Albany to William Harper (Orkney)
     and Mary (Cree).

6   Karen Cochrane to Barbara Mitchell, email, 8 May 2015. Uncle Barney
     called his eldest daughter "Chook," a "term of endearment in Cree,"
     he claimed, but I have been unable to authenticate this. Although
     the word does not seem to be Cree or Bungee, he, unlike his female
     siblings, acknowledged his Cree ancestry.

7   Daisy Turner, in *Moose Factory Cree* (7), translates the numbers one to
     four in Cree as "*pay yuk, ne sho, nei s to, nay ow*." These do not sound
     like Vivian's rendition, but perhaps she is mis-remembering. "Noot
     Shey" may be Bungee, a Red River dialect that is a mixture of Scots,
     Gaelic, Orkney, Cree, Ojibwa, and Saulteaux/French. Dr Lorraine
     Mayer, editor of the *Canadian Journal of Native Studies* informed me
     (email, 24 August 2015) that a Norway House speaker said that Happy
     New Year was *oh chay mih kee si kow*, and "oh chay" sounds similar to
     "noot shey." See also www.thecanadianencyclopedia.ca on "Bungee."

8   Bob Campbell, letter to author, 21 Dec 2000.

9   Weston 1. Pearl Weston, whom I never knew, was my fourth cousin.

Chapter One

1   "War Horrid War," *St. James's Chronicle*, 26 March 1778. 17th & 18th
     Century Burney Collection Newspapers (hereafter cited as Burney
     Collection).

2   There were different groups of Montreal-based traders. Before the
     Seven Years' War (1756–1763) the French bourgeois traders and their
     hired voyageurs, who had traded as far west as the Rockies, were called
     the Canadians. Some Anglo-American traders from New York and
     Pennsylvania also worked through the Montreal traders. After the British
     won the war, independent Scots and English traders began organizing
     their trade through Montreal. They were often referred to as Pedlars. The
     two groups can be referred to collectively as Montreal traders. Several
     of the various partnerships amalgamated into the NWC in 1779.

3   Ruggles, "Governor Samuel Wegg," 10.

4   William Tomison was born around 1739 in the Orkney Islands and died
     there in 1829. He began working as a labourer for the HBC in 1760 and
     rose to become inland master and chief factor of York Factory.

5   Matthew Cocking (1743–1799) from York, England, entered the HBC's
     service in 1765. Between 1772 and 1777 he gained experience inland
     travelling with the Indigenous people. He was master of Cumberland

House in 1775, master of Fort Severn in 1777, then, in 1781–1782, temporary chief of York Factory, before returning home in August 1782. He had "three mixed-blood daughters" (Spry, "Cocking, Matthew") born to three different Cree wives at the posts where he was master.

6 Tyrrell 17.

7 Henley House had been established on the Albany River in 1743; however, it was considered "a trading station" and not a permanent outpost (Ruggles 32).

8 Hearne 158. Hearne mentions "Messrs Francis [Franceway], Patterson [Charles Paterson], Homes [William Holmes], and [Peter] Pangman" being about 150 miles above Cumberland House on the Saskatchewan River. Two miles above Basquia (The Pas) are "Bruse [William Bruce], Blondal [Barthélemi Blondeau], Cutes [James Tute]." He is also aware of Joseph and James Frobisher and Lewis Primeau at Frog Portage (p 120).

9 Hearne 156–7.

10 Hearne 161.

11 HBCA A.4/3, 25 March 1778.

12 HBCA A.5/2.

13 William Wales, "Journal of a voyage…to Hudson Bay…," *Philosophical Transactions of the Royal Society* 60 (1770): 100–36, quoted by Rita Griffin-Short in "The Ancient Mariner and the transit of Venus," 177.

14 Coleridge, *The Rime of the Ancient Mariner*, part one, lines 51–4 and 59–62.

15 HBCA A.6/8, fol. 118d.

16 HBCA A.64/1, 15 April 1778.

17 HBCA A.4/3, 22 April 1778.

18 Tyrrell notes that the HBC told him, "So far as we have been able to ascertain, Philip Turnor, when he entered the service in 1778, was the first person specifically engaged by the Company in the sole capacity of 'Surveyor'." (Tyrrell 63).

19 Tyrrell 68. A chief factor would earn £100; a labourer would earn £6 or £8. In London in 1781, Turnor's wage was comparable to what a man skilled in engineering would receive, although Turnor was given lodging, food, and clothing from the company, which might amount to about £30 or £40 per annum.

20 HBCA A.5/2.

21 HBCA A.5/2, HBC to Betty Turnor, 4 February 1786.

22 Weston 3.

23 Keys, 10 August 1992.

24 SRO, Q/SB 1799 M/122, 137–142; Q/SB 1776 M/166–170.

25 "Staffordshire Enclosure Acts, Awards and Maps," Staffordshire and Stoke on Trent Archive Service, 2007, 2.

26 Randall 43–53.

27 Exuperious Turnor's will is found at The National Archives of the UK: Prob11/1885 Image 463/438. His burial record comes from Ancestry.com: 7 August 1836 at Lambeth. Another clue that unites this Exuperious to Philip Turnor is the name, Mr Cox. Exuperious's daughter, Harriet, married into the Cox family as noted in the will, and, according to the London Minute Book (HBCA A.1/46), on 14 March 1787 Betty Turnor was paid fifteen pounds by "Bill to [not legible] Cox on Acct of Philip Turnor her son."

28 Genealogical information was obtained from Ancestry.com: London Metropolitan Archives, Saint Mary, Battersea, Composite register: baptisms and burials, Feb 1700–Sep 1778, P70/MR2, Item 012.

29 HBCA A.5/2, Edward Jarvis, chief at Albany, to London Committee, 25 May 1783.

30 Turnor 218.

31 Davis 22; Ruggles, *A Country*, 130.

32 Ruggles, *A Country*, 132.

33 Ruggles, *A Country*, 44–5.

34 Tyrrell 68.

35 Griffin-Short 177.

36 Newman 146.

37 Ruggles, *A Country*, 15–16.

38 HBCA A. 64/1, 20 May 1778.

39 Ruggles, *A Country*, 15–16. See also Turnor's list of what was saved and lost on his first journey: Turnor 204.

40 HBCA C.1/382, 29 May 1778.

41 They are dated circa 3100 BCE and the earliest remains circa 6800 BCE.

42 Bligh was sailing master on board the *Resolution* and was made commander of the *Bounty* in 1787. The mutiny on board the *Bounty* took place in 1789.

43 HBCA C.1/382, 19 July 1778.

44 HBCA C.1/382.

Chapter Two

1 Although Tyrrell claims that John Turner is "probably" a brother of Philip (263), I have found no evidence to support this. John's name is always spelled with 'er', they do not come from the same location in England, and he is never mentioned as a relative.

2 Tyrrell 30.

3 J. Brown, *Strangers in Blood*, 55.

4 See Tyrrell, "Appendix B: Humphrey Marten," 592–7; and Pannekoek, "Marten, Humphrey."

5 See Graham, *Graham's Observations*, 249–50; and J. Brown, "Partial Truths," 61–2.

6 Tyrrell 5, 10: Edward Luitet (or Lutit/Loutit) was inland along the Saskatchewan River in 1766, and he accompanied Robert Longmoor inland in 1777–1778. He does not appear to be related to Low Loutit, who was the first Loutit in my family to join the HBC (on 14 April 1835).

7 HBCA B.239/a/76, 6 September 1778.

8 HBCA B.239/a/76.

9 Turnor 204.

10 Robert Longmoor (Longmore, Longoar. See Hearne 97): Longmoor, probably born in Edinburgh, Scotland, was in the HBC service from 1771–1812. Wintering among the Cree, building canoes, steering his own canoes, he was an asset to the HBC in the opening of the Saskatchewan River area (Rich, "Longmoor, Robert").

11 Tyrrell 13.

12 Hearne 97.

13 The York boat was developed in the mid-1700s based on an Orkney design. It was typically 12 to 14 metres long with a flat bottom and a pointed stern and bow. Though it could carry three times the load of a large northern canoe, it was heavy to portage.

14 Hearne 102.

15 Tyrrell 67–8.

16 Tyrrell 69.

17 Tyrrell 218; Turnor 222.

18 Rich, *Cumberland*, 309.

Chapter Three

1 Turnor 198. This entry and the one below (note 6) are replicated with the indentation, the spelling, capitalization, and punctuation as they appear in Tyrrell's 1934 volume, which is an accurately printed version of Turnor's (or the "Writer's") handwritten record of his journal. For the sake of consistency and ease of reading, subsequent entries and quotations will be amended to conventional standards.

2 Turnor 198. Tyrrell notes that William Lutit (Loutit, Lewtit) joined the HBC as a labourer in 1770 and journeyed inland in 1776–1778 and in 1781. No place of origin is given by Tyrrell, although he notes two other William Lutits who were from the Shetlands.

3 Turnor 199.

4 Sara Schechner (Curator, Collection of Historical Scientific Instruments, Harvard University), to Barbara Mitchell, email, 19 and 20 July 2016. Belyea, *Peter Fidler*, 14.

5 Hearne 161.

6 Turnor 199.

7 Turnor 199. See also Ruggles, *A Country*, 262.

8 The Governor and Committee Agenda Book for 19 May 1778 (A.4/3) notes a bill for Messieurs Dollond for a sextant and night glasses (£20.9) and also an item, "a sextant for Mr Turnor," so he may have been using a smaller model of one of Dollond's sextants on his first journey.

9 Turnor 200.

10 Turnor 201.

11 Turnor 203.

12 Turnor 204.

13 Turnor 204.

14 Turnor 208.

15 Hearne 170.

16 Tyrrell 68; Turnor 208.

17 See Turnor's comparison of the difference in trading practices between Cumberland House and Gloucester House (Turnor 274).

18 HBCA B.239/a/76, 2 October 1778.

19 Barthélemi Blondeau was a French Canadian trader who had been inland since 1772. From 1776-1779 he was at Sturgeon Fort with Peter Pond (Tyrrell 159).

20 The Cree inhabit areas from Quebec to Alberta and form the largest Indigenous group in Canada. Though all these groups of Cree speak a form of Algonkian, there are different dialects and a Swampy Cree might not recognize the Plains Cree dialect. Obviously there was a great need for interpreters and Turnor, at this point, could not understand much, if any, of the Cree language. See: www.thecanadianencyclopedia.ca/en/article/cree.

21 See Hearne's account in Tyrrell, 176-82.

22 Turnor 251.

23 Sources for imagined conversation: Rich, *Cumberland*, 266, 268; for Walker see S. A. Smith, "Walker, William"; and Tyrrell 215-16; for Tomison see Nicks, "Tomison, William"; and Tyrrell 581-91; for Hansom see Tyrrell 239-40.

24 Turnor 215.

25 For help in understanding the procedures used in obtaining longitude, see Sobel 92; and Ruggles, *A Country*, 263-4. Turnor took a number of readings for Cumberland House (during this visit and one in 1790) and came to the mean measurement of 102° 13' 32" W longitude as published later in his pamphlet, *Result of Astronomical Observations*.

26 Rich, *Cumberland*, 267.

27 Rich, "Longmoor." Longmoor helped establish Cumberland House with Hearne in 1774. Longmoor did not get to Eagle Hills in 1778 but wintered at a Montreal trader's house near Silver Grove, Saskatchewan, and then he established Hudson House. Longmoor was eager to go to the Athabasca region, but circumstances prevented that and he remained

master at Hudson House, then established Manchester House in 1786 and, from 1787 to 1792 was second in command at Churchill.

28   A writer transfers the post journals and correspondence to fair copy and keeps the accounts. Walker (circa 1754-1792), an Englishman, went inland in 1775, learned Cree, and advanced quickly as he was ambitious, articulate, and literate. He was master of Hudson House between 1781 and 1786, and then of South Branch House in 1787. Although he and Marten and Tomison had their differences at first, in 1791 Tomison recommended that Walker should succeed him as inland chief (S. A. Smith, "Walker, William"; Tyrrell 215).

29   Meat from deer, moose, elk, or bison would be beaten and dried in strips over a fire or in the sun. Some would be carried that way (beat meat) and some would be pounded to a fine powder, then mixed with the rendered fat from the animal to make pemmican. Sometimes berries, such as saskatoons, were added but not always. The pemmican would be packed in rawhide bags and would last a considerable time.

30   Charles Isham (circa 1754 -1814) had an English father, James Isham, and a Cree mother. He was educated in England and then apprenticed at Severn House for seven years. From 1775-1787 he journeyed inland. He returned to England for a year and then resumed his duties as a canoeman, labourer, interpreter, and master of several inland houses, including Swan River from 1790-1793 (Tyrrell 173; J. Brown, "Isham, Charles Thomas").

31   Rich, *Cumberland*, 287.

32   William Holmes, of Irish descent, traded out of Montreal, and was in the Saskatchewan River area in 1774 (Ray, "Holmes, William"). He formed a partnership with Robert Grant, a Scotsman, around 1777 (Tyrrell 218). John Cole, a New Englander, who first traded out of Montreal, joined the HBC in 1772, returned to the Montreal traders in 1773, and was employed by Peter Pangman in 1779 (Rich, "Cole, John"; Tyrrell 124, 224).

33   Imagined conversation based on Turnor 218-19, 235.

34   Waden (also Waddens) was born in Switzerland and arrived in New France around 1755. He became an independent fur trader around 1772, went north to Athabasca territory, and was killed at Lac la Ronge in 1782 (Cooper, "Waddens, Jean Etienne"). Little is known about Gibosh (Tyrrell 220), also referred to as Geboch (Tyrrell 224) and Gebosh (Tyrrell 225). He might be the father of the NWC trader Louis Guiboche.

35   Tyrrell 220.

36   Turnor 220.

37   In a 1780 letter, Tomison described Holmes as "a proud saucy fellow" who threatened the HBC servants in a "daring insulting manner" (Williams 93).

38   Peter Pangman (1744-1819), from New Jersey; Charles McCormick, born in Ireland; Booty Graves, an Englishman, who began working in the trade

with Peter Pond as early as 1765; and Robert Grant, from Scotland, were in an alliance at Fort Montagne d'Aigle (Eagle Hills) in 1778.

39   Turnor 223. Made Beaver (MB) was the currency of trade and referred to a prime skinned and stretched beaver pelt. Trading goods and other animal skins were given a value in terms of one Made Beaver. Values fluctuated according to the quality of goods and their availability. According to a record kept at Albany Fort in 1733, one gallon of brandy was worth one MB; one gun was worth ten to twelve MB; one brass kettle was worth one MB (Newman 47-8). Other animal skins were measured against this standard: one bear or one large otter skin was each worth two MB.

40   Turnor 223.

41   Sturgeon River Fort near Blondeau's house.

42   Imagined conversation based on Turnor 225-8.

43   Turnor 226. Laudanum was opium mixed with alcohol. It was used to treat pain, nervousness, rheumatism, and other afflictions; but it was a dangerous drug, and an overdose could be lethal.

44   Turnor 226.

45   Imagined conversation based on Turnor 227-8. Glover credits Turnor with clarifying the details of this event in his journal (first published in 1934) and explaining why the Montreal traders fled (Glover, xlix-l).

46   HBCA A.11/116, Turnor to London Committee, 15 September 1779.

47   Turnor 226 and 228.

Chapter Four

1   Turnor 252.

2   Tyrrell 234.

3   Turnor 233.

4   Pond arrived at Cumberland House in July 1779 (after Turnor had left), and he told the master, William Walker, about the Methy Portage and about the great abundance of furs he had brought out, some 80,000 beaver skins. Peter Pond (circa 1739-1807) was born in Connecticut and worked in the Detroit area before arriving on the Saskatchewan River in 1776, where he wintered at Sturgeon Fort. In 1778-1779 he was on the Athabasca River forty miles from Lake Athabasca, and in 1782-1783 at Île-à-la-Crosse. He traded in that country until 1788 and drew two important maps, in 1784-1785 and 1787, depicting the fur trading areas from the Great Lakes to the Arctic Ocean and the Rocky Mountains. He was a partner in the NWC. (Tyrrell 218; and Gough, "Pond, Peter").

5   Tyrrell 27-31. Hearne reached the mouth of the Coppermine River and the Arctic Ocean in July 1771. MacKinnon, "Hearne, Samuel."

6   Turnor 235.

7   Turnor 235. Malchom (Malcolm, Malcom) was born in the Orkney Islands about 1754 and died in 1799. He joined the HBC in 1774 as a labourer, went inland in 1778, and was temporary master at Hudson House in 1778 and 1780, and then at Cumberland House in 1783 and 1788–1789. He had a 'country wife' and two children (J. Brown, "Ross, Malchom"; Tyrrell 598).

8   Turnor 236–7. Mitchell Oman was born in Stromness, Orkney Islands, around 1753 and entered the HBC in 1771 as a labourer. His title was "canoeman" from 1784–1799 (Tyrrell 237). Magnus Twatt was born in the Orkney Islands around 1751 and entered the HBC's service in 1771, shortly after becoming a carpenter and canoe builder. In the 1790s he took charge of Cumberland House and Carlton House (Tyrrell 237). The James Spence referred to here is likely James Spence Sr. (1754–1795), labourer (Tyrrell 235).

9   The spelling of Indigenous personal names and of rivers and lakes varied in Turnor's text, in the company's correspondence and post journals, and in Tyrrell's notes. Sometimes hyphens were used between syllables, as in Cuta-bo-lin-wan (Tyrrell 241) or Bus-kes-cag-nes Lake (Tyrrell 243). Sometimes there were apostrophes or spaces. Often the word was written whole, without any separations. I have standardized the variations by employing the latter system, that is, writing it whole. It is about this point, as Turnor is heading into the Hayes River system, that he begins providing Indigenous names for rivers and lakes. See Tyrrell (238) for Turnor's first recording of a Cree name for a Lake ("Kis-ke-pe-te-sheak Sheak-quan-ish").

10   Turnor 240–1.

11   Tyrrell 242.

12   On his last journey to Chatham House in 1792, Turnor thought, "no European has been up the Saskatchewan River between this [the mouth of the Grass River] and the South track to Cumberland House," that is, between where the Grass River empties into the Nelson River and the mouth of the Echimamish River (Turnor 568).

13   Tyrrell 245.

14   Tyrrell 245: "Thus, as far as we know, they were the first Europeans to survey this route to York Factory…." Although the route had been noted previously in 1757 by Joseph Smith and Joseph Waggoner, two HBC servants who were employed to investigate the number of Canadian settlements inland, it had not been accurately surveyed for their descriptions were "crude and laconic" (Thorman, "Smith, Joseph").

15   Turnor 246.

16   Tyrrell notes that in 1793 David Thompson referred to the rock as Painted Stone Portage (246).

17   Turnor 249.

18 Belyea suggests that this simple structure reflects Indigenous mapmaking practices: "His [Turnor's] maps feature the same beadlike sequences of lakes and rivers that [Moses] Norton, [Andrew] Graham and [Samuel] Hearne drew, and that recall the extreme selectivity of Native cartography" (77).

19 There are some differences between the two maps that Turnor prepared after his first journey inland. G.1/21 is on a linen-like background and is a cleaner copy. G.1/22 is on a blue backing and has a number of either penciled or faded India ink numbers along the lower Nelson where the route was so difficult they had to track and portage numerous times. Also, the two cartouches are slightly different, although both are signed by Philip Turnor. The blue-bordered map has "Falling into" in larger script, but has slightly less elaborate scrolling. Did both maps go home to England, or did one stay at York Factory to help the men along the route? Warkentin and Ruggles point out that "Turnor's astronomical observations are almost perfect," but that his map is "generalized" (98).

20 Turnor 252.

21 Turnor 253–4.

22 Turnor was seemingly unaware that flat-bottomed boats had been used between Albany and Henley House since 1746. See John A. Alwin, "Uncelebrated Boats of the Albany."

23 HBCA A.11/116, Turnor to London Committee, 15 September 1779.

Chapter Five

1 Turnor 262.

2 Turnor 263.

3 John McNab (circa 1755–circa 1820), from Scotland, entered the HBC service as a surgeon for Albany Fort in the fall of 1779. He was at Albany for three years, then master at Henley House for five years. He returned to Albany until 1799 and, after a year in England, returned as chief at Churchill and then at York Factory. He was retired in 1810. He had a Cree wife and four children ("McNab, John, Dr.," Biographical Sheets).

4 Turnor 264.

5 Turnor 264.

6 John Favell entered HBC service as a writer in 1754 and was stationed at Albany, where he remained, except for his time at Henley between 1774 and 1780 ("Favell, John, Jr.," Biographical Sheets).

7 Thomas Atkinson was in the HBC service from 1775 to 1781. In 1777 he established Wapiscogamy House ("Atkinson, Thomas," Biographical Sheets).

8 Turnor 265.

9 HBCA B.3/a/77a, 19 May 1780.

10   Turnor 265.

11   Turnor 269; J. Brown, "Sutherland, George." Though Sutherland's health was compromised for a couple of years, he continued to move up in the HBC, taking charge of York Fort in 1794–1795. However, he and Tomison did not agree on inland policy, and he retired in 1799.

12   Turnor 277-8.

13   Turnor 270.

14   John MacDonald, Turnor's three-times-great-grandson, saw this inscription while on a canoe trip and reported it to the historian A. S. Morton in 1931 (quoted in Weston 15). Weston, a cousin of MacDonald, was either told about the letter or saw a copy, but no further information is available. The reference to a "large rock" is from Turnor (270).

15   Moose Factory Register, quoted in J. Brown, *Strangers*, 76. St. Andrew's Parish Register indicate that Charlotte and James were officially married on 17 October 1844 (Weston 42).

16   Turnor 271-2.

17   Turnor 273.

18   Turnor 274-5.

19   See "Kipling, John" and "Favell, John, Jr.", Biographical Sheets, and www.redriverancestry.ca. Kipling had a wife and child in England and, eventually, two Cree wives, with whom he had three children. Favell had four children with his Cree wife.

20   Carter 10, 31, 115. Carter indicates that "the marriage laws of Plains Aboriginal people were complex and flexible," allowing for polygamy (with little objection from the wives), divorce, and remarriage (10), but she also states that "we have few sources that shed light on the perceptions of the Aboriginal wives in these relationships" (31). Brown writes that wife-lending and exchanging were allowed, polygyny accepted but not promiscuity, and that the British "misrepresent[ed]" these Indigenous practices because they did not understand "the controls that went with it" (Brown, *Strangers*, 60).

21   The Mercator projection map was developed by Gerardus Mercator in 1569 and was the map used in most schools until relatively recently. It is a rectangle shape with parallel lines of longitude and latitude, unlike the spherical maps in which the lines of longitude and latitude narrow towards the poles. Though the Mercator map misrepresents size for landmasses nearer the poles, it is a simple, clear map that is easy to read for navigation purposes and served Turnor well.

22   HBCA G.1/23.

23   Turnor 280. Roads refers to a body of water, less protected than a harbour, where ships anchor when the harbour is too shallow, or anchor to wait for wind, or to transfer cargo.

24   Turnor 281.

25   HBCA A.11/44, Turnor to London Committee, 18 September 1780.

26   Turner 37.

27   "Turnor, Philip National Historic Person." Plaque designated by the Historic Sites and Monuments Board, 1973. Erected and maintained by Parks Canada.

28   HBCA B.135 a/65, 15 October 1781.

29   Turner 28.

Chapter Six

1   HBCA B.135/b/11, 17 May 1781.

2   The *Nautical Almanac and Astronomical Ephemeris*, along with its companion pamphlet, *Tables Requisite*, were published annually. The *Ephemeris* contained printed tables giving the position of astronomical objects (the stars and planets) at regular intervals of time. Complicated computations were made from these tables to establish longitude.

3   Ruggles, *A Country*, 51.

4   Turnor 285.

5   A log tent was a temporary A-frame log structure with no foundation or cellar. This one at Rupert's River was twenty-four feet long by eighteen feet wide, with one partition.

6   Rich, *Cumberland*, 101.

7   The first bateau, a wooden flat-bottomed boat, was used in 1746 by James Isbister on the Albany River up to Henley.

8   Wapiscogamy was renamed Brunswick House in September 1782 (Tyrrell 76).

9   John Thomas to Edward Jarvis, 22 February 1781. Quoted in Rich, *Moose Fort Journals*, 331–2.

10 HBCA A.5/2, London Committee to John Tomas, 15 May 1782.

11 Turnor 289.

12 Rich, *Moose Fort Journals*, 365–70.

13 HBCA A.6/13, London Committee to Edward Jarvis, 16 May 1781.

14 HBCA A.5/2, London Committee to Turnor, 25 May 1781.

15 Turnor 291.

16 Huck 116–19.

17 Turnor 290.

18 Turnor 290. The devil may refer to "the Paueehnsuk" described by Hap Wilson, who reports that many individuals encountered extraordinary experiences in this area. These "little creatures" cause bad dreams and "play tricks" (Wilson 138–9).

19 Wilson 138.

20 Turnor 290.

21 HBCA B.135/b/11, John Thomas to Edward Jarvis, 7 June 1781.

22   He observed the Missinaibi settlement at 48° 29' 42" N and longitude 84° 02'
      15" W (Turnor, *Result*, 8); Tyrrell observed it at 48° 28' 30" and 83° 28' (Tyrrell
      296). Thus Turnor was only about one and a half miles out on his latitude.

23   Turnor 297.

24   Huck 118–19.

25   Turnor 299. The names of the portages are supplied by Tyrrell in his
      footnotes.

26   Turnor 300–1.

27   Turnor 310.

28   Wapiscogamy, called Brunswick House in 1782, operated fully as an HBC
      post until 1791. In 1788, New Brunswick House was built on Brunswick
      Lake, closer to Lake Superior, and took over the trade from Brunswick
      House in 1791. It operated until 1879.

29   Turnor 305.

30   Turner 18. In her *Moose Factory Cree* dictionary Turner translates river
      as "sei pei."

31   Turnor 306.

32   Tyrrell 307; see map, G.1/1, 1782/83.

33   Turnor 308.

34   Turnor 309.

35   Turnor 310.

36   HBCA A.11/44, Turnor to London Committee, 17 September 1781.

37   Turnor, *Result*, 6, 10, 76.

38   Rich, *Hudson's Bay Company*, 99.

Chapter Seven

1   Turnor's journal from 7 August 1781 to 14 October 1782 (fourteen months)
      is missing, so we have no personal record of his time at Moose Fort or of
      his successful journey to the Abitibi. However, London did receive a copy
      of the journal, and wrote on 25 May 1783, "have read over your Journal
      of a Journey to the Abbitiby." Entries in Moose Fort correspondence fill
      in the story.

2   HBCA B.135/a/65, 5 November 1781.

3   Chichehennis is also spelled Chickahenish and Chichahanish.

4   Turnor 275.

5   The line "give us good measure in cloth" and some other details of the
      trading procedures are taken from James Isham's account in *Andrew
      Graham's Observations on Hudson's Bay 1761-91*, as presented in Ray and
      Freeman, *"Give Us Good Measure,"* 54-75. Umfreville also presents a
      trading scene, 28-32.

6   See Turnor's remarks about women, Turnor 275; and see J. Brown,
      Strangers, 63.

7   See Podruchny, "Tender Ties," 247–86; and Van Kirk 31-3.

8   Fidler 549.

9   Dorothy Turner to Barbara Mitchell, email, 28 October 2009.

10 Weston 36.

11 Joseph Turner's house is now at 2 Museum Street, Moose Factory, in the Centennial Park. See "HBC Worker's House—Turner House," Canada's Historic Places, www.historicplaces.ca.

12 HBCA B.135/b/13, Cocking to Jarvis, 12 August 1782.

13 Hackett 113–16.

14 Newman 345.

15 HBCA B.135/b/12, Hutchins to Jarvis, 4 March 1782.

16 HBCA B.135/b/12, Hutchins to Jarvis, 4 April 1782.

17 HBCA B.135/b/12, "Instructions for Mr Philip Turnor Moose Fort from Edward Jarvis," 22 May 1782.

18 HBCA B.135 b/12, Turnor to Jarvis, 3 June 1782.

19 Only under the greatest stress does Turnor invoke God. He does so when he is afraid the ship is not coming with the years' supplies ("if it please God to send us a ship this year…," 20 August 1780); here at Sextant Falls; and when he is starving at Île-à-la-Crosse ("pray God send it well over…," 22 March 1791).

20 The eighteenth-century Enlightenment is marked by rationalism, individualism, scientific curiosity, and a break with political and religious tradition.

21 HBCA B.135/a/55, "Mr John Thomas's Remarks on his Journey to the Abbitiby Settlements," 7 August 1774."

22 HBCA B.135/b/12, Turnor to Jarvis, 3 June 1782.

23 Tyrrell 75.

24 Tyrrell 75. Tyrrell describes Turnor's route back to Moose Fort and comments that Turnor proceeded north "over a number of lakes and portages in country as yet unexplored."

25 Tyrrell 75.

26 Rich, *The Fur Trade and the Northwest to 1857*, 159.

27 Williams 89.

28 Tyrrell 595.

29 Williams 87n3.

30 HBCA A.11/44, Turnor to London Committee,16 September 1782.

31 HBCA B.135/b/13, 23 September 1782.

Chapter Eight

1   HBCA B.135/b/13, Thomas to Turnor, "Instructions," 30 September 1782.

2   Other men whom Turnor met over the course of his career in Rupert's Land had Cree families: Atkinson had a family of two sons and a

daughter, one son who was sent to England to be educated; Matthew Cocking had a family (to whom he left money); Charles Isham, English-Cree, had four children; Ferdinand Jacobs had a son and a daughter; Edward Jarvis had an English-Cree wife and a son who was educated in England; Humphrey Marten had numerous liaisons with the daughters of the leading Home Guard; Malchom Ross had a wife and two children who accompanied him on his travels to the Athabasca country with Turnor and Fidler in 1791.

3   Rheumatism in the eighteenth century was a broad term covering inflammation of joints, gout, sciatica, and acute rheumatism. Acute rheumatism, later known as rheumatic fever, was the most serious, as it involved cardiac problems.

4   HBCA B.23 a/6, 6 December 1782.

5   HBCA B.23/a/6, 5 March 1783.

6   HBCA B.135/b/13, Turnor to Thomas, 10 March 1783.

7   HBCA B.3/k/1. His suggestions are fragmented and impossible to read.

8   HBCA B.135/b/13,13 April 1783 and 19 May 1783.

9   HBCA B.135/b/13.

10   HBCA B.135/b/13, Turnor to Thomas, 9 June 1783.

11   HBCA B.23/a/6, 9 June 1783.

12   HBCA B.135/6/13, Jarvis to Thomas, 26 June 1783.

13   The Seven Years' War (1754-1763) between the major powers of Great Britain and France culminated in the Treaty of Paris in 1763, in which most of France's territory in eastern Canada was ceded to Great Britain.

14   HBCA B.135/a/66, 28 July 1783.

15   HBCA B.135/b/13, Thomas to Jarvis, 8 July 1783.

16   The Treaty of Paris, signed on 3 September 1783, ended the American Revolutionary War.

17   HBCA B.135/a/66, Thomas to Jarvis, 28 August 1783.

18   HBCA G.1/1.

19   HBCA A.5/2, London Committee to Mr. Maugenest, 25 May 1783.

20   Edward Clouston, an Orkney man, entered the HBC service in 1779 and worked as a servant to Edward Jarvis. He accompanied Turnor inland in 1783 and worked with him until 1785. He carried on as writer or was in charge of small posts until his retirement in 1798 ("Clouston, Edward," Biographical Sheets).

21   HBCA A.5/2, London Committee to Turnor, 25 May 1783. Germain Maugenest (1764-1792), an independent Montreal fur trader, worked in the Lake Nipigon and then Sturgeon Lake areas from about 1770-1779, at which time his debt to Ezekiel Solomons, a Montreal fur trade entrepreneur, caused him to turn to the HBC. He was approved by the London Committee, granted a salary of £100, and expected, with his knowledge of the Canadian trade, to be of great assistance in expanding

HBC trade. However, he was not effective as a master, although his advice on trade goods and packing proved helpful (see Thorman, "Maugenest, Germain").

22   HBCA A.5/2, London Committee to Turnor, 25 May 1783..

23   HBCA A.11/44, Turnor to London, 30 September 1783.

24   HBCA B.135 b/14, Thomas to Turnor, 9 October 1783.

25   See Turnor's comments of 31 July 1780: Turnor 274.

26   HBCA A.11/44, Thomas to London Committee, 24 April 1784. He is responding to a "private letter" from them requesting him to write up "every important business" of the last company year.

Chapter Nine

1   HBCA A.5/2, London Committee to Maugenest, 23 May 1783.

2   Turnor's journals are missing from March 1784 until October 1785, so there is no account of the details of his preparation for Abitibi or the journey itself, except what is mentioned in his five letters of that period and in the Moose Fort journals and correspondence.

3   HBCA B.135/b/14, Turnor to Thomas, 17 June 1784.

4   HBCA B.135/b/14, Thomas to Turnor, 18 June 1784.

5   HBCA B.135/b/14, Turnor to Thomas, 8 July 1784.

6   HBCA B.135/b/14, Turnor to Thomas, 8 August 1784.

7   HBCA A.11/44, Turnor to London Committee, 8 August 1784.

8   HBCA A.11/44, Turnor to London Committee, 8 August 1784.

9   HBCA A.11/44, Turnor to London Committee, 8 August 1784.

10   HBCA B.135/b/14, Turnor to Thomas, 8 August 1784.

11   HBCA B.135/b/16, Thomas to Turnor, September 1784.

12   HBCA B.135/b/16, Turnor to Thomas, October 1784.

13   After considerable investigation it remains unclear what relation Exuperious is to Philip—possibly a cousin or an uncle.

14   HBCA B.135/b/16, Turnor to Thomas, October 1784. See also Rich, *Moose Fort Journal*, 110.

15   HBCA B.135/b/16, Turnor to Thomas, 20 March 1784.

16   HBCA B.135/b/16, Thomas to Atkinson, 9 June 1785.

17   HBCA B.135/b/16, Thomas to Turnor, 4 June 1785. If Turnor drank all this by himself and by the time he left on 27 July 1786, he would have consumed about five ounces of spirits per day.

18   HBCA B.135/d/55. A list of servants' bills drawn in 1785-1786 shows that around September, Turnor owed £3 10s. for rum. Maugenest owed the same. Other servants' bills showed under a pound spent on brandy. Not only did Turnor enjoy his drink, but, apparently, he had to pay for it himself while he was at Moose Fort.

19   HBCA A.5/2, London Committee to Turnor, 11 May 1785.

20 HBCA A.5/2, HBC to Mrs Betty Turnor at Mrs Jeffrys, No 22 Deal End, Birmingham, 26 May 1785. No further information about Turnor's mother has been discovered. She could have moved from Laleham or from Battersea to stay with a relative in Birmingham.

21 HBCA B.135/d/54, 22 September 1785. On the "Register" of servants' bills drawn, Turnor states that "for my own use" he draws "the Balance of my Wages," payable to Thomas Hutchins. Turnor had met Thomas Hutchins at Albany in 1779. In 1782 Hutchins retired to England and became corresponding secretary to the company.

22 These men were William Beckwith, William Johnson, Mathew Tate (who entered the service in 1774), John Johnson, and Robert Yoston, about whom there is no available information.

23 Tyrrell 80. Tyrrell writes that Turnor "gives no farther information as to the identity of the Master or Clerk of this hitherto unknown trading-post." However, Elaine Mitchell provides the names: Donald McKay was master at the House (which was called by them Langue de Terre) and his brother Angus was a clerk (Mitchell 28).

24 HBCA B.135/b/17, Turnor (writing from Waratowaha) to Thomas, 18 February 1786.

25 Though Mr. Patrick Cloney, surgeon, is referred to a number of times as a member of the Moose Fort Council since at least 1782, the only other information I found in the Turnor material and post journals is that he, along with Turnor, was accused of excessive drinking in May 1786, and that he must have returned to England in the fall of 1786, for he is reported as returning to Moose Fort on 6 September 1787.

26 HBCA B.135/b/17, Thomas to Turnor, 5 April 1786.

27 HBCA B.135 b/17, Thomas to Jarvis, 7 April 1786.

28 HBCA B.135/b/17, Thomas to Turnor; "Instructions," 22 May 1786.

29 HBCA B.75/a/1, 27 July 1786.

30 HBCA A.5/2, HBC to Betty Turnor, 4 February 1786.

31 HBCA A.5/2, London Committee to Turnor, 24 May 1786.

32 HBCA A.5/2, London Committee to Jarvis, 24 May 1786.

33 HBCA A.5/2, London Committee to Turnor, 24 May 1786.

34 HBCA B.135/b/17, Thomas to Turnor, "Instructions," 12 September 1786.

35 HBCA B.135/b/17, 19 October 1786.

36 HBCA B.75/a/2, 28 December 1786.

37 HBCA B.135/b/18, Turnor to Thomas, 8 March 1787.

38 HBCA B.135 b/18, Thomas to Turnor, 28 May 1787.

39 HBCA B.135/b/18, Turnor to Thomas, 1 July 1787.

40 HBCA B.135/b/17, Thomas to Turnor, 22 May 1786.

41 HBCA A.11/45, Thomas to Governor and Committee, 5 September 1787.

42 HBCA B.135/a/72, 9 July 1787.

43 Mitchell 29, 231–3. James Grant was in charge of Fort Timiskaming (Upatchawanaw) and wintered there from 1787–1793.

44 HBCA, A.11/45, Thomas to Governor and Committee, 5 September 1787.

45 HBCA A.11/45, Thomas to the Governor and Committee, 5 September 1787.

46 Weston 1.

47 Weston 1, 17.

Chapter Ten

1 *General Evening Post*, 13–16 October 1787. Burney Collection.

2 *St. James's Chronicle*, 16–18 October 1787. Burney Collection.

3 *Whitehall Evening Post*, 15 October 1787. See also *The Chronicle*, 15 October 1787, and *London Advertiser*, 15 October 1787. Burney Collection.

4 Rude 2.

5 The final mention of Betty Turnor in the HBCA is on 14 March 1787 in the London Minute Book: "Betty Turnor … Bill to [first name undecipherable] Cox on Acc't of Philip Turnor her son" for £15 (HBCA A.1/46).

6 London Metropolitan Archives, X055/001: according to her christening record, Elizabeth Hallett was born on 7 March 1752 to Thomas and Elizabeth Hallett in Battersea.

7 Wales (1734–1798) and Maskelyne (1732–1811) were well acquainted. Maskelyne had become a member of the Royal Society in 1758, observed the transit of Venus at St. Helena in 1761, and was appointed Astronomer Royal in 1765. From 1766 Wales conducted observations and computations for Maskelyne, and Maskelyne selected Wales to go out to Hudson Bay in 1768–69 to observe the transit of Venus. The two men would have met regularly at the Royal Society.

8 Plumb 191.

9 Hearne retired to England in August 1787 due to poor health and because he felt criticized by the company for his management of Fort Prince of Wales. However, in his retirement he consulted with the company and worked on the manuscript of his journey to the Arctic, which was published three years after his death. He died in November 1792 in London.

10 Ruggles, *A Country*, 52.

11 Turnor refers to the people who lived in what is now the Northwest Territories as "northern Indians" or Chipewyan. They speak Athapaskan. Today they are called Dene or Denesuline and include Chipewyan, Tlicho, Yellowknives, and Slavey who occupy the land from Lake Athabasca, north to Great Slave Lake, and east to Wollaston Lake and to Churchill.

12 Fry 126.

13   Genealogical information was obtained from Ancestry.com: banns were published 22 February 1788, and on 13 June 1788, "Philip Turnor of this Parish, Bachelor and Elizabeth Hallett of this Parish, Spinster were Married in this Church by Licence…." Source Citation: London Metropolitan Archives, P70/MRY2, Item 036, Saint Mary, Register of Marriage.

14   "Battersea," *The Environs of London, Volume 1, County of Surrey*, 1792, 26–48, accessed 4 November 2012, www.british-history.ac.uk/report.aspx?compid=4537.

15   "House of Lords," *London Chronicle* 13 February 1788. Burney Collection.

16   Carnall and Nicholson 5. Hastings was acquitted in 1795. Doubts had been cast about his guilt, England had turned its attention to war with France, and public interest had waned.

17   Fry xxii.

18   HBCA G.2/11.

19   HBCA A.1/46, fol. 162; Ruggles, *A Country*, 52.

20   Tyrrell 86. Turnor's contract of May 1789 states that he was "aged 36 years, [of] the Parish of Laleham in Middlesex."

21   Plumb 192. The King was suffering from what historians now think was porphyria.

22   HBCA E.3/2, "Memoir of a Map of the Lands around the North Pole by Alexander Dalrymple 1789," 97.

23   HBCA E.3/2, "Memoir of a Map," 99.

24   Though Dalrymple did not realize that Hearne was referring in his calculations to Lake Arathapescow, that is Great Slave Lake, rather than Lake Athabasca, Hearne still had made an error in longitude.

25   Fry 204.

26   The following conversations are based on comments from West, "Introduction," Vol.1, viii–xi; and West, Vol. 2, *The Diary of James Wright*, 21–2, and Vol. 3, *The Diary of John Baine*, 28–30.

27   Baine and Wright were "accurate" and "keen observers." All comments in quotation marks in this section are taken from West, Vol. 1, "Introduction," viii–xi; Vol. 2, *The Diary of James Wright*, 21–2; and Vol. 3, *The Diary of John Baine*, 28–30.

28   Austen 236.

Chapter Eleven

1   HBCA A.11/117, Turnor to London Committee, 9 June 1790.

2   HBCA A.11/117, Turnor to London Committee, 3 September 1789.

3   HBCA A.5/3, London Committee to Elizabeth Hallett, 26 October 1789.

4   Nicks, "Thompson, David."

5   Moreau 72–3.

6   It is likely that, in today's medical terms, he had congestive heart failure that led to edema and failure of such organs as the liver.

7   HBCA A.11/117, Turnor to London Committee, 9 June 1790.

8   Peter Fidler was born 16 August 1769 in Bolsover, Derbyshire, and died 17 December 1822 at Dauphin Lake House, Manitoba. In April 1788 he signed on as a labourer for the HBC. He must have received some formal education, for he was soon assigned to South Branch House as a writer. After completing the journey northward with Turnor, he was sent back to the Saskatchewan River area where he travelled to the foothills of the Rockies. He continued mapmaking and surveying, built Carleton House, travelled into Athabasca Country, and established Nottingham House on Lake Athabasca in 1802, where he stayed, under duress from the NWC, until 1806. Although he was listed as surveyor on the Servants' Lists from 1794, he was formally appointed to that position in 1810 and his salary was raised to £100. Between 1812 and his death, he surveyed lots at the Red River Settlement, amidst harassment from the Metis, and, finally, became chief trader at Brandon and Dauphin Lake Posts.

9   HBCA B.239/b/50, Colen to Turnor, 20 July 1790. Barbara Belyea points out in *Peter Fidler* (3) that, even before signing up with the HBC, Fidler owned three books on astronomical navigation, so he was more experienced than Thompson.

10   HBCA A.11/117, Turnor to London Committee, 9 June 1790.

11   David Malaher and Andreas Korsos, digitizers of the 1826 Thompson map, to Barbara Mitchell, email, 9 and 16 August 2015.

12   Broughton 216. As Peter Broughton points out, Turnor deliberately adjusted his mirrors so they were non-parallel, thus creating an index error that he could then account for in his computations.

13   HBCA A.11/117, Turnor to London Committee, 9 June 1790.

14   HBCA A.11/117, Turnor to London Committee, 9 June 1790.

15   HBCA B.239/b/50, Turnor to Colen, 10 June 1790.

16   HBCA B.239/b/50, Turnor to Colen, 10 June 1790.

17   Alexander Mackenzie (1764–1820) first worked in the Montreal offices of Gregory, MacLeod & Company, and in 1785 was assigned to the Churchill River department at Île-à-la-Crosse. This company joined with the NWC (which had been officially established in 1783 by Frobisher and McTavish and others) in 1787 and Mackenzie was made second in command of the Athabasca area until Peter Pond left in 1788, at which point Mackenzie was put in charge. Patrick Small began trading in 1781 and in 1784 was a partner in the NWC. He was at Île-à-la-Crosse from 1784–1791, when he left the northwest for Montreal (Tyrrell 330). Angus Shaw was at Moose Hill Lake near Beaver River from 1789–1792, when he left to build Fort George on the Saskatchewan River (Tyrrell 358). William McGillivray (1764–1825), a partner in the NWC in 1790,

was responsible for the Churchill River area and had his headquarters at Île-à-la-Crosse. In 1791 he was put in charge of the Athabasca department and, in 1804, became head of the company (Tyrrell 317; Ouellet, "McGillivray, William").

18 Turnor 317. Hayes, in *First Crossing*, claims that "Though Mackenzie did not realize it, he had reached the Arctic Ocean" (106). Apparently Mackenzie had doubt because he was in the Mackenzie delta, not right at the sea. He was also not sure which island he was on. In *Voyages... to the Frozen and Pacific Oceans* (1801), according to Hayes, Mackenzie removed evidence of this doubt.

19 David Chapin points out that Pond's new map contained more errors than the 1785 map: "The new map [1787] also shifts most of the interior lakes and rivers farther to the west than the earlier one" (241). The new map shows Lake Athabasca 20 degrees farther west than it should be.

20 Hayes, *First Crossing*. Hayes says that "there were two sorts of errors that crept into Mackenzie's calculations: errors in latitude as he measured with his sextant, and errors of direction as he measured with his compass." In locating Whale Island, his most northerly point, Mackenzie was out by eighteen to twenty-three miles too far south (116). This was not a serious miscalculation; however, he did not fix longitude. He was not the first European to reach the Arctic Ocean overland but was the first to explore the Mackenzie River, one of the longest rivers in the world.

21 W. Kaye Lamb writes that Mackenzie's "shortcoming was emphasized, perhaps in a somewhat arrogant and embarrassing way, by Philip Turnor" ("Mackenzie, Sir Alexander"). Turnor's remarks were made in his journal entry and it is unlikely that he spoke as bluntly as he wrote; and, furthermore, while his remarks are pointed, they are true and obviously helpful, since Mackenzie acted upon them.

22 Hayes, *First Crossing*, 144.

23 Hayes, *First Crossing*, 11.

24 HBCA B.239/b/50, Colen to Turnor, 20 July 1790.

25 Turnor 322.

26 Dalrymple saw Hearne's map at the HBC and either saw or knew of Pond's maps. By comparing Hearne's and Turnor's calculations he was able to determine the degree of error in Hearne's calculation of Churchill from Lake Athabasca. He therefore reduced the estimate of distance by one-third (Fry 203; Binnema 112), locating the lake farther east, and would have provided Turnor with this information.

Chapter Twelve

1 Hugh Leask (Lisk) and Robert Garroch (Garrock, Garrett) were both from Orphir, Orkney Islands; Malcolm Grot (Groat) was from South

Ronaldsay; and Peter Brown from Stromness. They were all employed as labourers, canoemen, steersmen, and bowmen going inland (Tyrrell 327).

2   Turnor 331; Huck, "The Sturgeon-Weir River," 170.

3   Tyrrell (353) notes that, though it is difficult to tell exactly where Turnor's observations were taken, it would appear that his longitude position was between one and seven miles west of the correct position.

4   MacGregor 28.

5   Turnor 357.

6   HBCA B.9/a/1, 20 October 1790.

7   Turnor 359.

8   HBCA B.9/a/1, Journal of Malchom Ross, 6 December 1790.

9   Strips of deer, moose, or buffalo were dried over a low fire, and, when thoroughly dried, they were beaten between stones into jerky-like strips.

10 See Tyrrell's quotation from Ross, 360.

11 For similar reasons, just five and a half years later, David Thompson defected to the NWC to become their surveyor. Thompson left the HBC Bedford House on the west side of Reindeer Lake on 23 May 1797 and travelled to Alexander Fraser's post on Reindeer River. He felt that his superiors were not backing exploration in the Athabasca region and that he was going to be assigned a trading post rather than continue with his explorations. He was criticized by the HBC officers for breaking his contract. See Nicks, "Thompson, David."

12 Turnor 363.

13 HBCA B.239/b/52, Turnor to Colen, 22 March 1791.

14 Turnor 363.

15 Tyrrell 369.

16 Mr. Laurent Leroux built a house on Great Slave Lake in 1786 and he accompanied Mackenzie to Great Slave Lake on Mackenzie's journey to the Arctic (Tyrrell 370).

17 Turnor indicated that two canoes of "Southern Indians" were there "to hunt for them" (Turnor 370).

18 Conversation based on Turnor's remarks of 2 June 1791, combined with Ross and Fidler's remarks, quoted in Tyrrell 370–1.

19 Tyrrell 369. Tyrrell quotes from Alexander Mackenzie's letter to his cousin, Roderick Mackenzie, 1 June 1791.

20 Turnor 384.

21 Turnor 385. See also Fidler's comment that to return to the Methy Portage would have been "mortifying to the highest degree," quoted in Tyrrell 386.

22 Fidler, quoted in Tyrrell 386. Fidler was not the first to see the Athabasca oil sands, but according to MacGregor his description "is the earliest written record of seeing the world-famous Athabasca tar sands in situ" (32).

23 Ross, quoted in Tyrrell 385.

24 Turnor 388.

25 Turnor 398.

26 "His latitudes were quite accurate, the true latitude of (old) Fort Chipewyan being 58° 40' N, so that Turnor was about 5 km or 3 miles too far south." Hayes, *First Crossing*, 148.

27 In *First Crossing* Hayes writes, "The correct longitude is 110° 28' W, so Turnor was very close, about 5 km or 3 miles too far east" (148).

28 Turnor, *Result of Astronomical Observations*, 5.

29 HBCA B.9/a/1, Journal of Malchom Ross, 29 June 1791.

30 Turnor 400.

31 Turnor 400. Turnor simply translates the Cree name as "Slave Indian River." Though he does not offer any further explanation, this name has often been wrongly interpreted as referring to slave-like people. Keith Goulet, a fluent Cree speaker, interprets it as meaning "people from other lands, another place or peripheral regions" (Jennifer Brown to Barbara Mitchell, email, 31 March 2015).

32 The following October (1792), Mackenzie, just returned from England, took the Peace River on his route to the Pacific.

33 Turnor 405. The fifteen-mile stretch of the Slave River between present-day Fort Fitzgerald and Fort Smith, with its rocky islands, granite banks, and numerous falls, is now portaged.

34 HBCA B.9/a/1, Journal of Malchom Ross, 14 July 1791.

35 Tyrrell 413. They were about six to seven miles north of the present site of Fort Resolution.

36 Turnor 414.

37 Tyrrell 418. Tyrrell indicates that this river would be either the Back River or the Hanbury River. This imagined conversation is based on Turnor's journal notes (418–19).

38 Turnor 419.

39 Chesterfield's Inlet is at 63° 20' 27" N; Wager Bay is at 65° 30' N.

40 Turnor 420. Some of the confusion over the location of Lake Athabasca was caused by the name. Turnor labeled it Athapiscow or Athapescow Lake (from the Cree); Pond had labeled Lake Athabasca as Arabaska and situated it incorrectly about 150 miles from the Pacific; Samuel Hearne had labeled a large lake as Lake Arathapescow which was Great Slave Lake; but the London Committee and Dalrymple mistakenly thought these were the same lakes.

41 It is the tenth-largest lake in the world, measuring 300 miles (480 kilometres) in length.

42 These particular willows are endemic to this area. Their Latin name, *Salix turnorii*, is after Philip Turnor.

43 The Athabasca sand dunes stretch like a desert for 65 miles (100 kilometers) along the southern edge of the lake. The sand dunes were

formed during the end of the last glacial period and are about 8,000 years old. A point near Archibald River is named Turnor Point.

44 Turnor 429. As Adrienne Mayor points out, "tales of gigantic beavers figure in Native legends" and these were based on large fossil skeletons of "the Pleistocene beaver *Castoroides*," which averaged over six feet long (51).

45 Macdougall 30. Brenda Macdougall relates this legend and attributes its recording to Father Émile Peritot, an Oblate priest, who was in the area in the mid-nineteenth century.

46 Turnor 433.

47 Tyrrell 434.

48 Turnor 434.

49 Lake Athabasca is the eighth-largest lake in Canada and is 176 miles (283 kilometres) long.

50 Turnor 442.

51 HBCA A.11/117, Colen to London Committee, 24 September 1791: "it was his [Tomison's] intention to knock it [the Northern Expedition] on the head the first opportunity as well as Swan River—his meaning I judge to go no farther than stopping men from going that Journey." Tomison deliberately set out to distress Swan River, taking away every useful man and every canoe builder.

52 Ross, quoted in Tyrrell 445.

53 Turnor 455.

54 Fidler's journal, quoted in Tyrrell 526, 519, 536, 499, and 496.

55 Turnor 447.

56 Turnor 449. It is difficult to calculate this amount for this period, but it is somewhere between £20 and £100 sterling in the early nineteenth century.

57 Ross, quoted in Tyrrell 446.

58 Turnor 449.

59 Turnor 449–50.

60 Turnor 450.

61 Turnor 457.

62 Turnor 450.

Chapter Thirteen

1 Turnor 466.

2 Turnor 467.

3 HBCA B.9/a/1, Journal of Malchom Ross, 21 May 1792.

4 Maclaren "Alexander Mackenzie and the Landscapes of Commerce." Maclaren argues that William Combe was Mackenzie's ghost writer for *Voyages…through the Continent of North America, to the Frozen and Pacific*

Oceans (1801) and added the purple prose. See also Hayes, "Author's Note," *First Crossing*, 7.

5   Just east of Lac La Loche is a lake named after Turnor, originally called Lac des Isles. On its south shore is a village inhabited by about 400 Birch Narrows Dene.

6   Turnor 470.

7   Turnor 479.

8   Turnor 453.

9   Turnor 479.

10   Turnor 484.

11   Turnor 487.

12   Turnor 488.

13   HBCA B.239/b/52, Colen to Turnor, 12 July 1792.

14   Imagined conversation based on Turnor 450, 456, 457, 491, and on Turnor's letter dated 9 [19] July 1792 to the Council (HBCA B.239/b/52).

15   HBCA B.239/b/52, Turnor to Tomison, Colen and Council, 9 [19] July 1792. This is dated 9 July, but a response of 23 July refers to Turnor's letter of 19 July, so this letter must have been misdated by Turnor.

16   HBCA B.239/b/52, Turnor to Council, 23 July 1792.

17   HBCA B.239/b/52, Turnor to Colen, 24 July 1792. All quotations in this paragraph are from this letter.

18   Turnor 559.

19   Turnor 559. I have found no information on Linklighter (also spelled Linklater).

20   HBCA A/11/44, Turnor to London Committee, 30 Sept 1783.

21   Turnor 560.

22   Edward Wishart, from the Orkney Islands, was hired as a labourer in 1778. He travelled inland and in 1783 became a steersman and builder. In 1792 he went home, but returned in the same capacity in 1794 for one more year William Flett Senior, also from the Orkney Islands, entered the service as a labourer in 1773 and spent seven years travelling inland. After a year at home he returned as a canoeman and worked inland until 1794, when he retired home. No information was found on Andrew Codagill or on James Johnson/Johnston.

23   Turnor 560.

24   Turnor 567.

25   Tyrrell (483) thinks this NWC trader was William McKay, who traded in the Muskrat Country between Cumberland House and Split Lake, and who, in June 1792, was on his way to establish a house at the mouth of Reindeer River.

26   Turnor 225. At the time of the Eagle Hills attack Turnor wrote, "I have been well informed the French Canadians have often tried to set them [Indians] upon the Honourable Company's Servants without success."

27 Turnor 570.

28 Turnor 570.

29 Turnor 577.

30 HBCA B.239/b/52, Turnor to Colen, 24 July 1792.

Chapter Fourteen

1 Formerly known as the Peigan, a division of the Blackfoot nation.

2 Peter Fidler, quoted in Belyea, *Peter Fidler*, 116.

3 Fort Spitzee was a whiskey fort established about 1869 by T. C. Powers and Company, a group of free traders from Montana (*Leaves From the Medicine Tree* 168).

4 MacGregor 70-5.

5 Ruggles, *A Country*, 245. This map has been referenced but has not been located and, probably, is not extant.

6 HBCA G.2/13.

7 All quotations from this map are from the map found in the pocket at the end of Tyrrell's *Journals*.

8 Hayes, *First Crossing*, 148. Hayes suggests that Mackenzie would have known of Turnor's result either before he returned to Fort Chipewyan or at Fort Chipewyan, but in either case would have been able to take his own lunar distance now that he had received proper instruction while in England.

9 HBCA A.1/47, 12 December 1792.

10 "Currency, Coinage and the Cost of Living." A small family could live on £40 per annum, but a middle class family would want about £100.

11 Turnor 559-60.

12 He was censured, but sent out again in 1791, 1800, 1803, 1806.

13 *Evening Mail*, 18-21 January 1793.

14 Henry was born to Elizabeth Turnor's brother, Thomas Hallett, in Battersea, Surrey, circa 1773-1777. He joined the HBC in 1793 and spent his first winter with David Thompson at Holly Lake. Hallett had at least four wives and many children, four of whom married Peter Fidler's children. Hallett travelled with both Thompson and Fidler and took over Buckingham House in 1797. At Fort Edmonton in 1810, he and Robert Longmoor insisted on trying a Cree for attempting to steal HBC horses, found him guilty, and ordered him shot. This raised great concern and Hallett was suspended. He left to join the NWC and eventually retired to the Red River area, where he died in 1844. See www.redriverancestry.ca and Binnema, *Edmonton House Journals*, 470.

15 In 1794 Turnor published his *Result of Astronomical Observations* in which he advertised himself as a "Teacher of Navigation and the Lunar Observations, Prospect Row, Dock Head, Rotherhithe." The Surrey Land

Tax Records for that address indicate that Turnor paid tax of £1.15s on £14 for the period 1793, 1795 and 1796, 1798, and in 1799 it was empty (acknowledgement to researcher Harry Duckworth for locating the land tax records at ancestry.com).

16 The East India Company ship, *The Antelope,* was shipwrecked near Palua Islands in the South Pacific (now the Republic of Belau) in 1783. Captain Wilson became friends with the aboriginal chief, who requested that his son accompany the English back to England when they had their ship built. Prince Lee Boo arrived in England in July 1784 and just five months later, on 27 December 1784, he was dead from smallpox.

17 Walford 134–42.

18 Walford 134–42. At an average of 3 pence per week for one year he would make thirteen shillings and this amount for six boys would be nearly four pounds.

19 See "Appendix B" in Duckworth for a short biography (171–2). John Cornelius Vandriel worked as a clerk for the NWC. In the spring of 1790 Mackenzie asked him to make surveys of the route to the Grand Portage. The information was published in 1791 in John Long's *Voyages and Travels of an Indian Interpreter and Trader* and Turnor may have read this, or may have received the information from Dalrymple. Possibly he met Vandriel who, in 1793, signed a contract with the HBC.

20 The details on the front read: "Printed for A. Arrowsmith, Charles Street, Soho Square, by C. Buckton, Great Pulteney Street, Golden Square." A microfiche copy is located at the University of Toronto Library, CIHM no. 20799.

21 Overall the pieces varied from 79 to 93 cm (31 to 36.6 inches) wide and from 62 to 63.5 cm (24.4 to 25 inches) high, as measured by Ala Rekrut, Manager, Preservation Services, Archives of Manitoba.

22 Ruggles, *A Country,* 54. He writes that Turnor's graticule "was the most precise provided to that date for the region, a graticule that he himself had done so much to perfect."

23 Ala Rekrut, Preservation Services, HBCA, to Barbara Mitchell, email, 30 September 2015.

24 The ink colours have faded, but it would appear that Mackenzie's route was in red ink and Vandriel's and the "others" routes were in blue or green.

25 Ruggles, *A Country,* 58, writes that the "Genl: Map" was "a prime source for Philip Turnor in the compilation of his final manuscript map of 1794, and for Aaron Arrowsmith when he produced his historic map of British America in 1795."

26 Buckingham House was established by William Tomison in 1792 to compete with Fort George, the NWC house, located just one-quarter mile away. It is near present-day Elk Point, Alberta.

27 Fidler supplied Turnor with longitude and latitude values (dated 1792-1793) for the Red Deer River, the Askowseepee or Bad River (Bow River), two locations on the Stommixepisconneeheattatti or Bull Buffalo Pond River (Pekisko Creek), and for the North Saskatchewan River west of Buckingham House (Turnor, *Result of Astronomical Observations*, 13-14).

28 Turnor showed it meeting the Bow before the confluence with the South Saskatchewan at Empress, on the border of what are now Alberta and Saskatchewan.

29 Belyea, *Peter Fidler*, 107; MacGregor 66.

30 Turnor, *Result of Astronomical Observations*, 13.

31 HBCA G.2/32. This scope of latitude and longitude was highlighted for me by David Malaher, professional engineer, private researcher, and digitizer (with Andy Korsos) of the 1826 David Thompson map. It is not as large as David Thompson's 1826 map, which is over six feet wide and ten feet tall, but it is larger than Arrowsmith's 1795 map, which is about three feet by five and a half feet. It is unknown where Turnor found the space to handle such a large map. It could have been at the HBC offices, where there might have been a large committee table or floor space. Another possibility, suggested by David Malaher, was in a sails-making shop, where the sails were assembled on a large floor space in the loft. Or Turnor might have had enough space in his own location at Rotherhithe where he held his navigation school.

32 G. Smith, "Dayes, Edward (1763-1804)." Dayes had a solid reputation as a watercolour painter and draughtsman. He was well known for his view of Ely Cathedral in 1792. He taught watercolour techniques, stressing that the artist must not simply imitate nature, and he influenced many, including J. M. W. Turner.

33 Clayton, "Tomkins, Peltro William." It is uncertain which Tomkins, Peltro or Charles, did the script for Turnor's map.

34 Croarken, "Eighteenth Century Computers," and Nisbet 16-17.

35 Croarken writes: "In the worst case scenario, a single error in one digit in the *Nautical Almanac* could result in a navigational error of 60 miles, which could have fatal consequences if a ship was approaching land in poor visibility" ("Eighteenth Century Computers").

36 Cambridge, MS.RGO 4/324, fol, 35, 18 August 1794.

37 Cambridge, MS.RGO 4/325, 18 January 1796.

38 HBCA A.1/47,14 January 1795.

39 Baigent, "Arrowsmith, Aaron, the elder."

40 www.historicmapworks.com

41 As recognized by a number of authorities, Turnor's map was the foundation for Arrowsmith's 1795 map: Ruggles writes that, in 1795 Arrowsmith published his map, "A Map Exhibiting all the New Discoveries...," largely based on Philip Turor's final map (*A Country*, 60). Hayes, agrees (*Historical*

Atlas, 147), and Belyea writes, "Turnor's huge manuscript compilation was the base map for Arrowsmith's *Map Exhibiting all the New Discoveries*, the first state of which was published the following year" (*Dark Storm*, 45).

42   *The Morning Chronicle*, 13 March 1795, and also *The True Briton*, 13 March 1795, and *The Oracle and Public Advertiser*, 14 March 1795, Classified Ads. Burney Collection.

43   Hayes, *Historical Atlas*, 147.

44   Ruggles, *A Country*, 60.

45   Ruggles *A Country*, 60.

46   Cambridge, MS.RGO 4/325, 18 January 1796.

47   Cambridge, MS.RGO 4/325, 28 December 1796.

48   HBCA A.64/3, 13.

49   Ruggles, "Governor Samuel Wegg," 15.

50   "British Parliament/House of Lords," *Star*, 29 October 1795, Burney Collection.

51   Mary Croarken to Barbara Mitchell, email, 16 December 2007.

52   HBCA B.239/b/52, Turnor to Colen, 24 July 1792.

53   In inquiring about severe and recurring cases of rheumatic disease, I received a response by email on 7 November 2013 from Dr. Thomas Benedek, a rheumatologist and a historian of rheumatology, which read, "Of course, no conclusive answer to your question is possible. However, most likely your ancestor suffered recurrent bouts of rheumatic fever one of which affected his heart. Rheumatic heart disease affecting one or more heart valves eventually led to heart failure and death." Communication via Caduceus, an online information-sharing site of medical persons.

54   HBCA A. 5/4, Hudson Bay House to Turnor, 4 October 1799.

55   HBCA A. 5/4, Hudson Bay House to Turnor, 4 October 1799.

56   Cambridge, MS.RGO 4/324, Diary of "Nautical Almanac" work, 1 March 1800.

57   London Metropolitan Archives, Saint Marylebone, Register of Burials, Nov 1799–Aug 1811, P89/MRY1, Item 315. Citation found through Ancestry.com.

58   Cambridge, MS.RGO 4/324, Diary of "Nautical Almanac" work, 7 March 1800.

59   Cambridge, MS.RGO 4/324, Diary of "Nautical Almanac" work, 7 March 1800.

60   HBCA A.1/48, Minute Book, 26 March 1800.

61   Belyea, *Dark Storm*, 45.

62   The restoration of Turnor's 1794 map was begun by the Hudson's Bay Archives under Ala Rekrut in 2015. In May 2016 there was an entire session devoted to Philip Turnor at the Rupert's Land Colloquium with papers by Lisa Friesen, Archivist, HBCA; Ala Rekrut, Manager of Preservation, HBCA; Barbara Belyea; and Barbara Mitchell.

Epilogue

1   George Eliot, epigraph to Chapter 44, *Middlemarch.*

2   Holmes *xvi.*

3   Turnor 218.

4   Keats, "On First Looking into Chapman's Homer." Keats compares the revelation of the 'world' of Homer's poetry through Chapman's translation to the revelation of Uranus and the Pacific Ocean. Keats was mistaken that Cortez was the first European to reach the Pacific from the Americas; it was Balboa.

5   "Advertisement," *Result of Astronomical Observations,* 3.

6   Tyrrell 93.

7   Ruggles, *A Country,* 118: "The company established only two official full-time surveying and cartographic positions over these years, that of inland surveyor, held by Turnor...and that of company-colonial surveyor of Vancouver Island, retained by Grant and then by Pemberton, from 1849 to 1859."

8   Wilson 35.

9   Belyea speaks about the "very large proportion of the documentary record that says nothing at all about women's fur-trade roles" (*Dark Storm* 96); Wishart says that native wives seldom appear in the historical records (76); Macdougall writes that "women's names and even the locations and their cultural groups of origin are lost" (18); Carter writes that there are "few sources that shed light on the perceptions of the Aboriginal wives in these relationships" (31); and Jennifer Brown indicates that not only are source materials "never as complete as we would wish," but we are partial (biased) onlookers ("Partial Truths," 60).

10 Charlotte (Turner) Harper, Scrip Record, Library and Archives Canada, RG 15-D-11-8-a, vol 1321, claim number 117, www.collectionscanada.gc.ca.

11 Author's telephone interview with Isobel Loutit (three-times-great-granddaughter of Philip Turnor), 12 January 2007. In a recent article Niigaan Sinclair, assistant professor of Indigenous studies at the University of Manitoba, remarked: "one in two Manitobans has indigenous blood. In the end, we are who we think we are. Culture defines identity" (Macdonald, "Welcome to Winnipeg").

Bibliography

MANUSCRIPT SOURCES

Department of Manuscripts, University of Cambridge

MS.RGO.4/324 f. 35. Nevil Maskelyne. Diary of "Nautical Almanac" work. Records of work done for Nevil Maskelyne at the Royal Greenwich Observatory. 1794 onwards.

MS.RGO 4/325. Account Book for computers and comparers.

Hudson's Bay Company Archives, Provincial Archives of Manitoba, Winnipeg

SECTION A: LONDON OFFICE RECORDS

A.1/46–48. Governor and Committee Minute Books.

A.4/3–4. Governor and Committee Agenda Books.

A.5/2–5. Governor and Committee General Outwards Correspondence, 1776–1796.

A.6/12 13. Governor and Committee Official Outwards Correspondence, 1774–1786.

A.11/44–45. Governor and Committee Inward from Moose Factory, 1780–1796.

A.11/116–117. Governor and Committee Inward from York Factory, 1779–1782, 1787–1797.

A.21/1. Bills Payable, 1790–1797.

A.64/1 Governor and Committee Books, 1777–1782.

A.64/3 Cash Receipt Book.

A.64/7. Catalogue of Hudson's Bay Company Library, 1802–1819.

SECTION B. POST RECORDS

B.3/a/77a–78. Albany Post Journal, 1779 1781

B.3/k/1. Albany Minutes of Council, 1783.

B.9/a/1. A Journal of Occurrences on a Journey to the Athapescow Country by Malchom Ross Commencing Sept 13 1790 ending 17 July 1792.

B.9/a/1–3. Lake Athabasca Post Journal, 1790–1792.

B.9/a/2. Longitude and latitude observations by Malchom Ross for Isle a la Cross, Fort Chipewyan, Athabasca Lake and Slave Lake.

B.23/a/6–7. Brunswick House Post Journal, 1782–1784.

B.49/a/21–24. Cumberland House Post, 1789–1793.

B.75/a/1–2. Frederick House Post Journal, 1785–1787.

B.135/a/55. Moose Factory Post Journal, 1774.

B.135/a/65–69. Moose Factory Post Journal, 1781–1785.

B.135/a/70–75. Moose Factory Post, 1785–1789.

B.135/b/5–19. Moose Factory Correspondence, 1779–1787.

B.135/d/53–56. Moose Fort Account Book, 1783–1787.

B.198/a/24. Severn Post Journal, 1779.

B.198/a/25b. A Severn River Journal of a Voyage in the Sloop, 1779.

B.239/a/75–76. York Factory Post Journal, 1778–1779.

B.239/a/89–94. York Factory Post Journal, 1789–1792.

B.239/b/49–54. York Factory Correspondence Book, 1789–1793.

B.239/d/87–96. York Factory Accounts Books, 1790, 1792.

NOTE: I read the following four "Journals" of Philip Turnor's travels on microfilm.
I checked these microfilm versions of his original text against the transcribed
versions published by J. B. Tyrrell in Journals of Hearne and Turnor and
found Tyrrell's transcriptions to be accurate. For Turnor's other journeys I used
Tyrrell's published accounts:

B.3/a/77b. "A Journal of the most remarkable transactions and occurrences
from York Fort to Albany and Moose Forts etc from 17 September 1779
to 14 September 1780."

B.9/a/3. "Journal of a journey from Cumberland House North America in
latitude 53 56 ¾' north and longitude 102 13' west of Greenwich towards
the Athabasca country and back to York Factory 13 September 1790 to 17
July 1792." Includes Turnor's map drawn from Shewditheda's description.

B.49/a/8. "A Journal of the most remarkable transactions and occurrences
from York Fort to Cumberland House and from said House to York Fort
from 9 September 1778 to 15 September 1779."

B.239/a/94. "Journal of a journey from York Factory up Port Nelson River
commonly called the North River." 31 July 1792 to 24 August 1792.

SECTION C: SHIPS' RECORDS

C.1/382. Log of King George II, 1778.

C.1/390. Log of King George III, 1787.

C.1/392. Log of King George III, 1789.

C.1/904. Log of Prince Rupert, 1782.

C.1/1055. Log of Seahorse (III), 1792.

SECTION E: PRIVATE RECORDS

E.3/1–6. Peter Fidler journals of exploration and survey, 1792–1806.

SECTION G: MAPS

G.1/1. "Chart of part of Hudsons Bay and Rivers & Lakes falling into it by
Philip Turnor." Dated by Richard I. Ruggles: 1782–1783.

G.1/21. "A CHART of Rivers and Lakes Falling into HUDSONS BAY According to a Survey taken in the Years 1778 & 9 By Philip Turnor."

G.1/22. "A chart of Rivers and Lakes Falling into Hudsons Bay According to a Survey taken in the Years 1778 & 9 By Philip Turnor" (copy of G.1/21).

G.1/23. "A Chart of Rivers and Lakes between Albany Fort and Gloucester House as taken in the Year 1780 by Philip Turnor."

G.2/11. "A Chart of Rivers and Lakes above York Fort falling into Hudsons Bay According to an Actual Survey taken by Philip Turnor 1778 & 9 And of Rivers and Lakes above Churchill Fort Joining the Same taken from a Journal kept by Malcolm Ross and laid down by Philip Turnor." Dated by Ruggles: 1787–1788.

G.2/13. "Chart of Lakes and Rivers in North America by Philip Turnor those Shaded are from Actual Survey's the others from Canadian and Indian information." Dated by Ruggles: 1792.

G.2/32. "To the Honourable the Governor, Deputy Governor, And Committee of the Hudson's Bay Company This Map Of Hudson's Bay and the Rivers and Lakes Between the Atlantick and Pacifick Oceans Is most humbly Inscribed By their most obedient & dutiful Servant, Philip Turnor." [1794].

BIOGRAPHICAL SHEETS.
www.gov.mb.ca/chc/archives/hbca/biographical/index.html

London Metropolitan Archives, London, England
XO55/001, Records for St. Mary's Battersea.

Staffordshire Record Office, Stafford, England
Q/SB 1775, 1776, 1777, 1781, 1795, 1799, Records of the Staffordshire County Quarter Sessions mentioning the Turnors.

OTHER SOURCES

Alwin, John A. "Uncelebrated Boats of the Albany." *The Beaver* 305, no. 4 (Spring 1975): 47–53.

Anderson, Mark. *The Day the World Discovered the Sun.* Boston: Da Capo Press, 2012.

Austen, Jane. *Persuasion.* London: Penguin Classics, 1985. First published 1818.

Baigent, Elizabeth. "Arrowsmith, Aaron, the elder." *Oxford Dictionary of National Biography.* Oxford University Press, 2004. http://dx.doi.org/10.1093/ref:odnb/698.

Belyea, Barbara. *Dark Storm Moving West.* Calgary: University of Calgary Press, 2007.

——, ed. *Peter Fidler: From York Factory to the Rocky Mountains.* Canmore, AB: Ha Ling Design, 2016.

Bennett, J. A. *The Divided Circle: A History of Instruments for Astronomy, Navigation and Surveying.* Oxford: Phaidon, 1987.

Binnema, Theodore. *"Enlightened Zeal": The Hudson's Bay Company and Scientific Networks, 1670–1870.* Toronto: University of Toronto Press, 2014.

Binnema, Theodore, and Gerhard Ens, eds. *The Hudson's Bay Company Edmonton House Journals 1806–1821.* Calgary: Alberta Records Publication Board, Historical Society of Alberta, 2012.

Binnema, Theodore, Gerhard J. Ens, and R. C. MacLeod, eds. *From Rupert's Land to Canada.* Edmonton: University of Alberta Press, 2001.

Broughton, Peter. "The Accuracy and Use of Sextants and Watches in Rupert's Land in the 1790s." *Annals of Science* 66, no. 2 (April 2009): 210–29.

Brown, George MacKay. *Portrait of Orkney.* London: John Murray, 1981.

Brown, Jennifer S. H. "Isham, Charles Thomas." In *Dictionary of Canadian Biography.* University of Toronto/Université Laval, 2003–. www.biographi.ca.

——. "Partial Truths: A Closer Look at Fur Trade Marriage." In *From Rupert's Land to Canada,* edited by Theodore Binnema, Gerhard J. Ens, and R. C. MacLeod, 59–77. Edmonton: University of Alberta Press, 2001.

——. "Ross, Malchom." In *Dictionary of Canadian Biography.* University of Toronto/Université Laval, 2003–. www.biographi.ca.

——. *Strangers in Blood: Fur Trade Company Families in Indian Country.* Vancouver: University of British Columbia Press, 1980.

——. "Sutherland, George." In *Dictionary of Canadian Biography.* University of Toronto/Université Laval, 2003–. www.biographi.ca.

——. and Robert Brightman, eds. *"The Orders of the Dreamed:" George Nelson on Cree and Northern Ojibwa Religion and Myth, 1823.* Winnipeg: University of Manitoba Press, 1988.

Bumstead, J. M. *Fur Trade Wars: The Founding of Western Canada.* Winnipeg: Great Plains Publications, 1999.

——, ed. *Interpreting Canada's Past.* Vol. 1, *Before Confederation.* Toronto: Oxford University Press, 1986.

Carnall, Geoffrey, and Colin Nicholson, eds. *The Impeachment of Warren Hastings: Papers from a Bicentenary Commemoration.* Edinburgh: Edinburgh University Press, 1989.

Carter, Sarah. *The Importance of Being Monogamous.* Edmonton: University of Alberta Press, 2008.

Chapin, David. *Freshwater Passages: The Trade and Travels of Peter Pond.* Lincoln, NE: University of Nebraska Press, 2014.

Clayton, Timothy, and Anita McConnell. "Tomkins, Peltro William (1759–1840)." In *Oxford Dictionary of National Biography*, Oxford University Press, 2004-. http://dx.doi.org/10.1093/ref:odnb/27514.

Coleridge, Samuel. *The Rime of the Ancient Mariner*. In *Coleridge's Poetry and Prose*, edited by Nicholas Halmi, Paul Magnuson, and Raimonda Modiano, 59–99. New York: W. W. Norton & Company, 2004.

Cooper, J.J. "Waddens, Jean Etienne." In *Dictionary of Canadian Biography*. University of Toronto/Université Laval, 2003-. www.biographi.ca.

Croarken, Mary. "Eighteenth Century Computers." *Resurrection* 39 (2007). www.cs.man.ac.uk/CCS/res/res39.htm. Accessed 8 October 2014.

"Currency, Coinage and the Cost of Living." *The Proceedings of the Old Bailey*. www.oldbaileyonline.org/static/coinage.jsp. Accessed 17 November 2014.

Davis, Richard, ed. *Rupert's Land: A Cultural Tapestry*. Waterloo, ON: Wilfred Laurier University Press, 1988.

Davis, Wade. *The Wayfinders: Why Ancient Wisdom Matters in the Modern World*. Toronto: House of Anansi Press, 2009.

Dickason, Olive Patricia. *Canada's First Nations: A History of Founding Peoples from Earliest Times*. Toronto: McClelland & Stewart, 1992.

Duckworth, Harry W., ed. *The English River Book: A Northwest Company Journal and Account Book of 1786*. Montreal and Kingston: McGill-Queen's University Press, 1989.

Eliot, George. *Middlemarch*. Edited by Gordon S. Haight. Boston: Houghton Mifflin Company, 1956. First published 1871–1872.

Fenn, Elizabeth A. *Pox Americana: The Great Smallpox Epidemic of 1775–1782*. New York: Hill & Wang, 2001.

Fischer, David Hackett. *Champlain's Dream*. New York: Simon & Schuster, 2008.

Friesen, Gerald. *The Canadian Prairies: A History*. Toronto: University of Toronto Press, 1984.

Fry, Howard T. *Alexander Dalrymple (1737–1808) and the Expansion of British Trade*. Toronto: University of Toronto Press, 1970.

Glover, Richard. "Introduction." In *Cumberland House Journals and Inland Journal, First Series, 1775–79*, edited by Richard Glover, xiii–xciii. London: The Hudson's Bay Record Society, 1951.

Gough, Barry, M. "Pond, Peter." In *Dictionary of Canadian Biography*. University of Toronto/Université Laval, 2003-. www.biographi.ca.

Graham, Andrew. *Andrew Graham's Observations on Hudson's Bay: 1767–1791*. Edited by Glyndwr Williams. Introduction by Richard Glover. London: Hudson's Bay Record Society, 1969.

Griffin-Short, Rita. "The Ancient Mariner and the transit of Venus." *Endeavour* 27, no. 4 (December 2003): 175–9.

Hackett, Paul. *"A Very Remarkable Sickness": Epidemics in the Petit Nord, 1670–1846*. Winnipeg: University of Manitoba Press, 2002.

Hampson, Norman. *The Enlightenment.* Harmondsworth, UK: Penguin, 1968.

Hayes, Derek. *First Crossing: Alexander MacKenzie, His Expedition Across North America, and the Opening of the Continent.* Vancouver and Toronto: Douglas & McIntyre, 2001.

——. *Historical Atlas of Canada.* Vancouver and Toronto: Douglas & McIntyre, 2002.

Hilton, John. *Orkney: An Outline History.* Kirkwall, UK: The Peedie Press, 1997.

Hitchcock, Tim, and Heather Shore, eds. *The Streets of London: From the Great Fire to the Great Stink.* London: Rivers Oram Press, 2003.

Holdstock, Pauline. *Into the Heart of the Country.* Toronto: HarperCollins, 2011.

Holmes, Richard. *The Age of Wonder.* New York: Random House, 2010.

Hopwood, Victor G., ed. *David Thompson Travels in Western North America, 1784-1812.* Toronto: Macmillan of Canada, 1971.

Howse, Derek. *Nevil Maskelyne: The Seaman's Astronomer.* Cambridge: Cambridge University Press, 1989.

Huck, Barbara. *Exploring the Fur Trade Routes of North America.* Winnipeg: Heartland Publications, 2000.

Innis, Harold A. *The Fur Trade in Canada.* Toronto: University of Toronto Press, 1930.

Jenish, D'Arcy. *Epic Wanderer: David Thompson and the Mapping of the Canadian West.* Toronto: Doubleday, 2003.

Keats, John. "On First Looking into Chapman's Homer." In *The Norton Anthology of English Literature*, edited by M. H. Abrams, 1796. New York: W. W. Norton, Seventh Edition, 2001.

Keys, David. "Tests confirm authenticity of Roman silver." *The Independent* (UK) 10 August 1992.

Lamb, W. Kaye. "Mackenzie, Sir Alexander." In *Dictionary of Canadian Biography.* University of Toronto/Université Laval, 2003-. www.biographi.ca.

Leaves from the Medicine Tree. Preserved by the High River Pioneers' and Old Timers' Association. *The Lethbridge Herald*, 1960.

Macdonald, Nancy. "Welcome to Winnipeg: Where Canada's Racism Problem is at its Worst." *Maclean's* 2 February 2015: 16-24.

Macdougall, Brenda. *One of the Family.* Vancouver: UBC Press, 2010.

MacGregor, J. G. *Peter Fidler: Canada's Forgotten Explorer 1769-1822.* Calgary: Fifth House, 1998. First published 1966.

MacKinnon, C. S. "Hearne, Samuel." In *Dictionary of Canadian Biography.* University of Toronto/Université Laval, 2003-. www.biographi.ca.

Maclaren, I. S. "Alexander Mackenzie and the Landscapes of Commerce." *Studies in Canadian Literature* 7, no. 2 (1982): 141-50. https://journals.lib. unb.ca/index.php/SCL/article/view/7980/9037.

Mayor, Adrienne. *Fossil Legends of the First Americans.* Princeton, NJ: Princeton University Press, 2005.

McGillivray, Duncan. "*The Journal of Duncan McGillivray of the North West Company at Fort George on the Saskatchewan, 1794–5.*" Edited by Arthur S. Morton. Toronto: Macmillan, 1929.

McGoogan, Ken. *Ancient Mariner: The Amazing Adventures of Samuel Hearne, the Sailor Who Walked to the Arctic Ocean.* Toronto: HarperCollins, 2003.

McNab, David T. "Hiding in 'Plane' View: Aboriginal Identities and a Fur-Trade Company Family through Seven Generations." In *Hidden in Plain Sight: Contributions of Aboriginal Peoples to Canadian Identity and Culture*, edited by David Newhouse, Cora J. Voyageur, and Dan Beavon, 295–308. Toronto: University of Toronto Press, 2005.

Milloy, John. *A National Crime: The Canadian Government and the Residential School System, 1879–1986.* Winnipeg: The University of Manitoba Press, 1999.

——. *The Plains Cree: Trade, Diplomacy and War, 1790 to 1890.* Winnipeg: University of Manitoba, 1988.

Mitchell, Elaine Allan. *Fort Timiskaming and the Fur Trade.* Toronto: University of Toronto Press, 1977.

Moodie, D. W., and Barry Kaye. "The Ac Ko Mok Ki Map." *Canada's History (The Beaver)* 307, no. 4 (Spring 1977): 4–15.

Moreau, William E., ed. *The Writings of David Thompson.* Vol. 1, *The Travels.* Montreal and Kingston: McGill-Queen's University Press, 2009.

Newman, Peter C. *Company of Adventurers.* Toronto: Viking, 1985.

Nicks, John. "Thompson, David." In *Dictionary of Canadian Biography.* University of Toronto/Université Laval, 2003–. www.biographi.ca.

——. "Tomison, William." In *Dictionary of Canadian Biography.* University of Toronto/Université Laval, 2003–. www.biographi.ca.

Nisbet, Jack. *The Mapmaker's Eye: David Thompson on the Columbia Plateau.* Pullman, WA: Washington State University Press, 2005

Online Cree Dictionary. www.creedictionary.com.

Ouellet, Fernand. "McGillivray, William." In *Dictionary of Canadian Biography.* University of Toronto/Université Laval, 2003–. www.biographi.ca.

Pannekoek, Frits. "'Corruption' at Moose." *Canada's History (The Beaver)* 309, no. 4 (Spring 1979): 4–11.

——. "Marten, Humphrey." In *Dictionary of Canadian Biography.* University of Toronto/Université Laval, 2003–. www.biographi.ca.

Payne, Michael. *The Most Respectable Place in the Territory: Everyday Life in Hudson's Bay Company Service – York Factory, 1788 to 1870.* Revised edition. Ottawa: National Historic Sites, Parks Canada, 1996.

Podruchny, Carol. *Making the Voyageur World: Travelers and Traders in the North American Fur Trade.* Toronto: University of Toronto Press, 2006.

Plumb, J. H. *England in the Eighteenth Century (1714–1815).* Harmondsworth, UK: Penguin, 1950.

Raffan, James. *Emperor of the North.* Toronto: HarperCollins, 2007.

Randall, J. L. *A History of the Meynell Hounds and Country, 1780-1901*. London: Sampson, Low, Marston & Co., 1901. http://dx.doi.org/10.5962/bhl. title.25527.

Ray, Arthur J. "Holmes, William." In *Dictionary of Canadian Biography*. University of Toronto/Université Laval, 2003-. www.biographi.ca.

Ray, Arthur J., and Donald B. Freeman. *"Give Us Good Measure": an economic analysis of relations between the Indians and the Hudson's Bay Company before 1763*. Toronto: University of Toronto Press, 1978.

Rich, E. E. "Cole, John." In *Dictionary of Canadian Biography*. University of Toronto/Université Laval, 2003-. www.biographi.ca.

——, ed. *Cumberland and Hudson House Journals, Second Series, 1775-1782*. Introduction by Richard Glover. London: The Hudson's Bay Record Society, 1951.

——. *The Fur Trade and the Northwest to 1857*. Toronto: McClelland & Stewart, 1967.

——. "The Fur Traders: Their Diet and Drugs." *The Beaver* 307, no. 1 (Summer 1976): 42-53.

——. *Hudson's Bay Company, 1670-1870*. Vol. II, *1763-1820*. Toronto: McClelland & Stewart, 1960.

——. "Longmoor, Robert." In *Dictionary of Canadian Biography*. University of Toronto/Université Laval, 2003-. www.biographi.ca.

——, ed. *Moose Fort Journals 1783-85*, London: The Hudson's Bay Record Society, 1954.

——. "Trade Habits and Economic Motivation among the Indians of North America." In *Sweet Promises: A Reader on Indian-White Relations in Canada*, edited by J. R. Miller, 157-79. Toronto: University of Toronto Press, 1991.

——. "Turnor, Philip." In *Dictionary of Canadian Biography*. University of Toronto/Université Laval, 2003-. www.biographi.ca.

Robertson, Heather. *Measuring Mother Earth: How Joe the Kid Became Tyrrell of the North*. Toronto: McClelland & Stewart, 2007.

Rude, George. *Hanoverian London: 1714-1808*. Oakland, CA: University of California Press, 1971.

Ruggles, Richard I. *A Country So Interesting: The Hudson's Bay Company and Two Centuries of Mapping, 1670-1870*. Montreal and Kingston: McGill-Queen's University Press, 1991.

——. "Governor Samuel Wegg, 'Winds of Change'." *The Beaver* 307, no. 2 (Autumn 1976): 10-20.

——. "Hospital Boys of the Bay." *The Beaver* 308, no. 2 (Autumn 1977): 4-11.

——. "Mapping the Interior Plains of Rupert's Land by the Hudson's Bay Company To 1870." In *Mapping the North American Plains: Essays in the History of Cartography*, edited by Frederick C. Luebke, Frances W. Kaye, and Gary E. Moulton, 145-60. Norman, OK: University of Oklahoma Press, 1987.

Saul, John Ralston. *A Fair Country: Telling Truths about Canada.* Toronto: Viking Canada, 2008.

17th & 18th Century Burney Collection Newspapers. Gale Group. British Library.

Smith, Greg. "Dayes, Edward (1763–1804)." In *Oxford Dictionary of National Biography.* Oxford University Press, 2004. www.oxforddnb.com/view/article/7376.

Smith, Shirlee Anne. "Walker, William." In *Dictionary of Canadian Biography.* University of Toronto/Université Laval, 2003-. www.biographi.ca.

Sobel, Dava. *Longitude: The True Story of a Lone Genius Who Solved the Greatest Scientific Problem of His Time.* New York: Walker Publishing Co., 1995.

Spry, Irene M. "Cocking, Matthew." In *Dictionary of Canadian Biography.* University of Toronto/Université Laval, 2003-. www.biographi.ca.

Stewart, Iain. "Athabasca Sand Dunes." In *Encyclopedia of Saskatchewan.* Canadian Plains Research Center, University of Regina, 2005. http://esask.uregina.ca/entry/athabasca_sand_dunes.html.

Thompson, David. *Columbia Journals.* Edited by Barbara Belyea. Montreal and Kingston: McGill-Queen's University Press, 1994.

Thomson, Don W. *Men and Meridians: The History of Surveying and Mapping in Canada.* Vol. I, *Prior to 1867.* Ottawa: Department of Mines and Technical Surveys, 1966.

Thorman, George E. "Maugenest, Germain." In *Dictionary of Canadian Biography.* University of Toronto/Université Laval, 2003-. www.biographi.ca.

———. "Smith, Joseph." In *Dictionary of Canadian Biography.* University of Toronto/Université Laval, 2003-. www.biographi.ca.

Tyrrell, J. B., ed. *Journals of Samuel Hearne and Philip Turnor Between the Years 1774 and 1792.* Toronto: The Champlain Society, 1934.

Turner, Daisy. *Moose Factory Cree.* Cobalt, ON: Highway Book Shop, 1974.

Turnor, Philip. *Result of Astronomical Observations made in the interior parts of North America.* London: Printed for A. Arrowsmith, 1794.

Umfreville, Edward. *The Present State of Hudson's Bay.* Edited and with an introduction by W. Stewart Wallace. Toronto: Ryerson Press, 1954. First published in 1790.

Van Kirk, Sylvia. *Many Tender Ties: Women in the Fur-Trade Society.* Winnipeg: Watson & Dwyer, 1980.

Verner, Coolie. "The Arrowsmith Firm and the Cartography of Canada." *Canadian Cartography* 8, no. 1 (June 1971): 1–7.

Walford, Edward, ed. "Rotherhithe." In *Old and New London.* Vol. 6. London: Cassell, Petter & Galpin, 1878, 134–142. British History Online. www.british-history.ac.uk/report.aspx?compid=45271.

Wallace, W. Stewart, ed. *Documents Relating to the North West Company.* Toronto: The Champlain Society, 1934.

———. *The Pedlars from Quebec.* Toronto: Ryerson Press, 1954.

Warkentin, John H., and Richard I. Ruggles. *Historical Atlas of Manitoba, 1612–1929.* Winnipeg: Manitoba Historical Society, 1970.

West, John F., ed. *The Journals of the Stanley Expedition to the Faroe Islands and Iceland in 1789, Volumes 1–3.* Torshavn, Faroe Islands: Torshavn Press, 1976.

Weston, Pearl. *Across the River: A History of the Turner, Thompson, Campbell Families.* Regina: Print West Communications, 1995.

Williams, Glyndwr, ed. *Hudson's Bay Miscellany 1670-1870.* Winnipeg: Hudson's Bay Record Society, 1975.

Wilson, Hap. *Trails and Tribulations: Confessions of a Wilderness Pathfinder.* Toronto: Natural Heritage Books, Dundurn, 2009.

Wishart, Vernon R. *What Lies Behind the Picture? A Personal Journey into Cree Ancestry.* Red Deer, AB: Central Alberta Historical Society, 2006.

Descriptions and Credits for Maps and Figures

ORIENTATION MAPS

MAP 1   West of Hudson Bay and the Arctic Shores
MAP 2   The Nelson and Churchill River Systems
MAP 3   Between Lake Superior and James Bay

Permission to use these maps granted by Ross Hough, Cartographer, Queen's University. Originally printed in *A Country So Interesting* by Richard Ruggles, McGill-Queen's University Press, 1991. Adapted and amended for this publication by Julia Siemer, University of Regina.

TURNOR MAPS

PLATE 1   "A Ground Plan of York Fort in Hayes River America taken August 1778 by Philip Turnor," HBCA, G.1/109. N4439.

PLATE 2   "A CHART of Rivers and Lakes Falling Into HUDSONS BAY According to a Survey taken in the years 1778 & 9 By Philip Turnor," HBCA, G.1/21, 1779. N3503.

PLATE 3   "A Chart of Rivers and Lakes between Albany Fort and Gloucester House as taken in the year 1780 by Philip Turnor," HBCA, G.1/23, 1780. N4084.

PLATE 4   "Chart of part of Hudsons Bay and Rivers and Lakes falling into it by Philip Turnor," HBCA, G.1/1, 1782-83. N3636.

PLATE 5   "A Chart of Rivers and Lakes above York Fort falling into Hudsons Bay According to an Actual Survey taken by Philip Turnor 1778 & 9 And of Rivers and Lakes above Churchill Fort Joining the Same taken from a Journal kept by Malcolm Ross and laid down by Philip Turnor," HBCA, G.2/11, 1787-88 N4783.

PLATE 6   "Chart of Lakes and Rivers in North America by Philip Turnor those Shaded are from Actual Survey's [sic] the others from Canadian and Indian information," HBCA, G.2/13, 1792. N14763.

PLATE 7   The cartouche on the 1794 map: "To the Honourable the Governor, Deputy Governor, And Committee of the Hudson's Bay Company This Map of Hudson's Bay and the Rivers and Lakes Between the Atlantick and Pacifick Oceans Is most humbly Inscribed By their most obedient & dutiful Servant, Philip Turnor," HBCA, G.2/32, 1794. N4859.

PLATE 8   Author viewing Turnor's 1794 map for the first time. (Photo by Orm Mitchell, 2008).

Permission granted by the Hudson's Bay Company Archives for use of all images prefaced by HBCA.

FIGURES

FIGURE 1   Genealogical chart. (Chart by author on map, G.1/1).

FIGURE 2   1753 engraving of Fenchurch Street where Hudson's Bay House was located. (HBCA, N5415).

FIGURE 3   Eland Wood, Staffordshire, England, Estate of the Duchy of Lancaster, and formerly the hunting lodge of King George III. (Photo by author, 2011).

FIGURE 4   Three HBC ships, *King George II*, *Seahorse*, and *Prince Rupert IV*, at Gravesend, 1769. (Drawing by John Hood. HBCA,1987.363-S-438/59).

FIGURE 5   Login's Well, Stromness, Orkney. (Photo by author, 2002).

FIGURE 6   "Ship among the Icebergs." (From Robert M. Ballantyne, *Hudson's Bay or Every-day Life in the Wilds of North America...*, 1875, 13. HBCA FC3212.2B3).

FIGURE 7   York Factory in the 1770s. (Drawing by Samuel Hearne; engraving 1797. HBCA N5411).

FIGURE 8   A Group of Home Cree who lived on the Hayes River. Strips of caribou meat hang in the smoke above the fires. (From Edward Chappell, *Voyage to the Hudson's Bay*, 1817, 33, HBCA, N7602).

FIGURE 9   York Factory on Hayes River. (Photo by author, 2005).

FIGURE 10   Eighteenth-century surveyor's field compass by George Adams, London, similar to a compass used by Turnor. (Collection of Historical Scientific Instruments, Harvard University, DW0687).

FIGURE 11   Eighteenth-century brass sextant made by Peter and John Dollond, England, similar to one used by Turnor on his 1790–1792 expedition. (Collection of Historical Scientific Instruments, Harvard University, 0063).

FIGURE 12   Tracking on Steel River. (From Robert M. Ballantyne, *Hudson's Bay or Every-day Life in the Wilds of North America...*, 1875, 45. Engraving by Emile Antoine Bayard, HBCA N14844).

FIGURE 13   Cumberland House, 1858. In Turnor's time the main settlement building measured twenty-six feet by thirty-eight feet. (Sketch by John Fleming. Toronto Reference Library, *Landmarks of Canada*, JRR 2387).

FIGURE 14   Final pages of Turnor's first journal (September 1778 to September 1779). (HBCA, B.49/a/8).

FIGURE 15   Moose Fort, circa 1804. (William Richards, HBCA, N5302).

FIGURE 16   Albany Factory, 1804–1811. (William Richards, HBCA, N5303).

FIGURE 17   HBC post at Marten Falls, 1905 photograph. (Duncan Campbell Scott Fonds, Archives of Ontario, C 275-3-0-2 S 7534).

FIGURE 18   Author with Turner sisters, Myrtle, Dorothy, Trudy, and Sue, and their mother Daisy at Moose Factory. (Photo by Orm Mitchell, 2012).

FIGURE 19   Thunderhouse Falls on the Missinaibi River. (Photo by Dave Sproule, Ontario Parks).

FIGURE 20   Tikinagan or cradleboard. (From Robert M. Ballantyne, *Hudson's Bay or Every-day Life in the Wilds of North America...*, 1875, 49. Engraving by Hay Stafford Stead. HBCA, N8342).

FIGURE 21   Joseph Turner's 1863 house, on left, at Moose Factory Centennial Park Museum. (Photo by author, 2012).

FIGURE 22   Rick Isaacson canoeing Sextant Rapids (April 2012). (Photo from Rick Isaacson, Howling Wolf Expeditions).

FIGURE 23   Frederick House Plaque, Barbers Bay near Connaught, Ontario. (Photo by author, 2012).

FIGURE 24   St. Mary's Church, Battersea, Surrey (circa 1829). (From Thomas Allen, *History of the Counties of Surrey and Sussex*, Vol. 1, 446, Toronto Reference Library, AR 921.21 A48).

FIGURE 25   Île-à-la-Crosse: detail from Turnor's 1794 map. (HBCA, G.2/32. Photo by author, 2014).

FIGURE 26   Detour around Methy Portage via Red Willow River (Christina River): detail from Turnor's 1794 map. (HBCA, G.2/32. Photo by author, 2014).

FIGURE 27   Fort Chipewyan on Lake Athabasca: detail from Turnor's 1794 map. (HBCA, G.2/32. Photo by author, 2014).

FIGURE 28   "Shewditheda's map of Great Slave Lake, Northern Indian Lake and Esquimay river to the sea." Sketched by Turnor in his journal, 25 July 1791. (HBCA, N16157, B.9/a/3, fol. 83).

FIGURE 29   Turnor's astronomical observations, 18 August 1791, taken near mouth of McFarlane River on Lake Athabasca. (HBCA, B.9/a/3, fol. 93).

FIGURE 30   Final journal pages of Turnor's journey northward, 1790–1792. (HBCA, B.9/a/3, fol. 158-9).

FIGURE 31   Spitcheyee (Highwood) River running into the Bow River: detail from Turnor's 1794 map. (HBCA, G.2/32. Photo by author, 2014).

FIGURE 32   Author viewing Turnor's 1794 map for the first time. (Photo by Orm Mitchell, 2008).

FIGURE 33   St. Peter's Church, Selkirk. (Photo by author, 2005).

FIGURE 34   Nancy Ann Harper, great-granddaughter of Philip Turnor. This is the oldest photo in author's possession of one of Philip's descendants. (Family photo).

FIGURE 35   John Low Loutit, husband of Nancy Ann Harper. (Family photo).

Page references in *italic* indicate figures.

#

A

B

I

J